SHARPTON

A Demagogue's Rise

BY CARL F. HOROWITZ

ISBN: 0692277803
ISBN 13: 9780692277805
Library of Congress Control Number: 2014958508
National Legal and Policy Center, Falls Church VA

"Man lives *by* habits, indeed, but what he lives *for* is thrills and excitements. The only relief from Habit's tediousness is periodical excitement."

William James
"The Psychological Roots of War" (1904)

TABLE OF CONTENTS

PREFACE

Everyone loves a winner. Or as the late, unlamented Osama bin Laden often said: "People prefer a strong horse to a weak horse." It's a serious defect in the human psyche: No matter how unattractive the person, if he seems unstoppable, and even better, seems unstoppable while wearing a cloak of moral righteousness, he often is irresistible to a large group of followers. Even without any formal title or office, such a person seems to have a preternatural ability to persuade others to hop on his bandwagon. That's the essence of real power.

Reverend Al Sharpton has that kind of charismatic power. Having just turned 60, he can be said to have acquired as much of it as any living American. Given his track record for fomenting the worst sorts of crowd behavior, that is a scary thought. Yet it is an inescapable one. A hybrid of charismatic black American archetypes – the Bible-thumping minister, the street politician and the radical civil rights leader – he now wields influence on a magnitude that very few people of *any* race can claim. Sharpton is not a government official, yet the Obama administration regularly consults with him on racial issues. President Obama in 2011 and again in 2014, in fact, was the marquee speaker at the annual convention of his New York-based nonprofit organization, National Action Network (NAN), now claiming more than 70 chapters around the country. He is not a corporate CEO. Yet over the years he has persuaded some of the nation's largest corporations to donate funds to NAN, and, for a while, to pull out of their sponsorship of Don Imus' syndicated radio show. He is not a labor leader, yet he regularly coaxes donations to National Action Network from powerful unions. He is not a professional entertainer, yet he has gotten leading performing artists, such as Mariah Carey, Denzel Washington and Bill Cosby, to speak at NAN banquets. And though he still makes the news as much as ever, he's also been reporting it on MSNBC since August 2011.

A good many people in the upper reaches of American life simply can't be bothered with Sharpton's track record as one of America's most durable demagogues. Their attitude appears to be: Why deal with the past? He's grown. Don't we all? Thus, his admirers, especially in the media, in the past several years have spun a story that a "new" Al Sharpton has come to the fore. He's still an assertive alpha male, the argument goes, but he has evolved into a sensible pragmatist leading an overdue national conversation on race. The "old" Al Sharpton, the flamboyant corpulent loudmouth with the jumpsuits and medallions, is ancient Eighties and Nineties history. The cover story of the August 2, 2010 issue of *Newsweek* exemplifies this syndrome. Authors Allison Samuels and Jerry Adler manage to elevate Reverend Sharpton into an exemplar, however imperfect, of America's moral conscience in action. "It is, of course, the fate of people like Sharpton to be misunderstood, and his own tendency to get carried away while addressing a crowd has contributed to it at times...He is out there alone, still standing on the same principle he first enunciated in his housing project in Brooklyn: poor people have the same rights as rich ones, to justice in the streets and in the courts. If he didn't exist, we might, in fact, need to invent him."

Well, balderdash to that. While Sharpton has become more circumspect about how he phrases his public statements, he remains every bit as determined as he was 20 or 30 years ago to make life miserable for any white or group of whites, regardless of social position, whom he believes has visited injustice upon blacks. His accusations almost inevitably collapse under the weight of their own absurdity when exposed to the full range of facts. And even where he does make a credible case for an injustice having occurred, he does so by falsely projecting racial motive onto the wrongdoer. Yet his army of true believers, backed by more influential enablers, will never accept such criticism.

A bred-to-the-bone New Yorker, Sharpton lives to create drama. All it takes to get him to swing into action is a report of a white-on-black crime (which he assumes happened) or a black-on-white crime (which he assumes did not happen). Whether the storyline of a given campaign is true or false, what matters is manufacturing a pretext to take down the ostensibly white racist power structure in this country a few notches. Oblivious to what the general population thinks of him, Sharpton, aided by legal, political, religious and other allies, will jockey for position as an aggrieved black family's "adviser," often at the family's invitation. He then will organize marches, rallies, boycotts, fundraisers and other activities. During 2012-13, for example, Sharpton went the extra mile in an effort to incarcerate George Zimmerman, a mixed-race white Florida neighborhood crime patrol volunteer accused of murder in the shooting death in February 2012 of Trayvon Martin, a suspicious-looking black teen. Evidence indicated that Martin had been viciously beating Zimmerman until the latter pulled out, and used, his registered pistol in self-defense. Sharpton's campaign failed – and rightly so. The state case against Zimmerman was driven entirely by political pressure, not material facts. But the campaign helped generate an enormous groundswell of sympathy on behalf of Trayvon Martin, a person who frankly deserved none. Only weeks after the fatal shooting, Martin's parents appeared at the podium with Sharpton at the 2012 NAN convention in Washington, D.C. More recently, the same can be said of Sharpton's relentless denunciation of a justified police shooting death in Ferguson, Missouri of an "unarmed" violent black suspect and his close advisory role on behalf of the suspect's parents. Reverend Al was making the news even as he was reporting it on MSNBC.

Al Sharpton has no qualms about his modus operandi. As his goal is justice, the ends justify the means. The facts of a given case don't matter – or at any rate, don't matter nearly as much as the possibility of affirming an overarching narrative of black suffering and redemption at the hands of whites. All of Sharpton's "projects" over the past three decades follow this pattern, whether attempting to railroad New York

City "subway vigilante" Bernhard Goetz or discrediting the character of a white female jogger in Central Park beaten unconscious by a roving gang of predominantly black youths.

Such a person richly deserves opprobrium. Yet most of the criticism directed at Sharpton from both sides of the political spectrum has been ineffectual and often inept. His critics, be they politicians, journalists or Web message posters, almost invariably treat him more as a caricature than as a character. Nobody will deny that Sharpton revels in spectacle. But focusing on his bombast diverts attention away from his effectiveness. His critics typically see a blowhard street preacher riling audiences up or shaking targets down. What they *don't* see is his charisma, political street smarts and recommitment to an egalitarian civil rights vision that is now the coin of the realm even in certain provinces of the Right. They hear his speeches, but they're not really listening. And it is doubtful they have read any of his three published autobiographies.

Contrary to the conventional wisdom, this book argues that Sharpton *always* has had his eyes on social reform. Granted, it is consistently the wrong kind of reform, but it is reform all the same. Far from simply "wanting attention" or "just being out for himself" – a view, by the way, which many blacks held of Martin Luther King Jr. back in the day – Sharpton really does mean to be a transformative figure in American history. That's why he ran for president during 2003-04. That's why he holds National Action Network conventions every April. That's why he broadcasts his commentary on radio and TV shows. That's why he is on a first-name basis with hundreds of black clergy around the nation. That's why he evades taxes, all the better to save the money for supposedly higher purposes. On the surface, he appears as a loud, self-serving buffoon. But underneath, where it really counts, he is the essence of a committed radical civil rights leader. He seeks redistributive collective justice for blacks. And he means for whites to pay up. This is how he means to make history. A rebuke of Sharpton *and* his racially-driven revanchist vision is a necessity.

This book attempts to set the record straight about Al Sharpton and the underlying dishonesty of the larger project of anti-white radicalism masquerading as civil rights. And it seeks to do so thoroughly, with no cutting of corners. Two forces brought it into being.

First, the book, as common expression would have it, "wrote itself." That is, it already had appeared in primordial form as a report published in 2009 by the National Legal and Policy Center (NLPC) in Falls Church, Virginia, where I work as a policy analyst and editor. That rather lengthy work – lengthy, that is, for a background paper – itself was the result of several articles I had done on Sharpton. And since then, I have done many more articles on him. The Rev was a natural topic. NLPC for its more than 20 years of existence has existed for one overriding purpose: to promote ethics in American public life. Using various sources of information, the center makes every effort to hold public figures in government, corporations, unions and elsewhere accountable for potential and documented corruption. Back in February 2004, while Sharpton was still a presidential candidate (and more than a year prior to my arrival), National Legal and Policy Center filed a complaint with the Federal Election Commission pointing to various financial irregularities in his campaign. That May, about two months after he'd dropped out of the race, the FEC ruled that Sharpton had to return $100,000 in federal matching funds and forgo another nearly $80,000 for which he purportedly had qualified.

This ruling, as could be expected, made no impression on Reverend Al's behavior. Truly, he is a gift that keeps on giving. We live in a depraved world. But Sharpton, rain or shine, can be counted on to deliver threats, character assassination, misleading facts and outright falsehoods, all the while short-changing his creditors. I relate to him in roughly the same way that Hunter S. Thompson related to Richard Nixon. In a weird way, I have to thank him.

It was Sharpton's close association with the Obama administration that provided the impetus for expanding that report (which remains online at www.nlpc.org) into a full-fledged book. NLPC President Peter

Flaherty rightly was concerned about the high degree of influence Sharpton has exerted upon the administration, especially President Barack Obama and Attorney General Eric Holder. The ongoing saga of racial violence in Ferguson, Missouri attests to that influence. He originally had asked me to do an updated version of the paper. I thought this was a good idea. But in the process of expanding the manuscript, I came to realize in short order that the result would be something far longer than even the longest possible paper. I told Peter as much. After giving the matter some thought, he suggested making this into a book. I concurred. A book would give me the freedom to stretch out in ways simply not possible within the confines of a special report.

The second reason for this book's appearance is that nobody has written anything like it before. Sharpton's critics, to be sure, are legion. And they have gotten in plenty of licks. Yet in the end, they've barely laid a glove on him. That is because they work on the assumption that he is some sort of one-man freak show, far removed from the ostensibly "good" black mainstream. He's supposedly a leader with no followers, the argument goes. He's a chief without a tribe.

Critics from the Left, such as Wayne Barrett, Peter Noel and the late Jack Newfield, each for years associated with the *Village Voice*, are good examples of this syndrome. They happen to have done some excellent investigative reporting on Al Sharpton and his allies. And I refer to their work in this book. I've spoken with Barrett over the phone, and if it is possible, he finds Sharpton even more unappealing than I do. Yet such critics seem far less troubled by Sharpton's goals than by the methods he uses to achieve them. They hail the political progressivism for which he ostensibly stands, but view him as a sellout and a charlatan. Like so many whites on the Left, they kind of like Sharpton's views, but crave a sign from heaven that he's a changed man, and hence, no longer a source of embarrassment. Yet as Part III of this book argues in detail, he *has* changed his style. He's downright respectable, in fact. That's the whole problem in a nutshell.

On the Right, the territory from which I write, the output on Sharpton, I regret to say, also is wanting. With a few exceptions – Jay Nordlinger comes to mind – conservative authors usually take the easy route. They reduce Sharpton to a manic, cartoonish caricature removed from everyday black experience. This view is way off base. If Sharpton were even half as isolated from fellow blacks as claimed by pundits of the Right, he wouldn't have lasted on the national stage for 30 weeks, much less 30 years. The case for Sharpton-as-lone wolf typically amounts to little more than a laundry list of his distant past exploits, a "gotcha" highlight reel rendered in the tone of a high-strung Sgt. Joe Friday: *Tawana Brawley!...Crown Heights!...Freddy's Fashion Mart!* None of this has made as much as a dent on Sharpton. He has been "reminded" of all this and more at least a thousand times. And he has pat answers for every one of those campaigns.

The only real way to knock Sharpton off his throne is to examine each campaign in detail, both in content and context. As in a film *noir* storyline, where a hard-boiled detective seeks to unravel lies and alibis in a search for the smoking gun, this book tries to get the real story. And, conveniently, the facts *already* are out there for anyone taking the time to look. Repeatedly, Sharpton's version of events about a supposed atrocity dissipates once his projections, lies and omissions become transparent. In the end, it is details – and only details – that matter. Everything else is preaching to the choir.

This is a book about the public Al Sharpton. The private Al Sharpton is of relatively little concern here. Indeed, there isn't much in the way of a private life to dig up. As Sharpton himself readily admits, following the example of his original mentor, Adam Clayton Powell Jr., he prefers to expose himself. By doing so, he deprives his enemies of indulging that opportunity on their terms. His three book-length autobiographies alone make a biographer's job much easier. "To see what is in front of one's nose needs a constant struggle," George Orwell famously wrote. The facts of Al Sharpton's life are no secret. He's not hiding from them.

The struggle is to take what is in front of our noses and tell an alternative story. That's what this book is all about.

The intent is not character assassination. I made every effort to see the good in Al Sharpton. Yes, really. It cheapens any biographical work to reduce its principal subject to a depersonalized stick figure representing either total good or total evil. A biography, regardless of the perspective of the biographer, must get beyond shallow, histrionic "us versus them" pugilism and grasp the larger character arc. And Sharpton, though it pains me to admit as much, does have some good traits. He is by all reasonable appearances a decent father to his two daughters, both of whom are active in National Action Network affairs. He speaks out regularly against black "gangsta" culture and its accompanying misogyny. His focus on education is genuine; I've seen evidence of that in person more than once. And he is honest enough to admit that his values and personality were heavily shaped by his search for a surrogate father during preadolescence, his father having dumped his mother for a female who happened to be young Al's half-sister. He is more complex than the caricature typically offered by "Red State" propagandists.

That said, I find it impossible to look past Sharpton's unapologetic history of demagoguery and its effects on public discourse. Every time I begin to feel a twinge of sympathy for the man, he lets off another blast of loony accusations and contempt for rule of law rooted in anti-white animus. With the Reverend Al, the bad far outweighs the good. Distortion or omission of relevant facts; confusion of cause and effect; character assassination; rationalization of mob violence; advocacy of slavery reparations (from whites to blacks); and advocacy of economic collectivism – these are some of his defining traits. And taken as a whole, they render him a disastrous contemporary figure. Convinced of his righteousness, he will never change his ways. There is a possibility, however, that his sources of institutional support, especially corporations, will.

The book, as its title indicates, is about the rise of Al Sharpton to the top of American life. Those awaiting his fall, alas, will have to wait. Perhaps that will be part of a future edition. The three sections,

"Identity," "Projects" and "Triumph," present slices of Sharpton's life as part of what he sees as a Godly mission. They explain, respectively: 1) his identity and what came to define it; 2) his misleading campaigns over the last 30 years to create pretexts for mass protest and power seizure; and 3) his transformation into a dominant public figure. Truth, once again, is stranger than fiction. His transformation from street agitator to Obama administration shadow adviser, appalling as it is, fascinates for what it reveals not only about Sharpton and the people immediately around him, but also about our political culture.

This book thus can be seen as a critique of the cult of celebrity as well as a lengthy study in personal history and character. In America, perhaps more than in other countries, criminals can get a free pass if they have sufficient money, fame, friends and a good public relations agent. It worked for Sharpton's ultimate mentor, James Brown. During the course of his lifetime, Brown behaved in ways far worse than Sharpton, as this book will explain. But he was the Godfather of Soul, the hardest-working man in show business. All eventually would be forgiven. Through a combination of aggression, determination, charm and an absolute conviction of serving a higher purpose, Sharpton has worn down opponents and won admirers in much the same way. Many of his natural opponents no doubt have wondered: He must be doing *something* right to have lasted all these years. And his natural admirers, in response, more than ever see him as a "real man's man," to use Sharpton's own words in describing his initial boyhood hero, Adam Clayton Powell. I've been to several NAN conferences. I've seen the reactions of the audiences. Like it or not, their admiration for Sharpton is real.

Al Sharpton knows the psychology of the bandwagon, of why people root for the "strong horse" for no other reason than the fact of its strength. And though undeservedly, he has prevailed – at least so far. His own history is out there for one and all to see. Rebuke him, yes, but keep in mind that he does not care what anyone thinks of him. His mission, like that of all radical civil rights leaders, is social justice for blacks. And the ends always justify the means. Nothing will deter him.

And with powerful people protecting him, beginning with the current President of the United States, why shouldn't he play to win? This is his moment in history.

It is the responsibility of opponents of Sharpton, recognizing his corrosive effects on our political culture, to deprive him of his ultimate triumph. This book should be seen as an expression of the opposition.

Carl F. Horowitz
December 2014

PART I

IDENTITY

CHAPTER 1

"The Rev"

Reverend Al Sharpton, preacher, civil rights radical, inciter of crowds and celebrant of all things black, once upon a time routinely answered to the word "flamboyant." Back in the late Eighties and the Nineties, one could look it up in Webster's Dictionary and virtually anticipate an etching of Sharpton, his pompadour hair style in full bloom. But these days, the man known as "Reverend Al," or simply "the Rev," routinely is summarized by some even more disturbing words: "pragmatic," "respectable," "sensible" and "powerful."

When this work first appeared in the spring of 2009 in the form of a National Legal and Policy Center report,[1] Barack Obama had been U.S. president for all of several months. Few at the time anticipated that he would rely on Sharpton as his "go to" man, especially on incendiary race-related issues and events. But to those possessed of sound political instincts, not to mention a familiarity with Sharpton's life, Obama's close working relationship with Sharpton should not come as any shock. Sharpton's own presidential candidacy during 2003-04, while on the surface ludicrous, underneath was a masterstroke of political strategizing. It won Reverend Al the kind of influence in high places he had been craving for years. And as an "inside man" for the Obama administration, he has helped steer public policy more to his liking than he could have imagined, say, 15 years ago. As a result, he is now no longer simply one of the most powerful people in New York City; he is one of the most powerful people in America.

A self-described "refined agitator," Reverend Al still can be found leading civil rights marches and rallies. And while he doesn't necessarily manufacture riots, he remains adept at rationalizing them. His leap toward further refinement, and influence, took a huge leap in late summer 2011, when he became a full-time weeknight anchorman-commentator for MSNBC, now a subsidiary of Comcast (Comcast's acquisition of MSNBC not long before that, in fact, had more than a little to do with Sharpton). That someone with a lengthy track record of demagoguery can occupy such a position in a major news organization speaks of much wrong about our political culture.

Reverend Al has a lot of friends in high places. Many appear eager to share his concerns about the issues of the day. Having turned 60 on October 3, 2014, he celebrated this milestone during the two previous days by sponsoring an Education Summit at New York University under the auspices of his nonprofit organization, National Action Network, where teachers, community activists, civil rights leaders and nonprofit leaders discussed contemporary educational issues. He had major outside help. Corporate sponsors of the event included AT&T, Macy's, Viacom and Walmart. Union sponsors included the American Federation of Government Employees, the American Federation of Teachers, and International Brotherhood of Teamsters Local 237. Making an appearance at his October 1 birthday party at the Four Seasons Restaurant in Midtown Manhattan were prominent New York politicians Governor Andrew Cuomo, New York City Mayor Bill de Blasio, Senator Kirsten Gillibrand and Congressman Charles Rangel, plus singer Aretha Franklin and film director Spike Lee.[2]

Sharpton, some might say, has "mellowed." He's certainly acquired some extra lines on his face. His James Brown-inspired pompadour is shorter and graying. His loud track suits and medallions have given way to natty dress suits and ties. He's lost a lot of weight. And he's more circumspect about his choice of language when making public statements. Superficially, this amounts to change. Yet he remains a master of mass incitement for the cause of social justice. And having been rewarded by the pillars of society for his efforts, he has become a pillar in his own right. In this sense, he is at once less dangerous in appearance and more dangerous in influence. He's not just a strong horse; he's also a Trojan horse to anyone who can look beyond the next news cycle.

If Al Sharpton has a specialty, it is creating and rationalizing mass resentment among his fellow blacks, especially in the context of a criminal act, for maximum media coverage and eventual political surrender by people he considers to be white "racists" and thus a mirror of mainstream America. There are plenty of activists in this field, which mysteriously goes by the term "civil rights." But nobody does it quite like Sharpton. When the Rev gets his motor running, he can win air time and print space on almost any issue he wishes, thanks to the large number of people willing to indulge or march with him. And a lot of spectators, even if not necessarily siding with him, get a kick out of him. He may be a demagogue, but he makes for good news copy. If in a perverse way, he is fun. And fun means sales and ratings.

Think back, for example, to the spring of 2008. Barack Obama was still a U.S. senator from Illinois, consolidating his Democratic Party presidential campaign frontrunner position. Sharpton was preoccupied with a separate campaign on New York City streets. A State Supreme Court Justice had just acquitted three City police detectives, two of them black, on all counts related to the November 2006 shooting death of a young black man, Sean Bell, following a seven-week trial. The evidence of guilt was weak at best. The "unarmed" Bell, in fact, had tried to run over one of the cops with his car. But facts did not deter Sharpton. "This verdict is one round down, but the fight is far from over," he announced. "What we saw in court today was not a miscarriage of justice. Justice didn't miscarry. This was an abortion of justice...We are going to close the city down in a nonviolent, effective way."[3]

He made good on his promise – up to a point. On May 7, less than two weeks after the verdict, he and his followers blocked streets and entrances to the Triborough, Manhattan and Brooklyn Bridges. More than 200 marchers, including Sharpton and Bell's parents, were arrested. Sharpton and several other defendants would be convicted for disorderly conduct. Though the facts of the case fully justified the exoneration of the officers – as this book later will explain in detail – Bell's fate, the Rev insisted, could have been that of any young black man in America. The event to some extent made more headlines than the presidential campaign.

For 30 years, Sharpton has been in the national spotlight peddling his brand of racial justice. The Rev knows he is highly unpopular in many quarters. At times, he leads marchers into those quarters. That strategy led to his nearly being assassinated in 1991. But he has no regrets. As he would have it, American blacks are victims of persecution by whites and thus need his forceful voice. Through his campaigns, long on reckless accusations and short on cause-and-effect reasoning, he escalates the fury of his overwhelmingly black audiences, eager to have their sense of collective victimhood validated. Operating from National Action Network (NAN) headquarters at 106 West 145th Street in Harlem (Manhattan), Sharpton, when so predisposed, relentlessly plays offense against any white person, persons or organization who he believes has perpetrated, or turned a blind eye from, injustices against blacks. Though he won't say as much, his actions underscore a conviction that the ends justify the means. Thus, if he slanders the reputations of innocent persons (which he repeatedly has done) or evades taxes in an effort to bankroll his campaigns (which he also repeatedly has done), in his mind such actions are legitimate because his ulterior motive is laudable.

Al Sharpton's run as a Democratic candidate for U.S. president, which had no chance of yielding victory, seems a distant memory. But only the naïve believe that his political stock has not risen since – and largely as a result of that campaign. Indeed, he accomplishes far more now than that campaign ever did, whether as a TV news anchorman/commentator, syndicated radio talk show host, rally leader or de facto presidential cabinet member. He has a politician's keen sense that power is more than simply about holding formal public office. It is about winning concessions, using all available resources to induce changes in belief and behavior in others. And being persuasive, at least to his natural audience, he often gets results.

This raises a question: Who is making these resources available? Put more bluntly, who's been paying his bills? Much of the answer, as suggested earlier, can be found in the suites of large corporations. Here is a partial list of companies who have served as sponsors of National Action Network annual conferences over the years: Abbott Laboratories, Allstate, Anheuser-Busch, Best Buy, Citigroup, Colgate-Palmolive, Comcast, Continental Airlines, Daimler-Chrysler, Facebook, FedEx, Ford, General Electric, General Motors, Georgia-Pacific, Home Depot, Johnson & Johnson, Macy's, McDonald's, The News Corporation, PepsiCo, Pfizer, Sony Music, Verizon and Wal-Mart.

As is common with nonprofit organizations, NAN has different donor levels. But some corporate donors go that extra mile. Colgate-Palmolive, for example, several years ago admitted that it had given $50,000 in support of the 2008 NAN conference, held in Memphis that April.[4] In return for this generosity, NAN bestowed upon Colgate-Palmolive the honor of "Corporation of the Year." Even companies openly critical of National Action Network give generously. "They bash me at Fox News, but they sponsor my conference," Sharpton noted during NAN's 2012 convention, held in Washington, D.C.[5] Regrettably, he was right. The News Corporation, parent company of the "conservative" Fox News Channel, was listed in the program as a sponsor.

Corporations aren't the only source of institutional support. New York State Comptroller Thomas DiNapoli, whose agency at the time of the 2008 Memphis confab managed roughly $140 billion in public-employee pension funds, announced at that event his intent to earmark a share of assets to causes supported by Sharpton. That commitment earned him a "Keeper of the Dream" award. Labor unions, a natural political ally of Sharpton, also have made their presence felt. The American Federation of State, County and Municipal Employees (AFSCME), plus some New York City-based unions, Service Employees International Union (SEIU)

Locals 1199 and 32BJ, and the United Federation of Teachers (the lead affiliate of the American Federation of Teachers), were co-sponsors of that Memphis conference. A nonprofit group heavily subsidized by multibillionaire and three-term New York City Mayor Michael Bloomberg, the Education Equality Project, donated $110,000 to Sharpton in the fall of 2008.[6]

Al Sharpton can call upon top-tier individuals in politics, business, labor, broadcasting, entertainment, sports and philanthropy to lend their presence to National Action Network conferences and accompanying "Keepers of the Dream" banquet ceremonies. Featured speakers and guests of honor over the years have included James Brown, Mariah Carey, Bill Cosby, Newt Gingrich, Joel Klein, Spike Lee, Bill O'Reilly, Rosie Perez, Robin Roberts, Russell Simmons, Andrew Stern, Cicely Tyson, Denzel Washington, Jann Wenner and any number of Obama administration cabinet members. For good measure, Barack Obama himself has been a featured speaker, in 2007 as a U.S. senator from Illinois, and in 2011 and 2014 as U.S. president. In his 2011 speech before NAN, President Obama had this to say: "(I)f you do what civil rights groups like the National Action Network have always done, if you put your shoulder to the wheel of history, then we can move this country toward the promise of a better day."[7] If nothing else, Sharpton knows how to throw a party.

What is significant here is that by supporting Sharpton, these institutions and individuals effectively are admitting him to their ranks, enhancing his image and influence. During the Eighties and Nineties he was the *enfant terrible* of the civil-rights movement, a public relations agent's nightmare. But he has evolved into a respected media celebrity. He has published three autobiographies, respectively, in 1996, 2002 and 2013.[8] He served as guest host for the December 6, 2003 segment of NBC-TV's "Saturday Night Live," during which time he was an active candidate for U.S. president. During 2004-05, he hosted the Spike television network show, "I Hate My Job," a working stiff's version of Donald Trump's "The Apprentice." He has appeared as a guest actor in episodes of such popular television series as "New York Undercover," "My Wife and Kids," and "Boston Legal." For the last several years he's hosted a weekday radio talk show, "Keepin' It Real with Al Sharpton," which operates out of the studios of WWRL-AM (New York City), and is broadcast by the XM (satellite) and Radio One networks. In 2008 he appeared in a heavily-aired TV spot alongside conservative televangelist Pat Robertson to promote former Vice President Al Gore's anti-global warming campaign, "We Can Solve It." *Newsweek* magazine in August 2010 practically deified him in a cover story. His media earnings alone now are well into the hundreds of thousands and possibly as much as a million dollars a year.[9] His current net worth is roughly $5 million.[10]

Thanks to this image reinvention, Al Sharpton has become the nation's top civil-rights leader, a good deal more prominent than his fellow publicity-seeking civil rights activist elder, Jesse Jackson. But underneath this "new" Sharpton still lies the old one. From his Harlem headquarters ("House of Justice"), he pushes his varied campaigns under the tag line, "No Justice, No Peace." NAN has opened dozens of active chapters around the nation. Wherever he happens to be at any given moment, the peripatetic Sharpton hasn't forgotten how to go into attack mode, especially if the chosen target is white. He showed this in March 2012 when he traveled to Sanford, Florida to demand the conviction of a young mixed-race white man, George Zimmerman, who by all appearances had engaged in lifesaving self-defense the previous month against a violent black teenaged male, Trayvon Martin (as it turned out, Zimmerman's claim of self-defense was completely justified). Today's Al Sharpton no more hesitates to inflict extreme duress upon a person or community supposedly guilty of injustice toward blacks than the Al Sharpton of 20 or 30 years ago. To "the Rev," what always has mattered is maintaining the appearance that blacks are second-class citizens, all the better to secure affirmative actions slots, political favors, outsized jury awards and reparations on behalf of his people. Armed with moral indignation, selective facts, and contempt for rule of law, Sharpton relishes the opportunity to generate mass outrage over any incident appearing to confirm this appearance. He has a ready-made and large audience willing to hang on his every word.

Sharpton's modus operandi remains the same: 1) take details of a supposedly "racist" incident out of context; 2) recite them as evidence of how the deck is stacked against blacks; and 3) demand immediate and unorthodox steps to obtain "justice." He may pursue this approach with less bombast than during the old days, but he hardly has abandoned them. It speaks volumes about this nation's leaders that Sharpton not only coaxes donations from major corporations, but also has the Democratic Party's top tier virtually groveling for his endorsement. That is real power. But to understand how he got that power and how he maintains it, it is necessary to understand him as a distinct archetype.

CHAPTER 2

AL SHARPTON AS CIVIL RIGHTS RADICAL

Al Sharpton did not emerge from a vacuum. He has a recognizable context. To understand the man, one must understand his social type: the black civil-rights leader, and more to the point, the *radical* black civil-rights leader. Like mid-century figures such as A. Philip Randolph, Bayard Rustin, Whitney Young, James Farmer and most of all, Martin Luther King, Sharpton presses grievances and demand redress on behalf of his people. And like his somewhat older contemporaries, such as Julian Bond and Jesse Jackson, he has a hard, confrontational radical edge. Each of these people, past or present, has a distinct frame of reference: black victimization. And the victimizers are almost always white.

In a contemporary context, black victimization is a difficult if not impossible case to make. The denial of full rights to blacks, in the South or anywhere else in America, is a decades-old relic. Since the mid 1960s, blacks in no meaningful sense can claim they have been relegated to pariah status, a fact in large measure owing to increasingly tolerant white attitudes on race.[1] If crime rates are any guide (as they should be), the situation is quite the reverse. White crime victimization at the hands of blacks is far more common than vice versa.[2] And affirmative action, lately rechristened as "diversity," is set in stone. Blacks, legally, hold the upper hand.

Black civil-rights leaders, whether clergy or not, reject this account. Some might privately agree. But they know that to maintain credibility with their audiences, and remain employed, they cannot publicly admit as much. From their view, when blacks commit crimes, the offenders are reacting, consciously or not, to accumulated generations of injustice. Such behavior is thus "understandable," and as such, requires that whites make special allowances. Oppression of blacks is still a dominant reality, their argument goes. It's just more subtle now. In the world of the black civil rights leader, emotion, heavily driven by religious fervor, rules the day. And there is a large and often shockingly ignorant audience for this.

The equality that Sharpton and other civil rights leaders seek is one of results and not simply one of opportunities. However much they go to lengths to deny it, they already have achieved the latter. But they demand to know, why has equality of result not yet been achieved as well? They cannot accept that rule of law must take precedence over the impulse to smooth out collective disparities in income, wealth, educational attainment or some other social indicator. Nor can they accept that individual skills and character are what matter most in achievement. That there are extraordinarily successful and well-paid individual blacks in American life does not impress them either. Neither does the equally obvious fact that business elites in this country now practically jump over each other to hire blacks for top positions in a never-ending quest for "diversity." Equality, in the eyes of these activists, must be achieved *collectively* or it is meaningless. Even the appearance of indifference toward achievement of collective black equality of result is "racist."

This is arguably the primary reason why full-scale black riots over the last 50 years have occurred mostly outside the South, where expectation levels have been higher. Around late 1965-early 1966, with black rioting already having made its mark upon New York, Los Angeles and other major cities, political scientist James Q. Wilson saw the future:[3]

> *Negroes...are demanding that economic differences between Negroes and whites be eliminated. If the white liberal reformer is to be allowed to abolish the system by which political and economic progress was once made, then he must (many Negroes argue)*

replace it with something better. The Negro demand for economic equality is no longer...simply a demand for equal opportunity; it is a demand for equality of economic results. American politics has for long been accustomed to dealing with ethnic demands for recognition, power, and opportunity; it has never had to face a serious demand for equal economic shares. Thus, in the North as well as the South the principal race issue may be a conflict between liberty and equality. This may be the issue which will distinguish the white liberal from the white radical: the former will work for liberty and equal opportunity, the latter for equal shares. This distinction adds yet another complication to the uneasy liberal-Negro alliance.

This political behavior – radicalism superseding liberalism, while occasionally passing for it – has become the norm in the nearly 50 years since. "They (black civil rights activists) ended up rejecting the system," wrote British journalist Godfrey Hodgson in the Seventies. "But they began as believers in the liberal creed. These young revolutionaries started out convinced of the relevance of the Christian gospel, of the promise of America, and of the righteousness of the federal government. Fear, pain disappointment and betrayal changed them."[4] This interpretation is at once true and distorted. There was radicalization, all right, but it was far less justifiable than the author imagines. Rising expectations should not serve as a rationalization for crime. Moreover, many civil rights radicals, especially Sharpton, did not reject Christianity; they retrofitted it to their own anti-white animus. Many whites likewise became radicalized, recognizing that whole careers could be built upon trophy hunts for manifestations of veiled white racism, and accompanying "code words," that supposedly keep blacks down. To such people, Jim Crow, albeit of a nicer variety, is well and alive.

This psychology lies at the foundation of that strange contemporary god known as "Diversity." And this is Al Sharpton's frame of reference. For him, collective inequality constitutes a gross injustice, an ongoing

legacy of an evil past. Simple justice requires that whites provide com-
pensatory treatment to blacks, however much it might hurt, until the
nation as a whole reaches some undetermined point in the future at
which we all declare in unison: "Social equality has been achieved!"
Of course, this magic day will never come. Anyone can lie with statistics. Equally to the point, any white resistance to this march can be
explained away as "racism." Sharpton explained his position back in
2007, as the legal crisis in Jena, Louisiana (to be discussed later) was
becoming potentially lethal:[5]

> Martin Luther King, Jr., and others faced Jim Crow. We come
> to Jena to face James Crow, Jr., Esq. He's a little more educated,
> a little more polished, but it's the same courthouse steps used to
> beat down our people. And just like our daddies beat Jim Crow,
> we will win the victory over James Crow, Jr.

Paradoxically, Sharpton is also an advocate of black self-help and
moral responsibility. In the conclusion to his 2002 autobiography, *Al on
America*, he writes:[6]

> We have to be just as aggressive, just as hard on ourselves as
> we are on others. In fact, the only way we can have the moral
> authority to challenge others is if we first challenge ourselves. We
> have to be just as vocal about those who use racism as an excuse
> for failure as we are about the individuals and system that use
> racism to knock us down. We must take responsibility for our-
> selves. In a lot of ways we have become our own worst enemy.

On the surface, this quote is at odds with the previous one. Yet
there is no contradiction. In the first statement, Sharpton is denouncing white America for its legacy of oppression of blacks. In the second statement, he is calling upon fellow blacks to do their best in life,
lest they lend credibility to their white oppressors.[7] In each case, he

operates on the assumption that white racism is ever-present. The two sensibilities – denunciation of white injustice and exhortations to black excellence – go hand in hand.

What makes Sharpton truly radical is the incendiary manner in which he mates his racial identity and egalitarianism with the politics of confrontation. The man lives for manufacturing the appearance of a grievance, all the better to avenge it. Even where reasonable people would agree that a grievance is real, Sharpton makes sure to rub salt into the wounds to escalate white collective shame and black collective rage. Any slight committed against a single black, intended or not, thus becomes a grievous crime against *all* blacks. Should his activism produce troubling, even tragic consequences, he will portray himself a decent, misunderstood seeker of truth and justice. And should an interviewer remind him of some of those consequences, he will respond with aggressive evasion – it's all "in the past." A number of years ago, NBC's Tom Brokaw asked Sharpton if he would apologize for his role in the Tawana Brawley case, which centered upon the (false) accusation that several white men, including a police officer and a prosecutor, over several days in November 1987 repeatedly assaulted and raped a black teenaged girl in upstate New York. Sharpton, perhaps in part due to a defamation judgment against him, responded with assertions so unsupported, and unsupportable, that Brokaw dropped the subject.[8]

Al Sharpton, a slippery sort of alpha male, knows that his ability to connect with his audiences depends on his choreographed denials. To admit responsibility for his prior wrongdoing would undermine his credibility and discourage clients from coming to him. His self-anointed aura of moral and political invincibility enables him to become an "adviser" or "spokesman" for alleged victims and their family members, so much the better to line up or provide financial support, media coverage and legal representation. With his blindly loyal supporters in tow, he can make life miserable for the alleged perpetrator(s).

Sharpton's penchant for aggression and character assassination has won him many enemies. Even a certain number of blacks dislike him.

Yet remember this: Al Sharpton does not care what anyone thinks of him. As he puts it, "You cannot be a true leader if you care about what people think or say about you."[9] Even the prospect of assassination does not deter him. He received a glimpse of his own mortality in January 1991 when he was knifed by an angry white spectator prior to one of his by-then many marches through the Bensonhurst section of Brooklyn, N.Y. to shame that entire community over a 1989 murder of a black teen. Yet barely over a half-year later he had recovered enough to fan the flames of anti-white sentiment that led to a full-scale anti-Semitic black riot in Brooklyn's Crown Heights. The result was substantial property destruction, dozens of assaults, and the murder of an Orthodox Jew.

However black leaders emphasize unity among their own racial brethren, they also realize that as members of a minority group comprising only one-eighth of the U.S. population, it is to their advantage to celebrate racial pride in ways that potentially appeal to non-blacks. In this view, they can convey the view that supporting black civil rights is part of a larger struggle against oppression in all its forms. This cross-cultural egalitarianism thus assumes that the struggle of blacks is also the struggle of women, Hispanics, Asians, gays, lesbians, disabled, the unemployed – and seemingly everyone in the world other than white heterosexual males with high disposable incomes. Blacks, in this view, are a natural leading edge in promoting ecumenical progressivism. With noble-sounding rhetoric, a black civil rights leader can make headway as a unifying force, a "healer" of the nation's wounds.

Ecumenical Leftism has been the primary template for civil rights activism in this country from Martin Luther King onward. By establishing linkages with activists fighting for a more just society, one presumably less obsessed with profit and social status, blacks can achieve far more than if they were to fight alone. As victims of injustice, blacks should work with labor, feminist, environmental, gay rights and religious groups to wrest power and wealth from the unaccountable. King was an early proponent of this strategy. His ill-fated campaign in Memphis in

1968, as many know, was as much about union organizing (of city sanitation workers) as it was about racial equality. Al Sharpton, Jesse Jackson and other post-King civil rights paladins also have embraced this as a political strategy.

Jesse Jackson laid out the essence of this strategy in his wildly acclaimed speech at the 1984 Democratic Party national convention in San Francisco.[10] "My constituency," he remarked, "is the desperate, the damned, the disinherited, the disrespected, and the despised." He continued with this master metaphor:

> *America is not like a blanket – one piece of unbroken cloth, the same color, the same texture, the same size. America is more like a quilt: many patches, many pieces, many colors, many sizes, all woven and held together by a common thread. The white, the Hispanic, the black, the Arab, the Jew, the woman, the native American, the small farmer, the businessperson, the environmentalist, the peace activist, the young, the old, the lesbian, the gay, and the disabled make up the American quilt.*

This is the language of civil rights radicalism, a *faux*-populism holding America to be a glorious, diverse "quilt," "rainbow" or "mosaic" whose components serve as celebrations of demographic diversity. Underlying its litany of "excluded" groups of people is a deep animosity toward the idea that America should stand for anything in particular. As a microcosm of the world, we have no moral right to exclude any individual or group from the rainbow. No one component should be seen as more defining than any other. As applied to a political context, this vision necessarily undermines rather than promotes peace and harmony. By mobilizing disparate interest groups into pressing grievances against the larger power structure, it fails to recognize that many of these grievances will clash with one another – and that as government is pressed into the role of broker to mollify interest-group conflict, it necessarily aggressively grows in size and scope.

Al Sharpton embraces this view of social justice. At the 50th Anniversary for the March on Washington in August 2013, he declared: "As we fight for voters' rights, as we fight for jobs, as we fight for immigration, as we fight for equality, let us not try to limit the coalition. We need all of us together."[11] At the same rally, Rep. John Lewis, D-Ga., who actually had been one of the speakers at the original 1963 March on Washington, provided this slice of Rainbowspeak: "All of us, it doesn't matter if we're black, white, Native American or Asian-American. It doesn't matter if we're straight or gay. We are one family. We are one house. We all live in the same house."[12] Attorney General Eric Holder, as of this writing set to leave his post, spoke similarly at the rally. In favorably comparing the participants in 2013 with those of the 1963 event, he declared: "Their march is now our march. Our focus has broadened to include the cause of women, of Latinos, of Asian-Americans, of lesbians, of gays, of people with disabilities and of countless others across this great country who still yearn for equality, opportunity and fair treatment as we recommit ourselves to the quest for justice."[13] The Rainbow idea, in a sense, is the political realization of Maya Angelou's poem, "On the Pulse of Morning," which the author read at President Clinton's 1993 inauguration.[14]

Sharpton is a Rainbow radical. He is committed to social change in ways that overturn existing power and property relations, mobilizing opposition to those now holding power under the guise of "justice." He angrily rejects the idea that whites, even if they remain a majority, ought to play a dominant role in this country. And his radicalism is one of style, not just belief. Few public figures are so given to drawing wild conclusions in the wake of any report of a criminal act with racial implications. This recklessness springs from an implicit assumption that whites should be assumed guilty until proven innocent – the very antithesis of a functioning criminal justice system. Sharpton will twist or ignore facts until the storyline conforms to the preordained script.

In this respect, at least, the Reverend Al has veered away from his original employer and early mentor, Martin Luther King. To be sure,

King was a man of the Left. Yet he was not a hothead. He approached a given allegation of injustice against a black in a deliberate and rational manner. In his defining written work, "Letter from Birmingham Jail," King noted: "In any nonviolent campaign, there are four basic steps: collection of the facts to determine whether injustices are alive, negotiation, self-purification, and direct action."[15] Al Sharpton, unfortunately, has made a career habit of skipping Step Number One: He begins with an assumption that an accusation by a black against a white should be taken at face value. If he bothers to collect facts at all, it is to collect only those facts that bolster his guiding assumption – and even there, he will distort the context of events. Tawana Brawley is black and thus *must* be believed. Trayvon Martin, the Florida teenager who was shot to death while brutally assaulting a white neighborhood patrol volunteer, was black and thus his supporters' version of events *must* be believed. Sharpton has taken King's idea of direct action and injected it with rumor, hysteria and rioting. This is radicalism of an unusually pernicious sort – a radicalism that assumes values should shape facts rather than vice versa.

Never underestimate the role of black churches in all this. Black clergy, often joined by white clergy, long have played a central role in organizing disparate forces to advance the cause of civil rights. At the same time, they have their audiences in the proverbial palms of their hands. The black church style appeals to ecstatic emotions, replete with singing, shouting and escalating call-and-response audience participation. Their preachers *want* to lead. And their congregations *want* to be led. Churches long have heavily defined black communal life. The eminent black sociologist, E. Franklin Frazier (1894-1962), concluded in his posthumous book, *The Negro Church in America*, that "an organized religious life became the chief means by which a structured or organized social life came into existence among the Negro masses."[16] But Frazier also cautioned that black church leaders have an authoritarian relationship with their congregations in ways that preclude challenges from within. Its style is rarely adaptable to political debate. In their world, images of black suffering and redemption are utterly crucial. A wound inflicted on one black is a wound inflicted on all blacks. Veracity of facts matter less than feelings of righteous cleansing and redemption. While emotionally liberating, it is also intensely collectivistic. And in the world of politics, that can be highly dangerous.

Al Sharpton, an ordained minister by age 10, comes from this tradition. Say what one will about his manifold reprehensible campaigns, but Christianity – in a distinctly black voice – is the core of his existence. He will be the first to say that preaching to a congregation gives him more satisfaction than leading a political rally. He has numerous friends and allies among the black clergy, including National Action Network Chairman W. Franklyn Richardson. The frequent charge leveled by many on the Right – that Sharpton is a "fake Reverend" and a "fake Christian" – is pure wishful thinking. Such a charge is understandable given the desire to separate him from a putatively sensible black mainstream. But it won't work as political triangulation or as theology. It thoroughly underestimates his appeal to his core audience. For better or worse, Sharpton embodies black Protestantism. He knows which Bible passages and metaphors will inspire his audiences. That's why his bombast and cadence, while shot through with demagoguery, falls upon receptive ears. From the frame of reference of his audiences, he is speaking the truth to the salt of the earth. He is "telling it like it is."

Yet Al Sharpton speaks more than to just church congregations. He also speaks to the country. He views the second audience as an extension of the first. In each case, he believes he is on the side of righteousness and justice. In so doing, he has ingratiated himself into highest echelons of American life. Despite his history of character assassination, incitement to riot and financial impropriety, he now may be the most influential person in all of America, save for President Obama, and some corporate CEOs and entertainers. Calling him a rabble rouser will do no good. Sharpton will respond that Jesus of Nazareth, Adam Clayton Powell and Martin Luther King also were called rabble rousers in their day. And he will go about his mission, not caring a whit what one thinks of him.

Al Sharpton is tailor-made for the age of mass media. Manufacturing the appearance of injustice is a task made lot easier when television, newspapers and other sources of reports provide a selective lens, a validation of the view that holds blacks to be noble sufferers. This facilitates that one-sided chimera, a "national conversation on race." White corporate, labor, philanthropic and other elites, petrified of being tarred as "racists" or enemies of "diversity" (and of subsequent exile to the margins of public life), often yield to their accusers rather than vocally oppose them. Worse yet, they open their checkbooks as readily as they close their mouths. The term "civil rights" has become more weapon than high principle.

Sharpton has given civil rights radicalism an extra dose of street theater and menace. He may be "colorful" or "expressive" in the pejorative sense, but he should not be underestimated. To reach the pinnacle of power, one must have savvy, energy and an ability to size people up. And Sharpton, who *has* reached that pinnacle, has such traits in abundance. People who should know better often walk away as admirers. *New York Times* national political correspondent Adam Nagourney, reviewing Sharpton's 2002 book, *Al on America*, called its author "smart, articulate and eloquent...perceptive, funny and fearless." He added: "As anyone who has heard him talk from a pulpit can testify, Sharpton is a man with a heart and firm ideological beliefs...He has a command of politics that rivals some of the great New York party bosses. No less significant, he has an understanding of the way the press works that rivals more than a few city editors in this town."[17] The late New York City mayor, Edward Koch, who often feuded with Sharpton during his three terms in office during the late-Seventies and the Eighties, often calling him "Al Charlatan," adjusted his opinion years later: "Al Sharpton is maligned by a lot of people, but I happen to like him. He is a bona fide black leader, and by leader I mean someone who can say, 'I need people to mobilize and to picket,' and 5,000 people will come out."[18]

This book also believes in a need to mobilize – in opposition. It rests on the premise that while nobody is "all good" or "all bad," Sharpton is a lot closer to the latter than to the former. And the fact that he arguably has become more influential than any black civil rights leader in U.S. history – yes, even more than Martin Luther King – requires a methodical challenge to his legitimacy. He is a formidable opponent, far more so than some blowhard storefront preacher. That is why it is crucial to *build* a case against Sharpton. Reeling off a list of his greatest fits simply won't do. Building a case is not easy. There are reasons why he is the way he is. To put those reasons in context requires going back to his roots.

CHAPTER 3
EARLY YEARS, DEFINING INFLUENCES

It's a manifestation of human nature's dark side: Appalling and infamous lives provoke fascination. This certainly holds true for Al Sharpton. Countless people, including those who oppose him, can't seem to get enough of him. He's a public spectacle, a gladiator offering free info-tainment for the many – a break from their humdrum existence. His views aside, Sharpton's aggressive alpha male public behavior fascinates precisely because he so often gets away with it and remains unfazed. For that reason, he projects not just incredulity as well as invincibility. Many whites often have asked: Why is Sharpton so wild and crazy? Why can't he be a nice, *sensible* civil-rights leader like Martin Luther King? Actually, there are reasons why Sharpton is the way he is. And King, as we soon shall see, happened to be one of them.

Alfred Charles "Al" Sharpton Jr. was born on October 3, 1954 in Brooklyn, New York to Alfred Sharpton Sr. and his wife, Ada Sharpton. The father, a building contractor who in young Alfred's own words was a "slumlord," made enough money to move the family to a large home in the middle-class Queens neighborhood of Hollis. "At one point," young Al observed, "my father was doing so well he bought two Cadillacs every year, one for my mother, one for him."[1] The son wasn't poor, but he was rambunctious:[2]

I yelled when I was hungry. I yelled when I was wet. I yelled when all those little black bourgeois babies stayed dignified and quiet. I learned before I got out of the maternity ward that you've got to holler like hell sometimes to get what you want.

He would find an outlet for all that hollering early on. At age 4, he discovered he could preach. Encouraged by his parents, young Alfred was delivering sermons regularly at a local Pentecostal church, the Washington Temple of God in Christ. Dozens and even hundreds of worshippers would gather every Sunday to hear this "wonder boy preacher" speak the Word. By age 10, he was ordained as a minister by the church's pastor, Bishop Frederick Douglass Washington, himself a public figure with his own radio show. Sharpton by now was touring with gospel singer Mahalia Jackson, astonishing audiences with his Bible-thumping oratory. At school, Alfred would sign his homework with the title, "Reverend," annoying his teachers to no end. Reverend Washington expressed a fervent hope that this child prodigy one day would marry his daughter and become temple pastor.

It was not to be. And the main reason lay on the home front. Around 1963-64,[3] Alfred Sharpton Sr. left his wife for a younger woman. The added kick was that the woman happened to be his own stepdaughter – that is, his wife's daughter from a previous marriage. Young Alfred was dumbstruck; his dad and half-sister, Tina, had run off together. They would have a child, Kenny.[4] Meanwhile, Mrs. Sharpton and her two children from her second marriage, Alfred Jr. and Cheryl, found themselves struggling. They moved out of their Hollis home and into a cheap Brooklyn apartment. She worked as a maid, supplementing her income with public assistance. In short order, even sister Cheryl left to be with her father.

It is not at all unreasonable to suggest that Al Sharpton during this time hungered for a substitute father, as his biological father for all intents and purposes was out of the picture. Indeed, Sharpton freely admits as much. In his most recent autobiography, *The Rejected Stone*, he looked back:[5]

One day he (my father) was there, the next day he was gone.
I didn't understand the gravity of the incest, but I knew that
his act instantly transformed my life and traumatized our entire
family. My world flipped overnight. The whole ordeal almost
gave my mother a nervous breakdown, and it cast me out on a
lifelong journey to fill the hole he left in my heart and to search
for men who could act as stand-ins for the father I no longer
had.

Over the years young Alfred would find several such men, each in
his own way an ambitious, charismatic and narcissistic black male willing to stand up for himself.

The first such defining influence was Adam Clayton Powell, Jr.,
a Harlem clergyman, civil rights activist and eventually New York
Congressman.[6] Powell, who was born in 1908 and died in 1972, was
something of an enigma. He had extensive white ancestry, so much
so that at first glance it was easy to mistake him for Caucasian. Yet he
made his blackness into a calling. He distrusted whites and positively
loathed black "Uncle Toms" who took orders from them. Adam Clayton
Powell never took orders from anyone. And for decades, much of black
America saw him as a hero because of that.

Powell, who held a master's degree in theology from Columbia, became a public figure during the Depression. His father had been lead
pastor at Harlem's Abyssinian Baptist Church. Powell inherited the position in 1937. By then, he'd already acquired a reputation as the firebrand
chairman of the Coordinating Committee for Employment, a precursor
to Sharpton's National Action Network and Jesse Jackson's Rainbow/
PUSH Coalition. Through the committee, Powell organized mass meet-
ings, rent strikes, and threats of boycotts against white employers who
didn't hire enough blacks. The last activity proved especially effective
against the management of the 1939 World's Fair in New York, the City's
bus transit authority, and white owners of Harlem drug stores.

Politics was a logical next step. In 1941, Powell ran for New York City Council and won, becoming the first black ever to hold a seat. In 1944, he ran for Congress, campaigning for a new seat encompassing Harlem. Again, he won. Almost as soon as he arrived, Powell proved a formidable legislator, applying his taste for brinksmanship to a wide range of issues. He was instrumental – far more than people today realize – in generating support for progressive legislation, especially after becoming chairman of the House Education and Labor Committee in 1961. Many of President Kennedy's New Frontier and (especially) President Johnson's Great Society initiatives might not have come to fruition without Powell's persistence.

Adam Clayton Powell in 1966. (AP/Wide World)

Adam Clayton Powell, never one to duck combat on Capitol Hill, frequently came home to preach. At age 11, Al Sharpton became part of his audience. Having read a biography of Powell, he was determined to see him. He recalls the first encounter:[7]

I'll never forget to this day the first time I actually laid eyes on Adam Clayton Powell Jr. He walked out of the side door into the sanctuary in his robe, with that straight, long posture. He walked up those marble stairs to the semicircular pulpit. I thought I had seen God....He had this magnetism and this majestic air. He was very elegant, but at the same time defiant – a real man's man.

After the sermon, Sharpton screwed up the courage to seek a personal meeting. After persistent pleading with Powell's secretary, he met his idol face to face. And to Sharpton's own surprise, Powell recognized him, exclaiming, "Alfred Sharpton! Boy preacher from Brooklyn." The Congressman, it turned out, was a fan of F. D. Washington's radio program. It was the start of a long friendship. Young Alfred henceforth would be "the kid" in Powell's entourage.

Sharpton learned plenty of lessons from Adam Clayton Powell, but they weren't necessarily the right ones. Powell enjoyed flaunting his power, and the money that went with it, regularly shuttling between Washington and his island vacation home in Bimini, the Bahamas. The money for the good life came out of illegal withdrawals from committee funds – or so Powell's colleagues had determined following an investigation. The House Democratic Caucus in January 1967 stripped him of his chairmanship, and two months later, the full House of Representatives voted 307-116 to exclude him from their ranks. His seat now vacant, Powell campaigned the following month in a special election to get it back. He won. His House colleagues disallowed him from taking his seat. Powell promptly sued to rescind that decision, eventually winning in the Supreme Court in June 1969,[8] following his re-election the previous November. He emerged from self-imposed exile in Bimini and returned to Congress, minus his seniority. He ran for re-election in 1970, this time losing in the Democratic primary to Charles Rangel, who would go onto victory in the general election and retain the seat to this very day. Powell, meanwhile, died in April 1972 of acute prostatitis.

Sharpton defends Powell's legacy, despite the blemishes. He writes: "What I learned from Powell about leadership…is that you can't care what people think. Adam Clayton Powell did not care about being accepted by society." In a defining moment, he recalls advice Powell gave him sitting in a car:[9]

> *"Kid…Don't ever forget this: If you expose your own weaknesses, they can never use them against you. 'Cause can't nobody tell what everybody already knows. What might appear to be reckless behavior on my part is really defense. They can never threaten to expose me, because I expose myself.*

Powell also inculcated in Sharpton a hatred of blacks who projected weakness:[10]

> *These yellow Uncle Toms are taking over the blacks in New York. Don't you stop fighting. If you want to do something for Adam, get rid of these Uncle Toms.*

Nobody can doubt that Al Sharpton has taken these words to heart. The second great influence on Sharpton was Martin Luther King, Jr. Around age 13, Sharpton got his initiation into the world of civil-rights activism, working as a youth minister in the Brooklyn, N.Y. office of Operation Breadbasket, a multi-city boycott managed by King's Southern Christian Leadership Conference (SCLC) against white small business owners who failed to hire blacks or buy from black suppliers in certain quantities.[11] Sharpton on occasion did meet King, though the significance of the encounters wouldn't sink in until after the latter's assassination. He writes:[12]

> *I met Dr. King a couple of times. He knew me as "the boy preacher." When he would see me, he would say, "There goes that boy preacher!," and a big grin would break over his face. I*

felt good being a part of something he was involved in, and the loss (of his life) was definitely felt. But my mother's reaction – how hard she took it – confused me….

I understood her intellectually, but I didn't feel what she was saying until about a year later. I went to see a movie at the Loews Theater on Flatbush Avenue in Brooklyn. They were showing "King: From Montgomery to Memphis," a documentary on his thirteen-year career. At the end of the movie, Nina Simone sang this song: "Why? The King of Love is Dead." "Turn down your TV set; love your neighbor was his plea," and she asked, "What we gonna do now that the king of love is dead?" That's when it hit me…

What we gonna do? We couldn't just act like, now that King was gone, everything he worked for would stop. As Nina Simone sang her song, they showed Dr. King's funeral procession. There were horses carrying his body, a horse-drawn wagon with his casket in a glass case trotting through town. That image was all I could think about for days.

I sat there and made up my mind that there was something I had to do. I had to try and keep his legacy alive. I was only fourteen years old, but I knew I could do something, that I must do something. I went back to Breadbasket and asked if I could be youth director and began my journey to carry on Dr. King's legacy.

Some revisionism is necessary here. Sharpton's critics, such as journalists Juan Williams and Margaret Carlson, typically charge that he has "betrayed" Martin Luther King's vision. Where King was a selfless crusader who built bridges across humanity, goes the argument, Sharpton is merely a publicity-seeking buffoon who delights in tearing those bridges down.[13] This accusation isn't entirely false. King, at least, analyzed a situation dispassionately before swinging into action. Unlike Sharpton, he did not automatically take the word of a black individual or family declaring an injustice. King also steered clear of anti-Semitism;[14] Sharpton (though he vociferously denies it) more than once has encouraged it. King was modest in his tastes. Sharpton is flashy; he typically flies first-class and stays in deluxe hotel suites.[15] And King, if mainly because of the era in which he lived, challenged real injustices. Sharpton, by contrast, invents or exaggerates them.

But there are a number of considerations that undermine the "betrayal" line, which taken together, debunk the view held by a large number of naïve whites, especially on the Right, that Martin Luther King represented a Noble Exception in the world of civil rights activism. For starters, King's immediate family members are among Reverend Sharpton's staunchest allies. In 2001 King's now-deceased widow, Coretta Scott King, called Sharpton "a voice for the oppressed, a leader who has protested injustice with a passionate and unrelenting commitment to nonviolent action in the spirit and tradition of Martin Luther King, Jr." And King's oldest son, Martin Luther King III,[16] frequently has appeared with Sharpton at National Action Network functions and public protests. The younger King also co-hosted NAN's "Keepers of the Dream" awards ceremony in Memphis in 2008. Granted, one isn't automatically defined by immediate family members. Yet it is inconceivable that the elder King, were he alive today, would diverge from the rest of his family in any meaningful way on the issue of Al Sharpton. King might scold Sharpton from time to time, much as a father admonishing an impetuous son, but each would seek similar results.

Second, Sharpton's means are similar to those of King. Martin Luther King was Sharpton's first real employer. And Sharpton was a highly willing pupil. He learned from King the importance of *direct action* as a tool for negotiation. In "Letter from Birmingham Jail," King wrote: "(T)he purpose of direct action is to create a situation so crisis-packed that it will inevitably open the door for negotiation."[17] Is this not Sharpton's way? And like King, Sharpton maximizes events for dramatic effect, always with media coverage in mind. He also learned from King the value of networking, of building ties to labor, business, religious, philanthropic, and other types of organizations not normally focused on race, in order to advance the betterment of blacks. King, more than anyone else, used this strategy as a template for civil rights activism. Sharpton has worked with that template. He has not broken it.

Third and finally, Martin Luther King, like Al Sharpton, was a man of the Left. There is no getting around that. The notion that King was a "conservative" – and a Republican to boot – is one of those urban legends with a life of its own.[18] The record completely contradicts any such notion. From his graduate theology student years at Boston University onward, King very consciously drew upon certain traditions of socialism and pacifism to advance his idea of moral justice.[19] He came to support, and very explicitly, what we now call affirmative action and reparations, advocating large compensatory payments from whites to blacks.[20] His Poor People's Campaign, held in Washington, D.C. during May and June of 1968 in the wake of his assassination, amounted to a social welfare shakedown, replete with an Economic Bill of Rights and a makeshift "Tent City" on government property. And his commitment to pacifism was selective. When it came to world peace, Martin Luther King came to see the United States as the primary threat to it. His anti-Viet Nam war speech at Riverside Church in Manhattan on April 4, 1967, exactly one year prior to his assassination, was a nascent expression of the sort of Third World liberationist rhetoric that Jesse Jackson later would elevate into an art. The speech was highly eloquent, yet it testified to how far leftward King really leaned.

King's eventual heir to leadership, Jesse Jackson, would be another defining influence on Sharpton. Like Reverend Al, Jackson had gotten his civil rights career launch through King; he headed the Chicago office of Operation Breadbasket. On his visits to New York, Jackson on occasion would visit the group's Brooklyn office, headed by a Baptist minister, Reverend William Augustus Jones, eventually Sharpton's pastor until his death in 2006.[21] It was there where Sharpton and Jackson met. "I met the Reverend Jesse Jackson for the first time when I was about twelve years old," Sharpton recalls. "I was still very much the boy preacher in Brooklyn."[22] Jackson, whom Sharpton calls "my teacher," seemed impressive because he wasn't concerned about respectability in the conventional sense:[23]

> *He was in his late twenties, and right away we identified with each other. Jesse was younger than the other preachers of that time. He wouldn't even wear a suit and tie. Jesse always used to wear a medallion like Adam. And he sported the buck vest and a big 'fro.*
>
> *I later learned that he had been born out of wedlock and came from a broken home, like I did. He didn't come out of the seminary, wasn't one of those collegiate types. He wasn't like that. Jesse was regular....We just hit it off. I became his protégé. I started wearing medallions like his and I used to try to talk like him.*

Jackson also provided Sharpton with a job, making him national youth director of Operation Breadbasket in 1969. In 1971, near the end of that group's existence, Sharpton left to form his own nonprofit group, National Youth Movement (NYM). He openly acknowledged his debt to Martin Luther King and Jesse Jackson in his wide-ranging projects, which included urging black children in Harlem to participate in the then-new Christmastime black holiday of Kwanzaa; organizing and getting arrested at a sit-in demonstration at City Hall to demand summer jobs for black teenagers; getting arrested for sitting in front of the New York City Board of Education president during a protest; and leading a group of demonstrators along Wall Street who painted red "x" marks on office buildings which he claimed were fronts for drug dealing. Sharpton claimed that NYM had around 30,000 members in 16 cities and was effective in ridding the street of drug dealers. But Victor Genecin, a former New York State prosecutor and a now private-sector litigator, countered that the group was "never anything more than a one-room office in Brooklyn with a telephone and an ever-changing handful of staffers who took Al Sharpton's messages and ran his errands."[24]

Mentor and protegé in 2006. (AP/Wide World)

Sharpton and Jackson would continue their friendship over the years. "Jesse Jackson is probably the smartest person I know," Sharpton writes. "There's no one I know who has a more brilliant, fertile mind."[25] While the two have had their disagreements – Sharpton, for example, is far more sympathetic than Jackson toward black nationalists – they have wound up reconciling. When they first met, Jesse instructed Sharpton, "All you got to do is choose your targets and kick ass."[26] Sharpton has shown he's adept at both.

Throughout his career, Sharpton has emulated Jackson, going so far as to assemble a videotape library of his performances.[27] What Sharpton learned is that a combination of media-friendly ambition, intimidation and charisma can go a long way in extracting concessions from whites and covering one's tracks. For nearly five decades, Jackson has built a reputation as a leader by telling blacks, and eventually many whites, things they *want* to hear, whether or not these statements correspond to reality.[28] As much as Adam Clayton Powell and Martin Luther King, Jackson has displayed a gift for mobilizing audiences into action, while keeping the messy details of money and power in the background. This sounds like Al Sharpton, too, which is why a closer look at Jackson is in order.

Jesse Louis Jackson, Sr. was born in 1941 in Greenville, South Carolina. Like so many civil-rights leaders, from the beginning he has shown high fluency in the language of the street and the church. In the immediate aftermath of the King assassination in April 1968, Jackson, a newly self-anointed "Reverend," saw an opportunity to put his skills into practice, though by unorthodox means. He enlisted the help of a violent Chicago gang, the Black Stone Rangers, to intimidate local business owners into making "contributions" to Operation Breadbasket. Under the guise of promoting social justice, Jesse Jackson and his cronies, especially Black Stone Ranger leader Jeff Fort, ran what amounted to a robbery and extortion racket. Kenneth Timmerman, author of an exhaustive biography of Jackson, quotes a Chicago criminal justice official:[29]

> *Jeff Fort and the Jester would make the rounds of the small business owners, telling them that if they didn't contribute, 'We'll burn you down,' another official recalled. 'It was a shakedown, pure and simple. They called themselves community organizers. In those early days, Jackson boasted of his ties to the gangs. 'I get a lot of them to go to church. I baptized Jeff Fort at Fellowship Baptist Church,' he told one reporter.*

The Black Stone Rangers would change their name to El Rukn (Arabic for "The Foundation").[30] If this was part of an image makeover, it didn't work. Its leaders, including Jeff Fort, eventually were arrested and successfully prosecuted for murder, extortion, drug dealing and racketeering. With the Fort-controlled faction in federal prison, a new crop of thugs took over the El Rukns. One of those thugs was Noah Robinson, Jr., Jesse Jackson's half-brother. Robinson was an unusual character. A graduate of the University of Pennsylvania's Wharton School of Finance, he came to Chicago in 1969 to become full-time director of Operation Breadbasket's commercial division. Eventually building a multimillion dollar empire, his seemingly impeccable credentials ensured ample cover for El Rukn – and for himself and Jesse Jackson, the latter of whom now headed his own group, Operation PUSH (People United to Save Humanity).[31] "There was one very powerful reason why none of us spoke out more loudly against Jesse for all those years," remarked one local black minister. "It was fear of the long arm of the black mafia that Jesse's half-brother controlled."[32]

Years later, in September 1988, Robinson was arrested in Greenville, S.C. on racketeering, drug trafficking and murder-for-hire charges.[33] He and four co-defendants, each a ranking El Rukn leader, eventually were convicted by a federal jury on various charges, the most serious of which was the 1986 murder in Greenville of a former Robinson friend, Leroy "Hambone" Barber, and the subsequent attempted murder-for-hire of a business associate and a woman who had witnessed the Barber murder. Lawyers for the El Rukns managed to get the convictions thrown out, alleging prosecutorial misconduct, but in 1996 a federal jury again found the defendants guilty.[34] Jesse Jackson, ever the consummate politician, downplayed his relationship to his half-brother.

If Jackson has been circumspect about his underworld ties, he's been positively exhibitionistic in his friendships with present and former leaders of Third World dictatorships and terrorist movements, whom he sees as articulating legitimate grievances for the sake of people's liberation. Jackson at various points has drawn close to Fidel Castro (Cuba), Yasser Arafat (Palestine Liberation Organization), Charles Taylor (Liberia), Jose Eduardo Dos Santos (Angola), Ibrahim Babangida (Nigeria) and Robert Mugabe (Zimbabwe) – tyrants one and all – providing support for their causes and securing support for his own. Bill Clinton's election and subsequent re-election as U.S. president proved a boon to Jackson, who had grown close to him. In October 1997, Clinton's Secretary of State, Madeleine Albright, appointed Jackson "Special Envoy for the President and Secretary of State for the Promotion of Democracy in Africa." For years, he would enjoy virtual carte blanche in building a power base among African leaders, on occasion applying face-to-face shakedown tactics he'd practiced on Chicago's small merchants. He demanded and got, for example, a share of assets privatized by the government of Zambia.[35]

Jackson's religiously-themed hard-Left egalitarianism also would inform his views on domestic policy. No American welfare state, it seemed, was sufficiently large for him. Even the modest steps that Congress and the Republican White House took to curb federal spending were subterfuges for a war on the salt of the earth. Looking back on the Eighties, Jackson noted: "The Reagan years were devastating to us all. For eight years the lights were turned off."[36] This was errant nonsense,[37] but his audiences ate it up.

During the Nineties and beyond, Jesse Jackson has used his connections and financial backing to go on corporate treasure hunts. Texaco, Nike, Toyota and Anheuser-Busch have been among the companies who, following spurious accusations of racial discrimination by Jackson and his allies, have capitulated to exorbitant settlements. Jackson also took on the nation's citadel of public trading, the New York Stock Exchange (NYSE), through a new gambit, the Wall Street Project. Setting up shop rent-free in New York City's Trump Tower, Jackson coaxed large donations from such financial titans as First Boston, Merrill Lynch, Morgan Stanley and the Travelers Group in preparation for the project's grand opening of January 14-16, 1998. President Bill Clinton, Federal Reserve Chairman Alan Greenspan, Treasury Secretary Robert Rubin, and Donald Trump paid their respects to Jackson at the January 15 gala fundraising event on the NYSE trading floor, timed to coincide with Martin Luther King's birthday. It was the first in a continuing series of extravaganzas.

Al Sharpton learned his lessons well. Having observed Jackson sanitize his past by ingratiating himself with the pillars of American life, he figured he could succeed in this endeavor as well. Since "powerful" whites had shown themselves to be weak-kneed, Sharpton recognized that merely hurling an accusation of racism at them could reap rewards. A company could make its public relations problems go away by making a generous donation to National Action Network. Even better, its guilt-ridden top officials might come to accept Sharpton's views.

If Jesse Jackson was Al Sharpton's surrogate older brother, then James Brown was Sharpton's surrogate father. Brown, more than anyone else, came to define Sharpton's style and mission. As a child, young Alfred often would accompany his biological father to concerts by the late rhythm n' blues artist at the Apollo Theater in Harlem. He, like countless audiences, was entranced by Brown and his band's raw energy, precision playing and tight choreography. The recent film biopic, *Get on Up*, effectively captured the essence of Brown in his glory – and ugliness.[38]

Brown for a while actually lived in the same Hollis neighborhood where Sharpton was growing up. They met for the first time about a year after Sharpton's graduation from Brooklyn's Tilden High School. In his most recent autobiography, *The Rejected Stone*, he recalls the encounter:[39]

> *In 1973, when I was eighteen, James heard about my National Youth Movement and decided he wanted to help me raise money by doing a benefit concert. James seemed to really like me and took me under his wing. He started inviting me to his shows to help out, eventually bringing me all around the world with him and even appointing me as his manager because he knew he could trust me. Our relationship became like father and son. In fact, James's father, Joe Brown, once said I brought out the best in James because he wanted to live up to my admiration of him.*

Thus a lifelong bond was formed. The bond would grow closer early on when one of Brown's sons, Teddy, who was a member of National Youth Movement, tragically died in an auto accident. Sharpton would make Brown's musical revue the main focus of his social and professional life for the remainder of the decade, even as he set up NYM chapters around the country.[40] Through Brown, he met his future wife, Kathy Jordan, a backup singer with the band. Brown, in fact, was the person who convinced Sharpton to shorten his public name from "Alfred" to "Al." Years later Sharpton looked back upon those years as life-defining:[41]

> *(T)he person who had the greatest influence over me and is most responsible for the man I am today is James Brown. He had more impact on my life than any civil rights leader – maybe even more than my own mother. What I learned from him makes it possible for me to do the things I do today…(My) job was to carry his bag (of cash) around the country. But my real job was just to be his son. James Brown taught me about being a man. He gave me life skills that I never got from my own father. He taught me about self-respect, dignity, and self-definition.*

What Sharpton doesn't acknowledge is that his mentor, who died of natural causes at age 73 on Christmas Day, 2006, was highly deficient in any number of basic life skills. While it was hard to ignore Brown's prodigious talent and energy, it was impossible to look past his sociopathic tendencies.

"Dissent" was not a word in James Brown's vocabulary – at least if someone else was dissenting from him. He frequently would levy fines on band members for being late, missing notes, violating his dress code or engaging in back talk. This treatment eventually prompted a permanent walkout in 1969 of nearly all members of his longtime band, the Famous Flames. "James was bossy and paranoid," recalled former trombonist Fred Wesley. "I didn't see why someone of his stature would be so defensive. I couldn't understand the way he treated his band, why he was so evil."[42] Brown's bullying style also was manifest in his insistence upon an extreme formality of address. In *Al on America*, Sharpton favorably recalls a backstage incident on "The Tonight Show" in which Brown angrily ordered his band to pack up their gear and walk off rather than play; host Johnny Carson apparently had committed the cardinal sin of addressing the singer by his first name rather than as "Mr. Brown."[43]

With singer James Brown in 1982. (AP/Wide World)

Brown's behavior wasn't simply controlling; on many occasions it was criminal. During his teenage years in Augusta, Georgia, he'd done a stint in reform school for burglary. While one might overlook this, given his youth and extreme poverty, far less excusable were his frequent criminal acts well into adulthood. The best-known of these events occurred on September 24, 1988, several years after Sharpton had gone out on his own. High on PCP and armed with a shotgun, Brown terrorized attendees at an insurance seminar held in a building in Augusta that he owned. Tipped off, local police arrived on the scene. Rather than risk being arrested, Brown led police on a high-speed motor vehicle chase through the streets of Augusta, Georgia and eventually on Interstate 20 in Georgia and South Carolina until the cops managed to shoot out three of his tires. He was convicted of carrying an unlicensed pistol and assaulting a police officer, plus various drug and driving offenses. He received concurrent six-year sentences from Georgia and South Carolina, serving 15 months in prison and another 10 months in a work release program.[44]

Brown easily might have gone to prison for another 1988 offense. His then-publicist, Jacque Hollander, alleged that while riding with Brown in a van in South Carolina, the singer suddenly pulled her to the side of the road and raped her at gunpoint. Ms. Hollander, to her regret, did not file a criminal complaint until 2002. The judge dismissed the case on grounds that the statute of limitations had expired. Three years later, Hollander filed a civil suit, but again statute-of-limitation requirements precluded introduction of DNA and other evidence.[45] James Brown lucked out.

Brown also behaved rather badly at his Beech Island, South Carolina mansion, again emerging unscathed. His third wife, Adrienne Rodriguez, had him arrested for assault on four separate occasions, dropping charges in the first three instances before finally following through in the fourth (she would die in 1996 of natural causes).[46] Brown's old habits would die hard. His fourth wife, Tomi Raye Hynie, had him arrested in January 2004 after he'd pushed her to the floor during an argument. He pleaded no contest, but served no jail time. It wasn't just wives who had to be careful. On July 3, 2000, police were summoned to Brown's home after he brandished a steak knife at a South Carolina

Electric & Gas repairman, Russell Eubanks, and held him against his will. Eubanks had come to the estate in response to a report of a power outage. An officer from the Aiken County Sheriff's Office questioned Brown for about two hours, but did not arrest him.[47]

Brown even exercised his criminal impulses against a fellow prominent black rhythm & blues/soul artist, Joseph Arrington Jr., aka "Joe Tex."[48] James Brown and Joe Tex, who died in 1982, had a running feud going back to the mid-50s when each was affiliated with the King Records label. They frequently accused each other of ripping off material and stage moves. In the early 60s, Brown had the temerity to use Tex's estranged wife as a backup vocalist for a studio recording. The rivalry came to a head in 1963 after a concert in Macon, Georgia. They were on the same bill, with Tex opening for Brown. The promoter should have known better. During his set, Tex sarcastically mimicked Brown's familiar routine of feigning a collapse onto the stage floor, only to be resurrected to his feet by an assistant with a regal cape draped around his shoulder. Brown was incensed, especially given that Georgia was his home turf. After the show was over, Brown learned that Tex was attending an after-show party at a local nightclub. He was determined to meet him, gun in hand. Tex was there. So was one of Tex's allies, possibly a bodyguard. And that person likewise was armed. The two, after encountering each other, exchanged several rounds of fire. Several people in the audience were shot, though not fatally. Brown was never prosecuted.

Even putting the best face on all this, allowing for extenuating personal circumstances, Brown's pattern of criminal behavior was an outgrowth of his banana republic dictator personality. With James Brown, it was either his way or the highway. As not doing his bidding was a mark of "disrespect," Brown would have an instant rationalization for exacting retaliation against the "offender." His accumulation of wealth, fame and power did not mitigate this pattern. If anything, it reinforced it.

Sharpton might not have inherited Brown's propensity for spur-of-the-moment crime, but he did inherit his aggressive, preening narcissism. Like Brown, Sharpton always has had enormous difficulty understanding the practical limitations of power. As that related to his line of work, he cannot grasp that intimidating others in the pursuit of justice *is itself* an injustice. Nor can he accept that his mentor's legal problems were the result of real crimes. "James Brown in jail," Sharpton has remarked, "was the biggest cultural insult to a race that has ever happened."[49] Assault with a deadly weapon, aggravated assault and rape apparently don't qualify as a basis for going to jail as long as such acts involve James Brown.

What Sharpton grasped from observing Brown's life – or more accurately, averting his gaze upon that life – was that a person can get away with illegal or outrageous acts if he is sufficiently famous, talented, intimidating, or supportive of the "right" causes. In 2003, the State of South Carolina granted James Brown a full pardon for prior convictions. That same year, the Kennedy Center for the Performing Arts in Washington, D.C. honored him with a Lifetime Achievement Award. All was forgiven. He was, after all, James Brown.

Al Sharpton left the Brown entourage sometime in the early Eighties, although accounts differ as to exactly when.[50] It had been a long and productive apprenticeship. Now it was time to do his mentor proud. Through his National Youth Movement, Sharpton was going to take his brand of justice to a new level, loud enough for the whole country to hear. His identity and mission were set in stone. He knew who he was and what he had to do. Now it was time to shake things up. Opportunities would advent themselves soon enough.

PART II

PROJECTS

CHAPTER 4

MUSIC, MICROPHONES AND THE MOB

If Al Sharpton has seemed protected from the consequences of his illegal activities, perhaps that is because his secret employer for several years during the Eighties was none other than the Federal Bureau of Investigation. The FBI, aided by the New York City Police Department, had hired the Rev to gather information on suspected mobsters and associates, especially those connected to the Genovese crime family. This aspect of his history, well-known in fact though blurry in detail, came into much sharper focus in April 2014 with the publication of a lengthy article, "Al Sharpton's Secret Work as FBI Informant," on *The Smoking Gun* website.[1]

Sharpton, in a pre-publication interview, vehemently denied working as an informant. But the author, *Smoking Gun* editor/co-founder William Bastone, doesn't appear to be the sort of person to make up facts. And evidence suggests Sharpton did the FBI's bidding to avoid prosecution. From a moral standpoint, at least, it may have been the high point of his career. The people he went after – Mafia wise guys and associates – really *were* bad. That's more than can be said for his campaigns to railroad innocent whites into prison or prevent palpably guilty blacks from winding up there. Yet even here, his original intent may have been less to put away mobsters than to share in their profits.

Under the code name "CI (Confidential Informant)-7," Sharpton, beginning in 1983, collected extensive information for a joint FBI-NYPD task force. Based on that information, authorities were able to secure court authorizations to bug two Genovese crime family social clubs, including the Greenwich Village headquarters of family godfather Vincent "the Chin" Gigante, three cars, and more than a dozen phone lines. The information would be instrumental in securing many convictions.

As Sharpton spun the story to *The Smoking Gun*, the federal government was trying to suppress his brand of civil rights advocacy and possibly have him killed. His role was limited to initiating investigations of drug trafficking in black neighborhoods and of record company theft of black recording artist royalties. In this view, Sharpton was a heroic mole working for the government, a black Donnie Brasco.[2] *The Smoking Gun* had a different take: Sharpton was a crook who flipped for the Justice Department rather than risk being charged with a crime.

To understand Sharpton's role in this massive federal sting, it is necessary to understand that he had extensive connections to the record industry, a large segment of which long had been controlled by the New York criminal underworld. Fredric Dannen's now-classic 1990 book, *Hit Men*,[3] chronicles Mafia permeation of the industry. Sharpton had spent years at the top of the musical food chain with James Brown. By 1983, he wanted to expand the operations of his National Youth Movement. The Reverend knew all kinds of music people, many of them with a reputation as reprobates. Possibly, the feds believed, he could help get some convictions.

One of these potential targets was boxing and concert promoter Don King. A convicted murderer in his native Cleveland,[4] King made the most of his freedom after getting out of prison. He organized the "Rumble in the Jungle" heavyweight title bout between Muhammad Ali and George Foreman in Zaire in 1974. A decade later, he put the pieces together for the Michael Jackson/Jackson Five Victory Tour and negotiated an advertising deal with Pepsi on behalf of the Jacksons worth more than $5 million. But the loquacious King, with his trademark electric Afro hairdo, at the time also was a central figure in a federal investigation of corruption in professional boxing. William

Bastone argues that given his connections to King, Sharpton was in the thick of things:

> *(B)y any measure, Sharpton himself was a Mafia "associate," the law enforcement designation given to mob affiliates who, while not initiated, work with and for crime family members. While occupying the lowest rung on the LCN [La Cosa Nostra] org chart – which is topped by a boss-underboss-consigliere triumvirate – associates far outnumber "made" men, and play central roles in a crime family's operation, from money-making pursuits to more violent endeavors.*

> *For more than four years, the fact that Sharpton was working as an informant was known only to members of the Genovese squad and a small number of other law enforcement agents. As with any Mafia informant, protecting Sharpton's identity was crucial to maintaining the viability of ongoing investigations. Not to mention keeping him alive.*

But was this route voluntary? According to *The Smoking Gun*, it was not. The article quotes an FBI agent assigned to the Genovese squad: "He thought he didn't have a choice."

In essence, argues the author, Sharpton, seen by the feds as the quickest path to Don King, was entrapped by an undercover agent posing as a wealthy drug dealer/boxing promoter. During two separate occasions, Sharpton was caught on video negotiating his participation in a cocaine deal. In one case, he was with Daniel Pagano, a Genovese crime soldier and son of Joseph Pagano; the elder Pagano was knee-deep in music industry operations and had done a nearly seven-year stretch in federal prison for heroin distribution. In the other case, Sharpton was with Colombo crime family captain Michael Franzese. The undercover agent offered Sharpton "pure coke" at $35,000 a kilo. As the agent spoke, Sharpton nodded his head, saying, "I hear you." The Rev also responded favorably when offered a 10 percent finder's fee on behalf of other coke buyers.

FBI agents weren't fully sure if they had enough on Sharpton for a prosecution. But they did believe they could convince him to go to work for them. As Bastone tells it:

> *The FBI agents confronted Sharpton with undercover videos and warned that he could face criminal charges as a result of the secret recordings...In subsequent denials that he had been "flipped," Sharpton has contended that he stiffened in the face of the FBI agents, meeting their bluff bluster and bravado...In fact, Sharpton fell for the FBI ruse and agreed to cooperate, a far-reaching decision he made without input from a lawyer, according to sources.*

Thus, Al Sharpton, FBI informant, was born. Wearing a hidden microphone much of the time, he helped get the goods on a number of colorful characters. There was Joe Pagano, who in addition to racking up a long criminal record, allegedly controlled Sammy Davis Jr. and was engaged in various kickback schemes with several Columbia Records executives. Pagano also was a friend of comedian Rodney Dangerfield, who had performed at his son and daughter's weddings. And there was Morris Levy, who was the founder and head of Roulette Records. Levy, a heavy straight from central casting, ran the label as a profit center for the Genovese crime family. He was a power player in the New York record industry with a net worth that eventually exceeded $50 million. Much of that represented his cut from the $30 million to $40 million he had siphoned off from Roulette's biggest hitmakers, Tommy James and the Shondells.[5]

Most importantly, insofar as Sharpton was involved, there was Gambino crime family soldier Joseph Buonanno, owner of a record distribution business in Manhattan and several record stores. Sharpton had met with Buonanno on many occasions. And he was tight with a

Buonanno enforcer, Robert Curington, a convicted black drug dealer. Curington served as a mentor to Sharpton, eventually assuming the grand-sounding title of Vice President of Industrial Affairs for National Youth Movement. Mostly, that meant pressuring (i.e., shaking down) major record labels and concert promoters into spending more money in the black community. The pair in 1986 also lined up endorsements of black ministers for Sen. Al D'Amato, R-N.Y., who at the time was in a potentially tough re-election race against Democratic challenger Mark Green. They also intimidated Joseph Robinson, the debt-ridden founder of the hip-hop label, Sugar Hill Records, who had given Morris Levy a stake in the company in return for bailing him out. Curington, a one-time star running back at North Carolina Central University, on one occasion used his athletic prowess to land a punch against one of Robinson's sons as part of a debt collection effort.

When *The Smoking Gun* report came out, the *New York Post* tracked down Curington, now 72, at his Durham, North Carolina home and interviewed him.[6] Curington insisted that Sharpton's ulterior motive was to get a piece of a cocaine deal. "It was greed," said Curington. "He just wanted money." Sharpton on three separate occasions allegedly met with an apparent South American drug trafficker who in reality was an FBI undercover agent going under the fake name of "Victor Quintana." On the third visit, said Curington, the agent proposed offering Sharpton $35,000 per kilo. Curington recalled: "Al told me himself. He bit and took the bait." Sharpton strongly disputes this account, adding that if this recounting of events were accurate, he could have claimed entrapment. Yet Curington insists this was the way it happened. He recalled: "He (Sharpton) was like two people. He ran around trying to score money for his National Youth Movement. But you can't be an activist and an opportunist."

By the end of the Eighties, dozens of Mafia wise guys and associates pleaded guilty or were convicted at trial. The ringleader, Joe Pagano, died of natural causes in 1989, two months before a grand jury accused his son and several other individuals of loan sharking, extortion and other crimes. Prosecutors, as a result, refrained from acting on the indictment's allegation that the son, Daniel Pagano, "solicited the use of a bank account of the National Youth Movement" for the purpose of money-laundering. Al Sharpton controlled that account. One has to wonder what would have happened if the Rev were charged and called to testify. The course of American history might well have been different.

By this time, Sharpton already had moved on to more visible campaigns. The first of them would originate in a New York City subway car.

CHAPTER 5

SUBWAY VIGILANTE

By the mid Eighties, much of the New York City subway system had descended into disarray. Trains and infrastructure were aging; transit union demands were driving budgets to the brink of insolvency; vandalism was rampant; and violent crime was on the rise. On average, nearly 40 reported crimes occurred daily on the subways. Every New Yorker knew the situation had gotten out of control. And they knew that blacks and Hispanics were disproportionately driving it. Law-abiding subway riders were taking all manner of precautions, save for one that in almost all cases was illegal: carrying a gun. One man, previously a subway crime victim, was unimpressed.

The afternoon of December 22, 1984 was unseasonably warm. About 1 P.M., a white independent home-based electronics repairman, Bernhard Goetz, 37, boarded a southbound Manhattan IRT Express train at the 14th Street Station. He was about to make history.[1] Seated to his immediate right were four black youths – Barry Allen, 19; Troy Canty, 19; James Ramseur, 18; and Darrell Cabey, 19. Approximately ten seconds after Goetz had taken his seat Canty asked him, "How are you?" Goetz responded, "I'm fine." At that point the four youths signaled to each other. They got up and walked toward the seemingly hapless passenger, with at least two of them surrounding him. Canty, acting as the group's spokesman, instructed Goetz: "Give me five dollars." Goetz asked, "What did you say?" Canty repeated his words: "Give me five dollars." Goetz's response this time wasn't in the script. He stood up, drew a five-shot, J-frame, .38-caliber Smith & Wesson revolver from

51

under his blue windbreaker, and began shooting. He emptied all five bullets from the gun's chamber, wounding all four youths, two of them critically.

Only two passengers – women who briefly fainted – remained in the subway car besides Goetz and the four youths. A conductor, having heard the high-decibel commotion, came over to ask the women if they had been injured. They were not. Then he asked Goetz to hand over his gun. Goetz refused, stating, "They tried to rob me." The conductor left. Goetz, anticipating an arrest, quickly exited at the Chambers Street Station, rented a car, and drove to Bennington, Vermont where he buried his gun and windbreaker.

Word of the shootings and the physical appearance of the shooter quickly spread. Here was this quiet, unassuming white guy who stood up to a group of menacing blacks, daring to do in real life what only Charles Bronson had the guts to do a decade earlier in the movie, *Death Wish*. The mail pouring into Mayor Koch's office was running 80-to-1 in favor of this "subway vigilante." His anonymity would be short-lived. On December 31, 1984, Goetz, believing his capture was imminent, turned himself into Concord, New Hampshire police.[2]

Upon his return to New York, the camera-shy Goetz received a hero's welcome. Dozens of people, including comedienne Joan Rivers, offered to help pay his $50,000 bail. The Guardian Angels, a heavily black and Hispanic red-bereted volunteer crime patrol, spoke in full support of Goetz. *New York Daily News* columnist Lars-Erik Nelson favorably compared Goetz's volley to "the first shot fired at Lexington and Concord."[3] The *Chicago Tribune*'s Mike Royko had some choice words of praise:[4]

> *As some of you recall, a few months ago a couple of young men, seeking to increase their net worth, put a gun to my nose. That wasn't the first time I was robbed or mugged, but it was the closest I've come to croaking – either from a twitch of a trigger finger or my own fright.*

So as a recent victim, I have a different perspective than that of a reporter...

It goes like this: To hell with the questions. I'm glad Goetz shot them. I don't care what his motives were or whether he has all his marbles. The four punks looked for trouble and they found it. Case closed.

Further contradicting the notion that Goetz was motivated by "racism" were comments by sympathetic blacks:[5]

I'm black, and I was mugged twice by punks in Mt. Morris Park going to church services. What is a person to do when they can't even go to church without getting assaulted? It's time the decent citizens of all races stop this crime problem and give the police a helping hand.

Another letter read:[6]

I'm a black woman. I have been robbed twice, both times by blacks. I didn't feel safe because they were black boys or the fact that I recognized one of them and thought maybe they wouldn't hurt me...Bernhard Goetz didn't see black boys. He saw the color of fear, the color of his life being at stake.

A prominent black civil rights leader, Roy Innis, head of the Congress of Racial Equality, also expressed support: "Bernhard Goetz was about to be mugged and we know it. If I was there I would have done the same thing, with one possible difference – [the crooks] probably would have been dead."[7] Innis' anger was justified: A son of his had been murdered in a street crime; another nearly had met the same fate.

Some New York City blacks, however, were not sympathetic. Most prominent among this faction was Al Sharpton. With youthful followers in tow, he launched a full-court press against Goetz. He recalled:[8]

*So I called a news conference on the steps of City Hall and de-
nounced the situation... I went to his apartment house in (sic)
14th Street and immediately we started getting press coverage.
We held prayer vigils; we went to all the court proceedings. I
had learned those things from the civil rights movement, so to
speak...We had never gone to white people's houses or to their
neighborhoods to picket and march. We created drama.*

The drama would prove crucial after a grand jury announced on
January 25, 1985 that it would not indict Goetz except for illegal gun
possession. Sharpton continued to lead public demonstrations to railroad Goetz for more serious crimes. Possibly swayed by Reverend Al, the
New York Court of Appeals (the highest court in the state) reversed the
action, concluding that a reasonable person in Goetz's position would
not have resorted to violence. A second grand jury then convened, this
time indicting him for various felonies, including assault and attempted
murder.

Let us understand something about Goetz's "innocent victims." At
the time of the shootings, his four tormentors, all high school dropouts,
already had amassed a combined nine criminal convictions. What's more,
they admitted their purpose for boarding the train that day was to rob
a video arcade at or near Pace University. Robbery wouldn't have been
too difficult either, given that at least two of the youths were packing
sharpened screwdriver shanks. Moreover, the Goetz experience made
little subsequent impression on the career paths of three of the youths.
After his release from the hospital, James Ramseur raped, sodomized,
beat and robbed a pregnant 19-year-old woman on a Bronx building
rooftop, eventually receiving a prison sentence of between 100 months
and 25 years. Barry Allen would go on to commit at least two muggings.
Troy Canty continued his career as a petty thief. Only Darrell Cabey,
paralyzed from the waist down, was out of commission.

At his criminal trial, Goetz confessed to the shooting, but argued
that his action fell under New York State's self-defense statute. It proved

a sound strategy. In June 1987, a jury, consisting of 10 whites and two blacks, convicted Goetz on a weapons charge but not on any of the more serious charges. The jury believed the defendant acted reasonably, especially given that back in January 1981 he had been mugged and badly injured by three youths in a subway station. He applied for a gun permit not long after, but was denied. Goetz received a sentence of six months in jail, a year of psychiatric treatment, five years probation, 2,000 hours of community service and a $5,000 fine. The New York State Court of Appeals upheld the conviction the following year.

This seemed far too stringent a punishment, even assuming Goetz had committed a crime. And there was more to come. Representing Darrell Cabey, radical lawyers William Kunstler and protégé Ron Kuby already had filed a civil suit in 1985, well before the criminal case had been decided, charging that Goetz had acted recklessly and inflicted emotional distress on Cabey, possessed racial motivations, and was a drug user. Though evidence undercut such claims, a jury, after numerous delays, in April 1996 awarded Cabey a princely $43 million, almost as much as the $50 million his lawyers originally sought. Of this sum, $18 million represented compensation for pain and suffering; the other $25 million represented punitive damages. Goetz, obviously unable to pay, declared bankruptcy.[9] He lived in relative obscurity after that until he ran for mayor in 2001 and then public advocate in 2005, though to no significant effect. A vegetarian and animal-rights advocate, the mild-mannered Goetz sells and services electronics equipment through his company, Vigilante Electronics. You've got to give the man credit: He has a sense of humor.

Al Sharpton, by contrast, does not have much of a sense of humor – or a grip on reality. In his 2002 autobiography, *Al on America*, he called Goetz a "vigilante who shot two blacks on the subway who were allegedly trying to rob him."[10] Aside from the ironic undercount, Sharpton writes as if Goetz had boarded the train for the ulterior purpose of shooting blacks. As for the word "allegedly," it, too, was an understatement. Cabey at the civil trial admitted he and his friends had intended to rob

Goetz, whom they saw as "easy bait." It was Cabey and his friends, not Bernhard Goetz, who were possessed of an ulterior motive. Goetz's action, by any reasonable standard, constituted self-defense, not a "hate crime." But to Al Sharpton, the two concepts are identical – as applied to whites.

CHAPTER 6

A DEATH IN HOWARD BEACH

Even before the Bernhard Goetz criminal verdict, Al Sharpton had moved on to his next project: justice for three young black men attacked by a group of white teenagers in the Queens, N.Y. community of Howard Beach. One of the blacks had been fatally hit by a car while fleeing attackers. On the surface, Sharpton appeared to be in the right. The crimes were real. Yet key details, especially those downplayed by major media, revealed him once more to be a racial demagogue.

By the late Eighties, Howard Beach long had established itself as a stable, middle-class and mainly white community in southwest Queens located along Jamaica Bay. Though more provincial than Manhattan, it was hardly a den of "hate criminals" or "extreme right-wingers." Blacks, though small in number, lived here without incident. Woody Guthrie, the late folksinger of the Left, called the place home for years.[1] Yet the neighborhood suddenly gained a national reputation as an incubator of white racist brutes. Al Sharpton, more than anyone else, shaped that reputation.

It was a little before midnight on December 19, 1986. Four black men had been riding in a car through Queens when their car broke down in an isolated marsh-like area along Cross Bay Boulevard. Three of the occupants – Michael Griffith, 23; his future stepfather, Cedric Sandiford, 36; and Timothy Grimes, 20 – walked about three miles toward a commercial area in hopes of finding personal help or a pay phone; a fourth occupant, Curtis Sylvester, 20, stayed behind to watch the car. Around 12:30 A.M., the trio came upon an open restaurant,

New Park Pizza, at 156-71 Cross Bay Boulevard. A counter employee told the men there was no phone available for use. They ordered a few slices of pizza anyway.

Shortly after eating, two police officers walked in, responding to a call of "three suspicious black males." Convinced the call was unwarranted, they left. Just outside the pizzeria, however, lay a ticket to mayhem. A group of white teens, presumably enraged at the audacity of blacks eating at a pizzeria in a white community, accosted the trio. One allegedly asked, "What are y'all doing in this neighborhood?" After a heated exchange, one of the whites attacked the blacks. Grimes escaped uninjured. But the white teens got out of the car and chased Griffith and Sandiford through residential streets all the way to 90th Street, whose dead end abutted the Belt Parkway. The teens split into two groups, one chasing Griffith and the other chasing Sandiford. In seeking refuge from the mob, the Trinidad & Tobago-born Griffith crawled through a three-foot hole in a fence and ran onto the parkway. It was a tragic move. An oncoming motorist, a court officer named Dominick Blum, traveling at about 55 MPH, unable to stop or swerve, struck Griffith, killing him instantly. Sandiford, who had been running immediately behind Griffith, was captured by the mob and beaten. Feigning unconsciousness, after the attackers left, he crawled through a fence hole and staggered onto the Belt Parkway where police found him bleeding.

This abbreviated official storyline, when revealed to the public, was a shock to the nervous system. It served notice to New Yorkers and the rest of the nation that white vigilante violence was well and alive even in the most cosmopolitan of cities. Mayor Ed Koch added to the climate of moral indictment, calling the incident "a modern lynching" and "the worst crime in the recent history of the city." Among New York blacks, the fires of outrage erupted. Al Sharpton stood ready to supply the gasoline.

Sharpton first learned of the incident from a 3 A.M. call from a National Youth Movement worker, Derrick Geter.[2] Nicknamed

"Sunshine," Geter was a cousin of Griffith. "Reverend Al," he said into the phone, "they just killed my cousin out in Queens. Will you come over to the house?" Sharpton wrote down the address and came over. After talking to Mrs. Griffith and Cedric Sandiford, he quickly concluded this was "clearly a racial killing." Here was proof that New York was no improvement over the old South.

Now as a matter of principle, Sharpton always has refused to obey local laws requiring a permit to march. For him, marching in the street is a "human right." He practiced what he preached on December 27, 1986, a week after Griffith's death, leading an estimated 1,200 followers down the street in the heart of the neighborhood. Feckless city officials did not try to shut down the march. "I was standing there at the head of the march of thousands," he recalled, "...and I'm the one who has called the march. I had arrived as an activist."[3] Sharpton also organized a rally at Boys and Girls High School in Brooklyn and another in Manhattan, where demonstrators marched from a midtown hotel to Mayor Koch's apartment in Greenwich Village.

Sharpton's motive wasn't just about getting justice for one specific set of crimes. It was obtaining racial payback on a vast collective scale. And whites were the people with debts to pay. That the weight of public opinion at this point was with Michael Griffith and his friends was irrelevant to Reverend Al. So apparently was the quick reaction by the authorities. Police already had arrested the three main culprits – Scott Kern, Jon Lester and Jason Ladone – on murder and related charges. They would be indicted by a grand jury. Police made several other arrests as well. Sharpton, however, would not be mollified. This was his opportunity to put the entire Howard Beach community on trial, baiting them into acting like bigots. Aware ahead of time of this "Day of Outrage," many local residents lined the boulevard and took the bait, jeering and yelling hostile remarks, often in the form of racial epithets. Reverend Al thus had fulfilled his prophecy. Howard Beach now stood as a metaphor for white racism everywhere. A decade and a half later, he wrote that his actions were necessary for the healing to begin:[4]

In 1986, in New York City, a young black man was killed for being in the wrong neighborhood. In 1950 (sic), Emmitt Till was murdered, lynched, for being on the wrong sidewalk in Mississippi.

We haven't come that far.

To many in America, racism is a thing of the past. It's something that happened "back then." To millions of blacks in this country, it is something we live every day. We know it exists – much to America's detriment. We must begin to have an honest and open discussion about race in America.

The Griffith family and Cedric Sandiford, for their part, seemed uninterested in open discussion. Sharpton set them up with a pair of temperamental radical black attorneys, Alton H. Maddox and C. Vernon Mason, who urged them not to cooperate with Queens District Attorney John Santucci. The Queens D.A., they insisted, was prejudiced in favor of the defendants. Additionally, Maddox, without any evidence, accused New York City Police Commissioner Benjamin Ward of conducting a cover-up. That Ward himself was black[5] didn't matter to Sharpton or his legal eagles. The City's criminal justice system being racist, only a State-appointed special prosecutor would be acceptable.

After a few weeks of growing pressure from the city's black leaders, New York Governor Mario Cuomo yielded. On January 13, 1987 he announced that his chief anti-corruption investigator, Charles "Joe" Hynes, would be special prosecutor, armed with broad subpoena powers.[6] While Maddox and Mason at first objected to Hynes taking on the case – like Santucci, he presumably was white and a lackey of white-dominated state and city government – eventually they relented.

The wheels for prosecution now were in motion. On February 9, a state grand jury indicted 12 defendants in the Howard Beach case, including Kern, Lester and Ladone, whose original indictments had been dismissed because of non-cooperation by black witnesses. The jury selection and trial would be drawn out. Many witnesses would testify. On December 21, 1987, after a dozen days of deliberation, the jury delivered a verdict: Kern, Lester and Ladone were guilty of manslaughter and second-degree murder in the death of Michael Griffith. Prison sentences would come early the following year. Lester got the stiffest – 10 to 30 years. Kern received six to 18 years, while Ladone received five to 15 years. In all, nine of the dozen indicted defendants were convicted on a variety of charges related to Griffin's death.

Justice had been done. Or had it? Somehow things didn't add up. The defense had introduced a number of key material facts to the jury, which had been selected with racial-ethnic diversity in mind.[7] Queens might not have been Manhattan, but even white kids in Queens didn't go around picking up baseball bats looking for blacks, any blacks, to knock around. One of the principal defendants, the English-born Jon Lester, even recently had dated a black female. And why were Maddox and Mason so adamant about urging non-cooperation among their clients? Was there material evidence that could have made their clients appear less than noble?

Actually, there was quite a bit of material evidence that cast a shadow on the "white racist" narrative. Consider the following:[8]

- The incident had its roots *before*, not after, the arrival by foot of Griffith, Sandiford and Grimes at the pizza parlor. It was blacks who had accosted whites, not the other way around. White occupants of a car, consisting of several males and a female friend, Claudia Calogero, had been driving home. Suddenly, Griffith, Sandiford and Grimes, without warning, walked in front of the car. This prompted the white driver to yell, "What the hell. I almost hit you – get out of the way." The remark had no racial overtones. And it was reasonable. The pedestrians, not the driver, had acted recklessly. Were they white, the reaction by the driver almost certainly would have been the same.

- The blacks at this point became highly agitated. Sandiford later admitted he had said, "F**k you, honky." Miss Calogero testified that he banged on the car and stuck his head inside a window. Another witness in the car, Jon Lester, testified that Sandiford spat in his face. Worse, two of the blacks were armed and let the whites know about it. According to Stephen Murphy, the lawyer for one of the minor defendants, Michael Pirone, the supposedly benign Sandiford and Grimes each had a knife on them and flashed their weapon at the whites.

- The whites who chased Michael Griffith did not pursue him all the way to the Belt Parkway. Griffith had other means of escape. Indeed, some of the pursuers didn't learn of his death until hours later.

- According to a toxicologist testifying for the defense, an autopsy showed Griffith had a "near-lethal level" of cocaine in his system. In other words, his spatial judgment was impaired to the point where he was unable to make sound decisions regarding his own safety.

- Sandiford's attackers received first-degree assault convictions, though the assault itself produced only minor injuries. An NBC movie docudrama, "Howard Beach: Making the Case for Murder," airing initially on December 4, 1989, depicted him as suffering a severe concussion and requiring 67 stitches.[9] Yet hospital records indicated he had no concussion and required only five stitches.

- Jon Lester, the white youth who received the harshest punishment – 15 to 30 years – had a black girlfriend, Ernestine Washington, with whom he had broken up about a month before the incident. "Jon was railroaded," she later said, "for two reasons: the pretrial publicity and the fact that the judge knew the prosecution had to win because they were afraid the city was going to blow up."

What very easily could have sabotaged Special Prosecutor Hynes' case – and frankly should have – was the extensive involvement in the case by Sharpton's hand-picked lawyers, Alton Maddox and C. Vernon Mason. From the very start, this two-man black legion of doom, especially Maddox, saw Howard Beach not as a homicide, but as a metaphor for the murderous criminal history of white America. As such, they reasoned, there was no point in having Cedric Sandiford and Timothy Grimes cooperate with their tormentors. This assumption led to highly unethical legal conduct.[10] Maddox had persuaded Sandiford not to show up at a police suspect lineup. He also called for boycotts of all white businesses in the city, later narrowing down his targets to pizza parlors because the violence originated at a pizza parlor. Maddox also recklessly claimed that Dominick Blum, the motorist who accidentally killed Griffith, was part of a murder conspiracy; he demanded that Blum be arrested and his car impounded. He also accused investigators of conspiracy to deny Sandiford an opportunity to give his version of events. And he accused police of driving away from New Park Pizza, knowing a white gang was about to attack.

On no occasion did Maddox, Mason or Sharpton make any effort to retract these false and likely defamatory statements. They simply went about concocting new ones. It was all about racial incitement: On the day the Queens grand jury handed down the indictments sought by Special Prosecutor Hynes, Maddox addressed his own: "It was you black people marching and meeting and protesting all over the city who provided the fuel for these indictments."

Even some Left-leaning voices were disgusted with this legal chicanery.[11] *Village Voice* columnist Jack Newfield, long familiar with Alton Maddox, summarized him this way: "I have followed Maddox's career for years, and its most consistent themes have been hidden agendas, self-promotion and hatred of all law enforcement." Richard Emery of the New York Civil Liberties Union likewise remarked in an interview: "[Maddox's] methods are sabotage and the pursuit of racial division. He is very big on charges and very short on proof. That's a method we learned to despise during the McCarthy period. I will never work with him again."

None of this is to skirt around the fact that certain whites did commit crimes. Nor is it to deny that the use of baseball bats and a tree limb made the offenses all the more reprehensible. Prosecutions were warranted. Yet it is fair to say that the defendants' actions on some level were a response to their sense of being humiliated earlier that night by the blacks' menacing behavior. The notion that the whites were out-of-control "racists" on the prowl for blacks to beat up is nonsense. These youths were looking for *specific* blacks who earlier had criminally threatened them. But Sharpton and the Maddox-Mason legal team chose to believe that the entire Howard Beach neighborhood, supposedly a microcosm of racist America, ought to be put on trial. And they chose to antagonize that neighborhood and potentially undermine the prosecution with absurd and paranoid allegations. But fitting the facts to a preset conclusion is Sharpton's style. His choice of legal advisers reflected that.

The principals in the Howard Beach affair have left varying legacies.[12] Jason Ladone was released from prison in 2000. Jon Lester was released in 2001 and deported to Britain in 2001. Scott Kern was released in 2002. Kern and Ladone each have gotten married and have at least one child. The blacks haven't done so well. Cedric Sandiford married Jean Griffith, Michael Griffith's mother, in 1989. The union would be brief; Sandiford died of AIDS in 1991. Timothy Grimes would be arrested in July 1988 for shooting and seriously wounding his brother in Frederick County, Virginia. He was convicted in January 1989 and sentenced that April to 16 years in prison.[13] As of 2011, Grimes, a junior high school dropout who had amassed a criminal record even before the Howard Beach incident, had remained incarcerated for crimes he committed while in prison. The deceased Michael Griffith lives on – sort of. In November 1999, Mayor Rudolph Giuliani signed a bill designating a six-block stretch of Pacific Street in the Bedford-Stuyvesant section of Brooklyn as "Michael Griffith Street." As could have been predicted, this gesture of good will – some might call it capitulation – failed to impress Rev. Al Sharpton. At least New Park Pizza is still operating at the same location under the same name. Free enterprise lives.

Al Sharpton would go on to greater glory – in his own mind. During the Howard Beach trials, an alleged crime, this one in upstate New York, lay ripe for exploitation. The case would rocket Reverend Al, Alton Maddox and C. Vernon Mason to a wholly undeserved national cult-hero status of champion of the underdog. The most crucial aspect of the crime is that it never happened.

CHAPTER 7

THE GIRL WHO CRIED "WOLF"

Of all the campaigns that have defined Al Sharpton, one arguably sticks more than any other: his attempt to destroy the careers of several men, including a police officer and a county prosecutor, for their alleged 1987 abduction, beating and rape of an upstate New York black teenage girl, Tawana Brawley. Ms. Brawley, Sharpton and legal advisers Alton Maddox and C. Vernon Mason, were virtually inseparable during the entire media campaign, demanding arrests and convictions. A grand jury, however, after months of reviewing evidence, refused to indict. That was because there was nothing to indict. A decade later, a court slapped Sharpton, Maddox and Mason with a combined defamatory judgment of nearly $350,000.

Sharpton has remained unrepentant. Asked in a 1999 interview if he ever regretted his involvement in the Brawley case, he responded: "No. I think if I had to do it again I'd do it in the same way. I probably wouldn't have gotten into such a personal pissing contest with [New York State Attorney General] Robert Abrams. But I would do the whole thing again."[1] He later reiterated this view in his 2002 autobiography, *Al on America*. "For me," he wrote, "it (the Tawana Brawley case) defines my character, because I refuse to bend or bow – no matter the pressures. I took the word of a young girl, and if I had to do it over, I would do it again."[2] And in an April 10, 2007 interview with guest host David Gregory on MSNBC's "Hardball," Sharpton asserted, "I still don't apologize."[3]

Reverend Sharpton and his followers are free to entertain their illusions, but the body of evidence overwhelmingly leads to only one conclusion: Tawana Brawley made up her story. There were no assaults and or rapes. Her marks of physical trauma were self-induced. Nothing underscores Sharpton's lack of credibility more than his nonstop campaign to put the "assailants" into prison. The facts of the case, exhaustively reconstructed in the grand jury report[4] and a subsequent *New York Times* collaborative book, *Outrage: The Story Behind the Tawana Brawley Hoax*,[5] speak for themselves.

It was Saturday morning, November 28, 1987 in the town of Wappingers, Dutchess County, N.Y., about an hour's drive north of the Bronx.[6] Local residents were waking up to a horrifying discovery in their midst: a 15-year-old black girl, lying in a garbage bag, smeared with feces, clothing torn and burned, and covered with racial insults drawn in charcoal.

Mrs. Joyce Lloray, a resident of the Pavillion Condominiums, by chance had observed outside her apartment's sliding glass door a black girl climbing into a big green plastic garbage bag and then lying still on the cold, muddy ground. Mrs. Lloray called the Dutchess County Sheriff's Department. When officers and paramedics arrived, they found her in what appeared to be a ravaged state. The girl was named Tawana Brawley. And she had a story to tell. Unfortunately, the key parts of the plot were pure fiction.

Four days earlier, on November 24, Miss Brawley explained, she had skipped school to visit an ex-boyfriend, Todd Buxton, who was being held at the Orange County Jail in nearby Newburgh, N.Y. That evening she took a bus back to Wappingers, where she previously had lived with her mother, Glenda Brawley, in Apartment 19A at the Pavillion Condominiums complex; they now lived in the nearby Village of Wappingers Falls. According to Brawley, six white men, at least one of whom wore a badge, abducted her shortly after she got off the bus on her return trip, took her to a remote wooded area, and continuously sexually abused her for four days. Her physical appearance, at least, suggested her story was plausible.

Following the initial encounter with Miss Brawley, a sheriff's detective took her to St. Francis Hospital in Poughkeepsie, and requested that a rape examination be performed. He later was joined by a detective lieutenant, a detective who specialized in juvenile cases, a uniformed lieutenant, and other uniformed personnel. Dutchess County law enforcement officials clearly were taking this case seriously. Unfortunately, neither Tawana Brawley nor her family had any intention of providing help.

During the early evening of November 28 in the hallway of the emergency room, the boyfriend of Brawley's mother, Ralph King, was causing a commotion. According to several eyewitnesses, he yelled at the younger Brawley: "Don't talk to those white f**king cops, they're not going to help us. We're going to hire a lawyer and get all those white cops in court and make them tell us what they done." Three law enforcement officers and the emergency room physician all later testified to a grand jury that Mr. King, a nasty-tempered felon who had done seven years in prison for killing his wife back in 1970,[7] reeked of alcohol.

Not long after, Sharpton became the Brawley family "adviser." Quickly, he lined up Maddox and Mason to provide legal help, effectively snatching away representation of the girl from NAACP Legal Defense Fund lawyers. This was a crime beyond all imagination, Sharpton and his friends declared to anyone within shouting distance. Worse yet, they said, the government was covering for the assailants who included: Harry Crist, a part-time police officer in nearby Fishkill, N.Y.; Scott Patterson, a New York State Trooper; and Steven Pagones, a Dutchess County assistant prosecutor and a friend of Harry Crist.

Under enormous pressure from Sharpton and other "civil rights" leaders, Governor Cuomo appointed New York State Attorney General Robert Abrams as special prosecutor. Additionally, a Dutchess County grand jury convened to decide whether to recommend prosecution.

Sharpton instructed Brawley to refuse to cooperate with authorities, most of all, Abrams. To cooperate with Abrams, said Sharpton, would be as if "to sit down with Mr. Hitler." Alton Maddox declared, "Robert Abrams, you are no longer going to masturbate looking at Tawana Brawley's picture."[8]

The grand jury would spend seven months combing through police and medical records, and hearing the testimony of scores of witnesses. Sharpton, Maddox and Mason used this period as an opportunity to stage the ultimate media circus. Sharpton and his friends bused in protestors to the county courthouse on an almost daily basis, leading them in chants outside demanding punishment for the "real" criminals. Television and newspaper coverage was strong even if the evidence wasn't.

One target, Harry Crist, Jr., already was gone from this world. Only days after the announcement of the "hate crime," Crist, 28, reportedly despondent over the breakup with his girlfriend and the news of his ineligibility to become a New York State trooper, committed suicide by gunshot on December 1, 1987.[9] Al Sharpton announced to the world that Steven Pagones had murdered Harry Crist to keep his crime against Miss Brawley a secret. What's more, Sharpton, Maddox and Mason accused Governor Cuomo of protecting Pagones through his allegedly close connections to organized crime and the Ku Klux Klan. "Mr. Pagones and his organized crime cronies are suspects," Sharpton ranted on ABC's "Geraldo Rivera Show." Very publicly, at a March 1988 news conference, he accused Pagones of participating in the "assault" on Miss Brawley and, with the help of another assistant prosecutor, William Grady, of covering up the crime. "If we're lying, sue us, so we can go into court with you and prove you did it. Sue us – sue us right now."[10] Sharpton also demanded that Governor Cuomo immediately arrest these two "suspects." When asked for evidence of a cover-up, Sharpton answered, evasively, that they would reveal the facts only when the time was right. Cuomo and other state officials had the good sense not to oblige him.

But it was in the black churches – Sharpton's true element – where he let down his guard. Appearing with Tawana Brawley and one of her lawyers, C. Vernon Mason, at the Friendship Baptist Church in Brooklyn, the Reverend Al gave the audience his all.[11] As Brawley's mother walked among the crowd, Sharpton, alternating between pleading and shouting, declared of young Tawana: "Our proud African queen," the Rev declared. "She stepped out of anonymity, stepped out of obscurity, and walked into history." Comparing her to Rosa Parks and Fannie Lou Hamer, Sharpton bellowed: "If you can allow your daughters in your community to be raped and sodomized, the nothing else really matters. Some of us stood up and said enough is enough." As the congregation erupted in cheers, applause and shouts, Sharpton continued: "New York is Mississippi. The only difference between New York and Johannesburg is geography." And he wound up the event with a familiar call-and-response routine. "No justice!" he shouted. "No peace," the congregation responded in unison. "When do we want it?" asked Sharpton. "Now!" shouted back the audience.

The grand jury, mercifully, was not swayed by this melodrama. On October 6, 1988, its members released a 170-page report, based on more than 6,000 pages of testimony from over 180 witnesses and at least 250 exhibits. In highly forceful language, the report stated the case was a complete fabrication. Here are a few excerpts:

> We the grand jury of the Supreme Court, State of New York, County of Dutchess, empanelled on February 29, 1988, having conducted an investigation, and based on the preponderance of the credible and legally admissible evidence, conclude that the unsworn public allegations against Dutchess County Assistant District Attorney Steven Pagones are false, have no basis in fact and that he committed no misconduct, non-feasance or neglect in office.

> There was no medical or forensic evidence that a sexual assault was committed on Tawana Brawley. If a 15-year-old girl had been forcibly raped or sodomized by multiple assailants over a

*four-day period, there is a high probability that medical or foren-
sic evidence would have been found.*

*There is no evidence that a coverup occurred or was attempted in
this case. The actions of law-enforcement agencies and officials
were inconsistent with any attempt at a coverup.*

What, then, possessed Miss Brawley to go public with her "story?"
Since she chose to remain mum in the face of a grand jury subpoena,
nobody knew for sure. The most plausible motive, convincingly argued
in *Outrage*, was that having been grounded on the day she visited her
former boyfriend, she feared a beating at the hands of her mother's
boyfriend, Ralph King. She and her mother had staged an elaborate
abduction and assault to in hopes of keeping domestic peace.[12]

Al Sharpton, to this day, insists the crime was real. Yet all evidence
suggested this was a hoax. Consider the following facts:

- Brawley never backed up her initial allegations with an official
  statement – and even those allegations were sketchy and often
  self-contradictory.

- Unlike dozens of other persons, neither she nor her mother testified before the grand jury, even though they had been sub-
  poenaed to testify. Defying a subpoena happens to be a felony,
  which explains why they chose to relocate out of state, after receiving an estimated $300,000 raised by their "defense fund."[13]

- Forensic tests revealed no sexual assaults of any kind.

- Brawley exhibited no evidence of hypothermia, odd for someone supposedly held against her will outdoors for days during a
  time of year when temperatures regularly drop below freezing
  at night.

- Various witnesses swore they had seen her at parties in a nearby town during the period when she was "missing."

- Miss Brawley's mother was seen at the same residential complex, and only shortly before, at which she (Tawana Brawley) was seen getting into a garbage bag.

- Damage to the younger Brawley's clothing occurred inside her apartment. The grand jury report stated: "The items and instrumentalities necessary to create the condition in which Tawana Brawley appeared on Saturday, November 28, were present inside of or in the immediate vicinity of Apartment 19A."

- Renowned forensic psychiatrist Park Dietz, an expert witness, concluded, "Tawana Brawley's physical appearance when she was found is consistent with self-infliction and false accusation."

The June 1988 statement of a former Sharpton aide and bodyguard, Perry McKinnon, ought to have erased any doubts that this case was a hoax planned by Brawley and enabled her "advisers." A black Vietnam vet who had served as a police officer, private investigator and hospital security director, McKinnon made this astounding admission to investigators:[14]

Sharpton acknowledged to me early on that 'The Brawley story do (sic) sound like bullshit, but it don't matter. We're building a movement. This is the perfect issue. Because you've got whites on blacks. That's an easy way to stir up all the deprived people, who would want to believe and who would believe – and all [you've] got to do is convince them – that all white people are bad. Then you've got a movement…It don't matter whether any whites did it or not. Something happened to her…even if Tawana don't (sic) it to herself.'

McKinnon also alleged that Sharpton envisioned himself, Mason and Maddox taking over the city. In Reverend Al's own words, "We beat this, we'll be the biggest niggers in New York."[15]

Steven Pagones in 1998 after a jury awarded $345,000 in a defamation lawsuit against Sharpton, Alton Maddox and C. Vernon Mason. (AP/Wide World)

The grand jury's eventual refusal to indict would be a disaster for Sharpton, but he would not be deterred. At Pagones' press conference following the grand jury announcement, an uninvited Sharpton marched in, announcing, "Your accuser has arrived!" In the larger sense, he wouldn't leave. For years, Sharpton continue to hound Pagones, who remained the target of hate mail. Reeling financially, physically and emotionally, Pagones eventually sued Sharpton, Maddox and Mason in 1997 for defamation of character. In July 1998, after an eight-month trial, a state jury – four whites and two blacks – ruled that Sharpton,

Maddox and Mason had made a combined 10 defamatory statements[16] and ordered them to pay respective damages of $65,000, $95,000 and $185,000.[17] Sharpton refused to pay his share. With accumulating interest and penalties, the judgment against him rose to $87,000. Pagones had managed to collect a portion of that money by garnishing his income. Finally, in 2001 a group of wealthy black men, including lawyer Johnnie Cochran, New York City broadcasting mogul Percy Sutton and *Black Enterprise* magazine publisher Earl Graves, paid off the debt.[18]

As for Tawana Brawley, Pagones already had won a default judgment against her in 1991 after she repeatedly had ignored subpoenas. The presiding judge, however, waited until after the civil verdict to assess damages. In October 1998, New York State Supreme Court Justice S. Barrett Hickman ordered Brawley to pay Pagones $185,000. "It is probable that in the history of this state," wrote Justice Hickman, "never has a teenager turned the prosecutorial and judicial systems literally upside down with such false claims."[19]

Tawana Brawley wasn't about to pay. And she conveyed her refusal on the evening of December 2, 1997 at an event organized by Alton Maddox and attended by Al Sharpton, a time during which Pagones' defamation suit was active. Speaking before a wildly enthusiastic and overwhelmingly black audience at Bethany Baptist Church in Brooklyn's Bedford-Stuyvesant area, Brawley, having emerged from self-imposed obscurity, asserted that the original accusations were true.[20] "It happened to me, and I'm not a liar," she said. "What happened to me happens to hundreds of thousands of women every day." She gave no details of the actual sequence of events let alone an apology. Instead, she accused unnamed law enforcement officials of bribing people to pose as witnesses in order to portray her as a liar. She also denounced the "white press." Like Al Sharpton, Tawana Brawley had learned nothing and forgotten nothing.

Brawley's appearance actually was a disruption of an otherwise long descent into anonymity. In October 1989, at a ceremony at the Nation of Islam convention, the group's cult leader, Louis Farrakhan, bestowed upon her a Muslim name, Maryum Muhammad. During the 1989-90 academic year, she enrolled as a freshman at Howard University in Washington, D.C., her tuition covered by Alton Maddox's fledgling organization, the United African Movement.[21] Around this time, her mother, Glenda Brawley, facing a 30-day jail sentence for refusing to cooperate with a grand jury subpoena, moved out of state with her psychopath boyfriend, Ralph King. And not much has been heard from Tawana Brawley since. But she's no phantom either. As of late, she's been living in the Richmond, Virginia area, going under the name Tawana Gutierrez. And she still has the capacity to make the news. In August 2013, a Virginia state court ordered Brawley's employer, The Laurels of Bon Air, a Richmond nursing home, to garnish her wages in order to satisfy her debt to Pagones, by then in excess of $430,000, taking into account accumulated interest. Brawley/Gutierrez, who had paid Pagones $3,700 at that point, isn't likely to come close to paying off the full amount. Pagones' lawyer, Garry Bolnick, admits that the court order is mainly symbolic. "The only way we will get the money," said Bolnick, "is if some of her so-called supporters come up with it."[22] Good luck with that.

Tawana Brawley's legal advisers haven't been professionally active as of late. Alton Maddox in May 1990 was indefinitely suspended from practicing law by the New York State Supreme Court for refusing to cooperate with an investigation relating to his conduct in the Brawley case. He remains a radical activist today, contributing articles to black-oriented publications such as New York City's *Amsterdam News*.[23] C. Vernon Mason was disbarred by the State of New York in 1995[24] and became an ordained minister, serving as CEO of a nonprofit youth-mentoring group, UTH-TURN.[25] Equally encouraging, the target of their venom, Steve Pagones, became an assistant attorney general for the State of New York.

As for Sharpton, he continued his climb as a public figure. Only months after the Tawana Brawley campaign collapsed, he created what amounted to a reverse version of that campaign. In the Brawley campaign, he had falsely accused a group of white males of assaulting a black female. In the new campaign, he tried every tactic imaginable to exonerate a group of predominantly black male adolescents in New York City accused of severely beating and raping a white female. And this incident, unlike the one of Ms. Brawley's fertile imagination, was all too real.

CHAPTER 8

GOING WILD IN CENTRAL PARK

Her name was Trisha Meili. It would be nearly a decade and a half after her near-fatal group beating on April 19, 1989 before she could bring herself to announce her identity to the world as the "Central Park Jogger." No, Al Sharpton was not among those who had brutally assaulted her. But given his public demagoguery during the criminal justice process, he might as well have been.

Opened to the public in the late-1850s, Central Park is one of the world's finest tracts of urban parkland, possessed by great natural beauty and man-made amenities. But it also long has been a staging ground for New York City's criminal class, possessed by an abundance of hiding places from which thugs can prey upon unsuspecting victims. During the 1980s, the park became the focal point for a group crime known as "wilding." Roving packs of adolescents, teenagers and young adults, mainly black, would go lengthy assault and robbery sprees against random targets. In July 1983, at a Diana Ross concert, dozens, if not hundreds of black teenagers descended upon concert-goers and pedestrians, consummating an orgy of robbery, mugging and purse-snatching. In May 1985, black teenagers overran the Central Park March of Dimes Walkathon, attacking participants and stealing money, jewelry and other things of value. Sometimes individuals were targets, such as a man in 1988 bludgeoned to death. That latter year saw 622 of these pack attacks occurring throughout the city referred to family court.[1]

Trisha Meili, 28, was an attractive, athletic single white woman with a bright future. An investment banker with Salomon Brothers, she held two Master's degrees from Yale. On April 19, 1989 her decision to jog along her usual nighttime path through Central Park nearly cost her life. Sometime between 9 and 10 P.M., as she was running along an isolated traverse near 102nd Street adjacent to the North Meadow softball fields, a group of an estimated dozen or more youths accosted her, and proceeded to rape, sodomize and beat her with a pipe. After getting their fill of pleasure, they then dragged her about 100 yards from the scene of the crime and left her for dead. For several hours she lay in a coma until being discovered by two pedestrians. She then was rushed to Metropolitan Hospital, which listed the patient as having two skull fractures, severe hypothermia, and loss of more than half her blood.

Apparently, she wasn't the only person that night receiving a rude welcome. At least eight other people were attacked, though not as savagely, by members of a group that police said numbered between 32 and 41 members.[2] Aggressive police work soon led to arrests. Authorities charged six juvenile suspects with the attack against Meili: Steven Lopez, Antron McCray, Kevin Richardson, Raymond Santana, Yusef Salaam and Kharey Wise.[3] They also were charged with other attacks. All the defendants save for Salaam made formal confessions, and with a level of detail that couldn't have been faked. Yet within weeks they would retract their confessions, claiming they had been coerced. Another obstacle to a successful prosecution was that the DNA collected at the crime scene did not match that of any of the suspects. Prosecutors went ahead with the case anyway.

On the outside, intense pressure was growing for dismissal. Applying that pressure, more than anyone else, was Al Sharpton. Here was a woman, almost beaten to death, who in every way was the very antithesis of Sharpton's favorite non-victim, Tawana Brawley. Yet Trisha Meili was white. And her real – not imaginary – assailants consisted of several blacks and a Hispanic. And that made all the difference to Al Sharpton.

Reverend Sharpton and his followers heaped mounds of verbal abuse upon the woman throughout the proceedings. Sharpton's friend, the Reverend Calvin Butts of Harlem's Abyssinian Baptist Church (the late Adam Clayton Powell's church), declared, "There's no evidence to link them to the rape."[4] Ludicrously, Sharpton insisted that the victim's boyfriend was the culprit, leading crowds at courthouse rallies in the chant: "The boyfriend did it! The boyfriend did it!" In the spirit of compromise, Sharpton announced, "We're not endorsing the damage to the girl...if there was this damage." He also sought to have a psychiatrist examine the victim. "It doesn't even have to be a black psychiatrist," the Reverend added, unwilling to entertain the fact that following recovery from her coma, Miss Meili had no memory of the attack.[5] This didn't matter to the assembled black crowds, who screamed that she was "a whore," often mentioning her by name, which somehow had been leaked to, and published by, local black newspapers. When she came forward to testify, the spectators, which included defendants' family members, shouted her name, branded her a liar and accused her of being in the park to buy drugs. Sharpton's rent-a-mob also treated a white prosecutor, Elizabeth Lederer, in a similar manner.[6] As a final touch, Sharpton escorted the one and only Tawana Brawley to the trial and introduced her to the defendants, whom she greeted warmly. All in all, this was a repulsive performance even by Sharpton's standards. It didn't say too much for his followers either.

The defense team, which included William Kunstler and Ronald Kuby, wouldn't get its way. In two separate trials during 1990, racially mixed juries convicted McCray, Richardson, Salaam, Santana and Wise – collectively known as "the Central Park Five" – of rape and other charges, but not attempted murder. The defendants wound up doing at least five years of prison time. The sixth defendant, Lopez, pleaded guilty in January 1991.[7] The evidence for guilt was overwhelming. The defendants frequently made self-incriminating comments during testimony. Richardson's lawyer, Howard Diller, remarked after the trial: "They (the defendants) convicted themselves with their own statements. We could not overcome them."[8]

As time passed, the case gradually disappeared down the collective memory hole. Then, in 2002, lightning struck. A convicted rapist and murderer, Matias Reyes, serving up to a life sentence for other crimes, publicly announced that he, acting alone, had assaulted the Central Park jogger. DNA and sperm samples confirmed his participation in the attack. This opened up the charge once more that the original confessions had been coerced. District Attorney Robert Morgenthau, though not agreeing, notwithstanding recommended that all convictions be vacated. In December of that year, New York Supreme Court Justice Charles Tejada made the appeasement official.

Anyone thinking this turn of events invalidated the prosecution's case should understand several things. First, to vacate a prior conviction means to void it. It does *not* mean to exonerate the defendants. In other words, the prosecution *could* have asked for a retrial, but chose not to. Second, the accused youths very likely had committed other crimes during their wilding spree that night and thus could have been charged with them as well. Third, New York City police detectives vociferously had insisted that one or more of the defendants had been Reyes' accomplices that night. Reyes, in other words, did rape Meili, either while accompanying his friends or as a mop-up act. Fourth, Morgenthau's staffers blocked the police investigation. They prevented detectives from interviewing prison inmates and refused to release forensic reports and prison records. Morgenthau, a nonagenarian behaving far more like a politician than a prosecutor, had no desire for further action. Finally, his office almost certainly had acted illegally in dismissing the convictions.[9]

The case would remain alive long after in the form of a civil action. In December 2003, the five defendants sued the city, alleging their confessions were coerced. Each sought $50 million in damages. They were in continuous litigation with the City during the tenure of Mayor Michael Bloomberg, who should have summoned the will to tell the defendants and their lawyers to get lost. The election in November 2013 of Bloomberg's far-Left successor, Bill de Blasio, quickly broke the impasse. The new mayor early in 2014 announced that he was willing to settle.[10]

Even before the election of de Blasio, the defendants had acquired useful ammunition in the form of a misleading documentary film, *The Central Park Five*. Released commercially in November 2012, this widely and unjustly praised agitprop, directed by Ken Burns, his daughter Sarah Burns, and her husband, David McMahon, made a highly selective use of evidence to create the illusion that this was a latter-day Scottsboro Boys case. Supporters of the accused saw the film as irrefutable evidence of a frame-up, when in fact it was nothing of the sort.[11]

The case reached its conclusion on April 20, 2014. The City of New York announced that it had agreed to settle with the five defendants for a little over $40 million; an unnamed ranking City official announced the settlement.[12] Sharpton, with typical disregard for elementary facts, termed the tentative settlement "a monumental victory." He added: "It is also a victory in the community that stood with them from day one and believed in their innocence in this case. As supporters, we were viciously attacked for standing with them, but we were on the right side of history."[13] The deal still needed the approval of the City Comptroller and a federal judge, but with Al Sharpton still on the case, that wouldn't be hard to achieve. A federal judge made the deal official that September.

Actually, vindication had come from the victim, Trisha Meili, over a decade earlier. In 2003 the jogger revealed her name and life story in a book, *I am the Central Park Jogger*.[14] It would launch her career as an inspirational speaker. Meili may be a victim, but she's also a victor. It is she who is on the right side of history, not the thugs who beat her, nor Al Sharpton or the mindless mobs who hang on his every word.

CHAPTER 9

THE SIEGE OF BENSONHURST

If Howard Beach was Al Sharpton's testing ground for bringing a taste of hell to a predominantly white neighborhood, Bensonhurst was its fulfillment. Starting in the latter months of 1989, and continuing for more than a year, Sharpton and his followers besieged the heavily Italian-ethnic Brooklyn community to protest the murder there of a black teenager, Yusuf Hawkins.[1] Reverend Sharpton, and one of Tawana Brawley's lawyers, Alton Maddox, stage-managed the situation, serving as "advisers" to the victim's family, "protecting" the family from contact with police, prosecutors and white-owned media outlets. As with the Howard Beach and Tawana Brawley affairs, they were bent on completing controlling the public perception of the situation.

In Reverend Sharpton's recounting of events, a predatory white mob murdered an innocent black kid:[2]

> *In 1989, Yusuf Hawkins, a sixteen-year-old, was in Bensonhurst, Brooklyn, following up on an ad he had seen for a car. He got into an altercation with a gang of white boys, who accused him of talking to one of their women. They fought, and Yusuf Hawkins was shot to death.*

The reality was far more complicated. This was no Gotham City version of the Emmett Till murder. Sharpton, eager to tar the reputation of many for the sins of a few, didn't care.

It was a muggy Wednesday afternoon, August 23, 1989. A large group of young Bensonhurst white males had gathered in a schoolyard to discuss a problem. A local white girl, Gina Feliciano,[3] was turning 18 that day. And she was planning a party. Unfortunately, the party was shaping up to be a bloodbath. Let us backtrack a bit.

Gina Feliciano, to put it less than delicately, was white trash, a Caucasian equivalent of a black "gangsta." A bad-tempered crack addict and a high school dropout, she lived with her increasingly exasperated mother. The two constantly fought over her drug use and general behavior. Police had been called to the home on several occasions. The love-starved Ms. Feliciano at one time had a serious crush on a neighborhood fellow, Keith Mondello. The love was unrequited. A neighborhood woman, Carmen Mercado, recalled: "Gina believed that Keith was her boyfriend, or at least she wanted him to be. But he didn't want to have anything to do with her. He would joke with her sometimes, you know, play around. Keith had a girlfriend. He didn't need Gina."

In fact, it was hard to imagine any *anyone* in the neighborhood who needed her, especially since her crowd consisted heavily of black and Hispanic drug dealers. Unable to sink her hooks into Keith Mondello, she decided upon one Nick Nipitello, the estranged husband of a local Bensonhurst woman, Linda Nipitello. Mrs. Nipitello had grown tired of his erratic behavior. "I was just as glad that he was with her (Gina)," she said. "I didn't want him." The couple, however, had a seven-year-old daughter. And Nick often visited the home to see his daughter. The visits enraged Ms. Feliciano, who imagined Linda Nipitello to be a rival plotting to "steal" Nick away. The opposite was true, of course, but there was no reasoning with her.

By the summer of 1989, Gina Feliciano had grown more threatening toward Linda, telling to stay away from Nick "or else." In Gina's words: "I can have you taken care of just like that," waving her arm in a wide arc and snapping her fingers to the word "that." During one street confrontation in July, Linda Nipitello once again indicated her lack of desire for her husband. "Take him, go ahead and keep him," she emphatically told

Feliciano. "I don't want that no-good drug dealer in my house." Even that seal of approval didn't mollify Gina. Every time Nick visited his daughter, Gina would fly into a rage against Linda. During one chance encounter, she told Linda: "Try to get him back, you just try, and I'll blow your head off!" Not long after that, Linda Nipitello and a girlfriend, Elizabeth Galarza, were walking with Linda's daughter along Twentieth Avenue near 71st Street as they passed a pizza parlor. Suddenly, they heard a gunshot. The women and the girl hit the pavement for their own safety. Ms. Galarza, at least, managed to get a glimpse of a tall man with long blond hair and a moustache rapidly crossing the street. Nobody was able to pin anything on him or anyone else. And the cops suddenly grew disinterested when apprised that the incident likely was triggered by a love triangle of Gina Feliciano's fertile imagination.

The situation wasn't about to let up. Elizabeth Galarza began to receive menacing anonymous phone calls. In one instance, a male voice told her: "If you know what's good for you, you'll mind your own business." Galarza called police several times about this, but the cops brushed her off in a nice way. She was not imagining things. On several occasions, Galarza saw the man with the blond hair standing on the corner of Bay Ridge Avenue.

The reader by now may be grasping a salient point: Gina Feliciano and the company she kept were community nightmares. And that company consisted mainly of black and Hispanic gang members. Something had to give. And it did. On August 21, she and some Hispanics were outside Sal "the Squid" Mannino's candy store next to the entrance of her apartment building, smoking crack and playing a radio. Keith Mondello and several of his friends, noticing this, argued with Gina, and told the bunch to leave. They also said that her outside friends were scaring the community. Mondello added: "Stop bringing those niggers and spics around here or there's going to be trouble." His words were ugly, but however impotently, he was expressing legitimate and wide-spread frustration. Even the local Mafia guys weren't as brazen as the Feliciano bunch.

Gina Feliciano, as one could have been expected, took this directive rather badly. On August 22, furiously pacing up and down 20th Avenue, she periodically stopped into the candy store to make telephone calls to friends. Early in the day, she accosted the school crossing guard, Rose McNamara, unable to contain her rage. "I'm gonna show these white bastards who they're messing around with." McNamara, trying to calm her down, responded: "Gina, I thought you were going to go to school. Stop worrying about all this and go to school to be a secretary like you said you were going to do." Feliciano, a dropout not about to drop back in, furiously declined. This girl was *possessed*.

Feliciano would be celebrating her 18th birthday the following day. She already told a number of people about her plans for a party – her kind of party. There would be violence. She told Keith Mondello and Sal the Squid that she and her Hispanic friends were going to bring a large group of black friends to "beat the s**t out of all of yez." Mondello and Sal in turn relayed her message to the whole neighborhood. Mondello had seen some of these guys. They were big and dangerous-looking. One couldn't have too many reinforcements in a situation like this. They congregated outside a local school on 68th Street. A local female, anything but a lady, was about to lead a war on them. With cops seemingly downplaying the situation, the white guys felt they had no choice but to play defense. They had every reason to be frightened. Rather than go through legal channels, however, they decided on an Old School approach: Break out the baseball bats and golf clubs, and wait things out. If a rumble came to them, they would be ready.

The crowd at the school gradually grew. But the thugs whom Gina Feliciano had vowed to produce hadn't showed up yet. The crowd was getting restless. They didn't want to stand there all evening. A few of them who knew where Feliciano lived called up to her window. "Happy birthday, Gina!" they sarcastically chanted. "Hey, where are your nigger friends?" one fellow called out. "We're waiting." Queen Bee Gina opened her window, stuck her head out, and called down to them, appealing to their latent fear of sexual inadequacy: "The black guys are getting all the white meat, and you're not man enough!" The waiting game would continue. Then, around 9:30 P.M., the wait was over, but in ways nobody had anticipated.

Yusuf Hawkins wasn't anticipating a war. The black teen and three black friends from Brooklyn's Bedford-Stuyvesant neighborhood had just gotten off a subway train several blocks away, responding to a used car ad. Unfamiliar with the turf, they decided to walk toward their intended destination. Around the intersection of Bay Ridge and 20th Avenue, they would be spotted by Keith Mondello and about 30 other males, ready for a fight. "They're here!" said a local youth, Chris Lomuto. "Black kids are here!" At this point, the whole mob was thinking: *These must be some of the guys Gina Feliciano had warned us about.*

The group approached the four blacks and followed them, eventually surrounding them. "Is this them?" some members asked. At some point, someone yelled, "What are you niggers doing here?" When surrounded, Yusuf Hawkins and his friends explained they were looking for an address of the person advertising a 1982 Pontiac for sale. He even pulled out a piece of paper with directions. Some members of the group, including Keith Mondello, were awakening to the possibility that these weren't Gina's people – they were legit. One person, however, Joey Fama, wasn't convinced – or very patient about it. Holding a .32-caliber chrome-plated revolver, he reportedly yelled, "To hell with beating them up, forget the bats, I'm going to shoot the nigger." Another member of the group, James Patino, said "No!" But Fama, said witnesses, aimed his gun directly at Yusuf Hawkins and fired four times. Two of the bullets struck Hawkins, killing him almost instantly.

Police arrived on the scene. They recovered four emptied .32 caliber shells and seven baseball bats. No doubt this was a homicide. As eyewitness accounts enabled the cops to piece together a story, it became clear that it wasn't just the neighborhood about to blow; it was the whole city. And though the catalyst for the tragedy was a pathologically narcissistic female, the racial angle completely dominated the news. Here, by God, was Howard Beach *redux*, only on an even larger scale. White racism was alive in New York City after all!

The incident would provide fuel for all New York City politics. Ed Koch, three-term incumbent mayor, was in a fight for his survival. Seeking re-election, his opponent in the September Democratic primary was Manhattan Borough President David Dinkins, a black. Koch, a longtime civil rights supporter, was mortified that a hate crime such as this could happen under his watch. He denounced it in strong language. But the damage was done. However much he sought justice, enough voters had come to believe that he had overstayed his welcome and lost control of his city. Dinkins, a soft-spoken ex-Marine with a law degree, seemed a healing force. Quite naturally, he made Yusuf Hawkins into a campaign issue.

Another prominent local black, however, wasn't interested in speaking in a soothing voice. That was Al Sharpton. He believed that not only should the entire group of 30 or so youths stand trial, so should the whole neighborhood. Indeed, he called for putting all of white New York on trial. The facts said otherwise. This was not some white mob looking for a black, any black, to attack. This was a group of neighborhood people on alert for a very real threat of large-scale terror by a specific group of black and Hispanic drug dealers. Not everyone in the mob was white either. One of the youths who helped round up the bats for the group, Russell Gibbons, was black.[4] And several whites in the group had shouted at Fama *not* to use his gun.

In spite of this and other evidence, Sharpton and his cadres were convinced this was an unspeakable racial hate crime. And they used this presumption as a pretext for an endless campaign of menace. On a couple dozen of occasions, the Rev led demonstrators, many chanting and waving signs, on marches through the neighborhood. True to form, Sharpton refused to secure a city permit to march.[5] As with Howard Beach, he fulfilled his own prophecy. Unable to convince City Hall to enforce the law, local white residents taunted the demonstrators, on occasion throwing watermelons. Sharpton also fanned the fires on local talk radio, especially the black-owned WLIB-AM.[6] He also enlisted Yusuf Hawkins' father, Moses Stewart, as a team player, securing his permission to exert control over family communications with the outside world. Stewart, a follower of Nation of Islam leader Louis Farrakhan,[7] became a close ally of the Rev.

Sharpton wasn't the only incendiary leader. On August 31, 1989, a black revolutionary and career criminal, Robert "Sonny" Carson, led a riot. On August 31, 1989, a proclaimed "Day of Outrage," a mile-long procession of marchers blocked traffic on the Brooklyn Bridge, chanting, "What's coming? War!" Police at that point tried to keep the bridge open, whereupon marchers busted through the barricades and attacked. Some two dozen officers were injured in their attempts to make arrests.[8] Another local black power revolutionary, Viola Plummer, gave an incendiary speech, vowing, "From this day forward, for every black child that we bury, we are going to bury five of theirs."[9] Sharpton reportedly had nothing to do with this rally. But by refusing to criticize the event, intended as a memorial to recently-killed (in Oakland, California by a rival black militant)[10] Black Panther leader Huey Newton as well as to Yusuf Hawkins, Sharpton effectively was endorsing it.

On January 12, 1991, Sharpton's provocations nearly spelled his own doom. It was a typical demonstration day. Minutes before the march was to begin, he got out of his car to talk to some of the several hundred protestors assembled in the police-enforced staging area. As Sharpton turned to Moses Stewart, he suddenly felt something. That something was a knife plunged into his chest. He removed the knife and fell to the ground. People screamed. The Reverend's security detail grabbed and held the assailant, Michael Riccardi, and turned him over to police. Officers quickly put Sharpton in a detective car and rushed him to Coney Island Hospital. Despite the blood loss, he survived. When word of the stabbing got out, Sharpton's followers reacted with vengeance. Marchers appeared at the hospital, chanting, "Let's burn down Bensonhurst! Let's burn down New York!" Several black youths beat up an innocent white person on the train, exclaiming, "This is for Sharpton."[11] The Fruit of Islam, Louis Farrakhan's Nation of Islam paramilitary guard, stood watch over Sharpton in his hospital bed. New York City's black mayor, David Dinkins, elected in 1989 largely because of the fallout from the Bensonhurst shooting, paid a visit. So did Jesse Jackson.

Meanwhile, back at the Brooklyn courthouse, eight youths faced charges, including assault, rioting and civil rights violations. Brooklyn District Attorney Charles Hynes – the same Charles Hynes who had been special state prosecutor in the Howard Beach case – was determined to secure convictions of all involved. Five would be found not guilty. Joey Fama, the alleged shooter, though found not guilty of first-degree murder, was convicted of second-degree murder after an exhausting 11-day jury deliberation. He received a sentence of 32 years and eight months to life.[12] Before a separate jury, Keith Mondello, the alleged ringleader, was found not guilty of either murder or manslaughter, but was convicted for incitement, illegal possession of a weapon and other charges. He got a sentence of between 64 months and 16 years. John Vento was acquitted of murder and manslaughter, but was found guilty on a lesser riot charge.[13] He received an eight-year prison sentence. Joseph Serrano was convicted on a weapons charge (possession of a baseball bat) and received a sentence of 150 hours of community service. Pasquale Raucci was convicted of unlawful imprisonment, and sentenced to performing community service. Three other defendants – Charles Stressler, James Patino and Steven Curreri – were found not guilty as charged. Gina Feliciano, who *should* have been charged with something, was the substitute star witness for the prosecution after Vento, fearing local retaliation, had backed out. Her testimony helped put Keith Mondello away; he allegedly owned five guns and "can't wait for tonight."[14] Feliciano would get a certain measure of comeuppance in an unrelated matter. Just days after the Mondello guilty verdict in May 1990, she would be arrested by New York City transit police for fare-beating and crack cocaine possession inside a Brooklyn subway station.

Al Sharpton wasn't at all satisfied. He wanted *all* the defendants found guilty. In February 1991, a recuperating Sharpton declared, "The verdict in this case is an insult to all citizens of the nation, in particular the Hawkins family."[15] As for Michael Riccardi, Sharpton's would-be killer, he was convicted of first-degree assault in March 1992 and received a prison sentence of five to 15 years.[16] Much later, in December 2003, Sharpton would win a $200,000 out-of-court settlement with the City of New York, having claimed that the City had failed to provide sufficient police protection – never mind that he refused to secure official permission for his marches in the first place.[17]

Following his release from the hospital, Sharpton founded National Action Network, a nonprofit group that would supersede National Youth Movement. NAN would provide voter education, economic empowerment and other black-oriented programs. Had his brush with death caused him to see the light? Was this the dawn of a new Al Sharpton, favoring constructive engagement over intimidation? The time seemed right. The City of New York had its first-ever black mayor in David Dinkins, a self-described "racial healer" who likened his city to a "gorgeous mosaic." Was the Rev actually willing to fix the damage that he had played no small part in creating? Only months later, by his actions, he would resoundingly answer that question in the negative.

CHAPTER 10

RUNNING RIOT IN CROWN HEIGHTS

From outward appearances, Crown Heights, Brooklyn seemed a highly unlikely place for a riot. The mostly middle-income neighborhood has hundreds of well-preserved neoclassical town homes. Its main thoroughfare, Eastern Parkway, was modeled after the Champs-Elysees in Paris. The community long had been home to sizable Jewish and Italian ethnic populations. But starting roughly during the 1950s and accelerating thereafter, blacks, especially from the Caribbean, moved in. By the early Nineties, the area was at least 80 percent black. The remaining Jews, mostly members of the ultra-Orthodox Lubavitch sect, during the Seventies and Eighties lived in constant fear of crime, a fear justified in the face of frequent assaults and robberies at the hands of blacks. And during August 19-22, 1991, crime would occur in fast-forward mode. Acting on rumor and factual exaggeration, hundreds of blacks went on a rampage against neighborhood Jews, resulting in at least one murder, dozens of assaults, sporadic property destruction, and well over 100 arrests.

Al Sharpton insists to this day he had nothing to do with the riot. Given the material facts, that would be hard to accept.[1] He did proclaim: "If the Jews want to get it on, tell them to pin their yarmulkes back and come over to my house."[2] While that statement alone undercuts his assertion, there is an underlying story. A number of commentators over the years have assumed that because Sharpton made this statement around the same time as the riot, his purpose was to incite a riot in progress. In fact, he uttered these words on August 18, 1991, one day *before* the riot.[3] To understand the riot, then, one must understand the larger context.

During the late Eighties and the early Nineties, New York City was the epicenter of a virulent black nationalism. A combination of rapid black population growth, welfare dependency, crack cocaine addiction and trafficking (and accompanying conspiracy theories about who "really" was behind it), the incorporation of black studies curricula at all levels of education, the commercial success of Afrocentric cultural expression, the increasing public profile of Al Sharpton, and most immediately, the candidacy and subsequent election of David Dinkins as the city's first black mayor, created a perfect storm for possible revolution in the streets. Agitprop hip-hop recording artists Public Enemy for some reason caused black and white music critics alike, not to mention millions of fans throughout the country, to swoon with delight over their belligerent, incendiary raps. Spike Lee's brazenly anti-white 1989 movie, "Do the Right Thing," made a similar impression upon film critics.[4] Sonny Carson, the convicted kidnapper and extortionist who led the August 31, 1989 "Day of Outrage," followed up that effort starting in early 1990 with a highly menacing and protracted black protest boycott of two Korean-owned green grocers in the Flatbush section of Brooklyn.[5]

Amid this maelstrom of racial triumphalism was the chairman of the black studies program at City College of New York, part of City University of New York (CUNY), Leonard Jeffries Jr.[6] The Columbia-educated Jeffries, by virtue of being black and apparently nothing else, had parlayed his sense of racial grievance into an academic career starting in the early 70s. And by 1991, despite still having no publications, not to mention a teaching style barely distinguishable from incitement, he had become a public figure. Jeffries hated whites at least as much as he loved blacks. For him, all of Western civilization was one long act of white supremacist theft and destruction of noble African-derived cultures. The best that the world had to offer owed almost solely to black benevolence and creativity; the worst owed to white cruelty and perfidy.

Blacks were "sun people" – warm, communal and friendly. Whites, by contrast, were "ice people" – cold, violent and murderous. Jeffries was a black revolutionary crank in academic drag. Yet at CUNY, it could be said that he was in the right place.

He would prove an influential revolutionary and academician. In the late 1980s, whether out of timidity, naivete or both, New York State Commissioner of Education Thomas Sobol tapped Jeffries to serve on a panel that would explore ways to expand the focus on multicultural-ism in K-12 public education. The final 1989 report, "A Curriculum of Inclusion," bore Jeffries' input. Students of color, noted the authors, have been victims of "intellectual and educational oppression" as a result of curricula reflecting "systematic bias toward European cultures and its derivatives." So inflammatory was the overall tone that renowned histo-rian Arthur Schlesinger, another panel member, refused to endorse it. The project would be shelved, though a more conciliatory report, "One Nation, Many Peoples: A Declaration of Cultural Independence," would be released in its place in 1991.

On July 20, 1991, Leonard Jeffries graduated from minor to major public figure. In a speech before the taxpayer-financed Empire State Black Arts and Cultural Festival in Albany, N.Y., Jeffries blasted Jews as conspiring against blacks in every endeavor of life. Rich Jews, he as-serted, had been at the heart of the trans-Atlantic slave trade. Aided by the Mafia, rich Jews also supposedly controlled the movie industry in order to negatively portray blacks. And Jewish educators, needless to say, had thwarted the introduction of black studies curricula. During his two-hour broadside, he managed to get in pot shots at any number of prominent Jews, from Assistant Secretary of Education Diane Ravitch to Harvard sociologist Nathan Glazer to former New York City Mayor Edward Koch.[7] For weeks, local newspapers shone a light on this fanatic. The threat was real. But Jeffries also had his defenders. Among them was Al Sharpton. It was against *this* backdrop that Reverend Al issued his threat, "If the Jews want to get it on, tell them to pin their yarmulkes back and come over to my house."

David Dinkins, elected mayor in November 1989 over Republican Party nominee Rudolph Giuliani by about 2.5 percentage points after defeating three-time incumbent Ed Koch in the Democratic primary two months earlier,[8] was at once a beneficiary and a captive of this rising black-nationalist sentiment. Dinkins was black, but to the militants he seemed tame, an establishment Uncle Tom carrying the water for whitey. Eager, but not *too* eager, to prove his racial credentials, Dinkins passively endorsed the militants. While no one statement can be said to have triggered the Crown Heights riot, Sharpton's highly-publicized anti-Jewish remark of August 18, 1991 helped darken the gathering storm clouds. It would not take long for the storm to happen.

It was approximately 8:20 P.M., Monday, August 19, 1991. The leader of the Crown Heights Jewish Lubavitcher Hasidic community, Grand Rabbi Menachem Schneerson, was returning home in a three-car motorcade from his weekly visit to the graves of his wife and father-in-law, headed for the sect's headquarters at 770 Eastern Parkway. An unmarked police car with two officers inside and a rooftop light flashing headed the motorcade; Rabbi Schneerson's car was in the middle; and a Mercury Grand Marquis station wagon driven by a young Hasidic man, Yosef Lifsh, accompanied by three passengers, was in the rear. The vehicles were traveling at an average city speed. So far, everything appeared normal.

The situation suddenly became abnormal when the motorcade, traveling east on President Street, headed toward the Utica Avenue intersection. A Chevrolet Malibu traveling north on Utica also was headed toward the intersection. In response, Lifsh, 22, whose car had fallen behind the first two, ran either a red or yellow light (eyewitness accounts differed), in order to catch up. He swerved to avoid hitting the Chevy, but ran into another car. The impact caused Lifsh's Grand Marquis to career off the street, jump the curb and onto the sidewalk, knock down a stone building pillar down, hit a wall, and strike a pair of black children. They were seven-year-old Guyanese cousins, Angela and Gavin

Cato, playing in front of their apartment building. The girl and boy were injured, pinned beneath the car.

A bleeding Lifsh and his passengers exited the car and tried to lift their vehicle off the children. Quite obviously, this was no hit-and-run accident, let alone a premeditated act. Unfortunately, a group of black males sitting nearby didn't see things that way. Incapable of distinguishing between an accident and an act of aggression, the group suddenly turned on the impromptu Good Samaritans. A Lubavitcher passenger tried to call for emergency help on his cell phone, but he was physically assaulted and robbed before he could complete his call.

The situation was getting ugly – and fast. The police in the motorcade's unmarked lead car managed to dispatch other officers and an ambulance to the scene. At the same time, Hatzolah Ambulance Service, a privately-funded Hasidic operation, sent one of its own cars to the site. The Hatzolah and city ambulances arrived at roughly the same time. The angry crowd at this point had grown to about 150 to 250 persons, mostly black teenagers shouting "Jews! Jews! Jews!" Police ordered the city ambulance crew to remove the Hasidic men for their own safety. A second Hatzolah driver, his vehicle equipped with specialized trauma equipment, also arrived to help the crew working on Angela Cato. A city ambulance rushed Gavin Cato to Kings County Hospital, but it was too late. He died shortly after arrival.

Immediately, rumors circulated among blacks that "the Jews" had avoided justice. The first Hatzolah crew, with the full cooperation of police, allegedly whisked Lifsh off to safety and ignored Angela and Gavin Cato because they were black; that Lifsh was drunk, lacked a valid driver's license and was talking on a cell phone; and that Gavin Cato's father was beaten by police for interfering with the rescue. Each of these rumors was false, especially the first. *Police had ordered the private ambulance away for the owners' safety.*

And concerns over safety for Jews soon would be well-founded. Hundreds of blacks saw an opportunity to do what they no doubt had been fantasizing about. They threw debris, shattered windows, set fires and looted what appeared to be Jewish-owned stores. Black radio stations spread the word: It was party time. Soon enough, blacks from other neighborhoods arrived by subway in Crown Heights to join in. Many ran through the streets shouting, "Heil, Hitler!," beating and robbing Jews at random. One of the rioters later arrested, Charles Price, a heroin addict and convicted thief, exhorted a crowd to "take" Kingston Avenue because of its proliferation of its Jewish-owned businesses. According to an eyewitness, Price at one point shouted to the crowd, "I'm going up to the Jew neighborhood! Who's with me?" Another witness, a police officer, testified he heard him shouting, "Let's get a Jew."

Anyone not seeing a parallel between this and the Nazi government-instigated *Kristallnacht* against Germany's Jewish population on the night of November 9-10, 1938 simply wasn't being honest. Many older local Jews, themselves Holocaust survivors, saw the parallel. And the situation soon was about to get worse. Roughly around midnight, a roving gang of about a dozen to 20 blacks accosted a visiting Orthodox Jewish scholar from Australia, a doctoral student at the University of Melbourne in his late 20s, Yankel Rosenbaum. Though not a Lubavitcher, he looked like one, and that was all that the mob needed to know. Screaming "Get the Jew," the mob swarmed over him and beat him, fracturing his skull. Were that not enough, one of its members knifed him four times. Police on the scene radioed for assistance, mentioning that one of the attackers was wearing a red shirt and baseball cap. Shortly thereafter, one of the arriving cops found a youth answering to that description hiding behind a bush in a nearby yard. His name was Lemrick Nelson. And not only did Nelson look like the perp, but he also had a bloody knife and three blood-stained one-dollar bills that tests later showed were consistent with Rosenbaum's blood type. Nelson and four other suspects in the attack were taken into custody. Rosenbaum at least was able to identify Nelson, a student at Paul Robeson High School enrolled in a program for pupils with behavioral problems, was taken to the 71st Precinct in Crown Heights where he was advised of his rights. He then confessed to police that he stabbed Rosenbaum, though after having

had a beer or two. As for Yankel Rosenbaum, he was rushed by police and ambulance to Kings County Hospital in Brooklyn. He would
die from his wounds during the wee hours of the following morning at
roughly 2:25 A.M. Hospital staff, in fact, could have saved his life, but
overlooked a treatable wound.

When the dust from the pogrom settled, numerous businesses and
cars had been burned and nearly 200 persons had been assaulted and
injured. Fully 129 persons were arrested on a variety of charges; another
46 were issued court summonses. More than 90 percent of these individuals were black males under the age of 25.[9] Even after the riot, the
immediate and surrounding areas were far from safe. A couple weeks
later, on the night of September 5, several blocks from the Rosenbaum
stabbing, four black men surrounded the car of an Italian-American
motorist, Anthony Graziosi, 67, dragged him out of his vehicle (which
was at a full stop at a red light), robbed him, and then shot him to death.
Apparently, his full beard and dark clothing had marked him as Jewish.
The one person charged in the murder, Carl Jeffrey Daniels, told police
that he had participated in the robbery but had not fired off any shots.
Due to the unavailability or unreliability of witnesses, this would be a
tough case to prosecute, especially given that the jury consisted of 10
blacks and two whites. Daniels was acquitted in June 1992.[10] In another
instance, someone fired gunshots into a local synagogue. On February
6, 1992, Phyllis LaPine, a Hasidic mother of four, was repeatedly stabbed
to death by a black burglar while she carried groceries inside her apartment. The assailant, a 23-year-old career criminal, Romane LaFond,
would be convicted of murder by a jury that November.[11] On or about
the same day as the LaPine murder, a Lubavitch couple was beaten and
robbed by two black men yelling, "Jew, give me your money." About two
weeks later, a pair of black teenagers threw rocks and bricks at a school
bus with Jewish children inside.[12]

The City's black leadership didn't seem much interested in any
of this. But then, they didn't seem that concerned about those riotous nights and days of August 19-22, 1991. It's true that Mayor David

Dinkins and Police Chief Lee Brown dispatched some 2,000 police to the scene, but the effort proved insufficient. Dinkins also avoided calling the event a riot, at one point calling the criminals "demonstrators." He spent much of the time at the U.S. Open tennis tournament in Forest Hills, Queens. In November 1992, New York Democratic Governor Mario Cuomo issued an executive order authorizing State Criminal Justice Services Commissioner Richard Girgenti to conduct a full inquiry of the riot and surrounding events. The exhaustive two-volume report, released on July 20, 1993,[13] cited Dinkins and Brown for insufficient action against "the aggression of one group against another," but stopped short of accusing them of willfully pulling back on police assistance.

A portion of the press already had exonerated the rioters.[14] *New York Times* columnist Anna Quindlen, after visiting a housing project in Crown Heights, asked, recycling familiar Sixties-era "root causes" rationalizations: "What must you feel if you feel your whole life is a slur, if you read the handwriting on the wall of your existence ands the graffiti seem to say, 'Who cares?'"[15] A *New York Times* headline read, "Tension in Brooklyn; The Bitterness Flows in Two Directions."[16] The black New York City weekly newspaper, *The Amsterdam News*, didn't even bother feigning moral equivalence. Its headline read, "Many Blacks, No Jews Arrested in Crown Heights" – as if the arrests somehow were unrelated to criminal activity.

Then there was Al Sharpton, in a class by himself. He became involved in the situation when, while eating at a Harlem restaurant (with Alton Maddox), he received a call from Gavin Cato's father who wanted him as his adviser. This was the second day of the riot. Yankel Rosenbaum already had been dead for some 15 hours. But that hardly made Sharpton a misunderstood innocent. For one thing, he continuously has downplayed black wrongdoing, straining facts beyond credulity. In his 1996 book, *Go and Tell Pharoah*, he recalled, "Gangs of young Jews and young blacks were skirmishing throughout the neighborhood, and the Jews are getting the better of it because the blacks were not

102

expecting the attacks."[17] In *Al on America*, published in 2002, he wrote, again, in semiliterate fashion:[18]

> *Crown Heights happened when two kids were in front of their house playing in Brooklyn. A car jumps the curb and kills one of the kids. A private Jewish ambulance comes to take care of the driver of the car and leaves the two little children. The little boy dies and the driver flees the country. Violence breaks out. That night, Yankel Rosenbaum, a Jew, is killed…Violence erupted in Crown Heights, with Hasidic Jews on one side of Eastern Parkway throwing rocks and bottles, and those from the West Indian community on the other side throwing rocks and bottles.*

The Reverend Al had saved his eloquence – or what passed for it – back during the funeral service for Gavin Cato at Saint Anthony's Baptist Church in Crown Heights on August 26, 1991, one week after the riot began. It was clear that the estimated 3,000 blacks in attendance weren't there to mourn the passing of Yankel Rosenbaum. Fully aware of his audience's emotions, Sharpton was shameless in his manipulation of them. This was an injustice, he insisted, not an accident:[19]

> *The world will tell us that he (Gavin Cato) was killed by accident. Yes, it was a social accident. It's an accident for one group of people to be treated better than another group of people. It's an accident to allow a minority to impose their will on a majority. It's an accident to allow an apartheid ambulance service in the middle of Crown Heights. It's an accident to thin we will keep crying and never stand up and call for justice.*

This was the speech in which Sharpton, notoriously, made his reference to Jews as "diamond merchants." Yet contrary to popular misconception, the remark was not directed toward Jews in general, but toward a very specific group of Jews – and with a clearly conspiratorial view. "Talk about how Oppenheimer in South Africa sends diamonds to Tel Aviv and deals with the diamond merchants right here in Crown Heights," Sharpton told the packed congregation. "The issue is not anti-Semitism; the issue is apartheid."[20]

Sharpton at the funeral of seven-year old Gavin Cato, killed in car accident in Crown Heights, New York. (AP/Wide World)

Just in case anyone missed his menace, Sharpton declared that the black community "will not allow any compromise or sellouts or anything less than the prosecution of the murderers of this young man." He asked: "Have we lost all of our shame that even children are not above some crumbs from the table of people who have nothing but wickedness and hate in their hearts?" Reverend Al then poured on the sentimentality, assuring the audience that young Gavin Cato was in a better place.[21]

Don't worry…I prayed and called heaven this morning. The boy is all right. He's in the hands of an eternal God. In fact, they told me he was in the playroom. They introduced him to four little girls who got killed in Birmingham one morning. Yusuf Hawkins and Michael Griffith – they'll babysit him. Don't worry. They'll bring him over and introduce him to his uncle, Brother Malcolm.

Sharpton then revealed his own Afrocentric chauvinism in all its looniness:[22]

It's no accident that we know we know we should not be run over. We are the royal family on the planet. We're the original man. We gazed into the stars and wrote astrology. We had a conversation and that became philosophy. We are the ones who created mathematics. We're not anybody to be left to die waiting on an ambulance. We are the alpha and the omega of creation itself.

The Rev appeared to be confusing astrology with astronomy. And he didn't quite get around to listing the magnificent, albeit unknown African philosophers and mathematicians. Perhaps Leonard Jeffries could have provided some answers.

Sharpton would be loaded for bear at other times. Several days after the funeral – on the Jewish Sabbath, no less – he led about 400 marchers along the Eastern Parkway up to Lubavitcher headquarters, leading a chant, "Whose Streets? Our Streets," and "No Justice, No Peace." Non-Jewish whites weren't safe either. One of the protest signs read: "The White Man Is the Devil." A second riot very easily might have broken out. Al Sharpton wasn't about to discourage it. Indeed, according to one eyewitness, he had incited a crowd *during* the riot. In sworn testimony, a Hasidic Jew named Efraim Lipkind, a former resident of Crown Heights, stated that Sharpton was on the scene on the second night of rioting, whipping up the crowd. In Lipkind's words: "Then we had a famous man, Al Sharpton, who came down, and he said Tuesday night, 'Kill the Jews' two times. I heard him, and he started to lead a charge across the street to Utica (Avenue)."[23]

That leads us to the criminal justice phase. The Reverend Al, along with Cato family attorney Colin Moore, who himself had spoken at the funeral, played no small role in pressuring Brooklyn District Attorney Charles Hynes into convening a grand jury. The result, however, was not to Sharpton's liking. In October 1991, the grand jury charged Lemrick Nelson with the murder of Yankel Rosenbaum. The state's evidence against him was overwhelming. The victim (before he died, that is) had identified Nelson as the attacker. And Nelson had confessed to police during an interrogation that he was in possession of the murder weapon with the victim's blood. The grand jury, which consisted of 10 blacks, eight whites and five Hispanics, also declined to indict Yosef Lifsh, citing no credible evidence; Lifsh, in fact, had testified. Sharpton was his own worst enemy in all this. As the Cato family "adviser," he and Colin Moore persuaded the family not to cooperate with authorities.

Once the grand jury report came out only weeks after the riot, Sharpton and Moore, enraged that Lifsh had not been indicted, talked the Cato family into filing a civil damage suit. That they did – for $100 million. The problem is that Lifsh, for his own safety, reportedly had fled to Israel. Sharpton vowed to serve him with the papers in person. That September, he booked thousands of dollars worth of plane tickets for himself and his entourage (which included Alton Maddox) on an El Al Airlines flight to Tel Aviv. Despite this being Yom Kippur weekend, the Israelis were prepared. After going through Ben-Gurion Airport customs, Sharpton recalled being greeted by what "seems like the entire Israeli press corps." He related, "Then a woman...runs up to me and yells, 'Go to hell, Sharpton, go to hell.'" He responded: "I am in hell."[24] Lifsh, however, could not be located. Some sources suggested he might have been in Canada. At any rate, Sharpton's claim that the

Israeli government had an obligation to extradite Lifsh was nonsense because the U.S.-Israeli extradition treaty did not apply to civil cases.[25]

If the Rev's trip to Israel bore no fruit, neither, unfortunately, did the state's case against Lemrick Nelson. On October 29, 1992, a predominantly black and Hispanic 12-member trial jury, against a good deal of compelling evidence, found Nelson not guilty of murder. Afterward, several black jurors celebrated with Nelson and his lawyers at a local restaurant. The Rosenbaum family, properly disgusted at what appeared to be racially-charged nullification, persuaded U.S. Attorney Zachary W. Carter of the Eastern District of New York to indict Nelson in August 1994 for violating Yankel Rosenbaum's civil rights. Nelson's main defense was that he should be tried as a juvenile since he was likely to be rehabilitated.[26] Initially, U.S. District Judge David Trager ruled in Nelson's favor, but an appeals court overruled him in October 1995.

Prosecutors managed to win a retrial by jury. At the new trial, which began on January 16, 1997, court transcripts revealed that Nelson, according to prosecutor Alan Vinegard, "perceives himself to be the victim, and not the perpetrator." Nelson replied, "Damn right." On February 10, the jury declared Nelson guilty for wielding the knife that killed Rosenbaum. Over a year later, on March 31, 1998, Judge Trager sentenced Nelson to a 19-and-a-half-year prison sentence, plus five years of probation, for civil-rights violations. At sentencing, Nelson continued to insist he was innocent. "What about my civil rights?" he demanded to know of the court. "You violated my civil rights" – priceless commentary on the debasement of the term "civil rights."

Yet the case still had legs. On January 7, 2002, a three-judge appellate panel of the U.S. Court of Appeals for the Second Circuit overturned the convictions of both Lemrick Nelson and Charles Price, concluding that Judge Trager unconstitutionally had used race as a criterion for jury selection in achieving a higher proportion of whites on the jury than the state case had. Formally, this was true. But the purpose of achieving racial balance here was to *avoid* another racially-motivated jury nullification, not to replicate it. Through more racial balance, Trager, reluctantly, believed that a more informed verdict would result. That said, by 2-1, the appeals panel ordered Nelson and Price retried "before a properly chosen jury."

The second federal trial for Lemrick Nelson began on April 28, 2003. Though this jury, like the one in the state case, was heavily black, Nelson's attorneys feared a conviction. As such, they had an announcement: Their client was prepared to admit that he stabbed Rosenbaum, but that he was in a drunken state that evening and thus had been unaware of his actions. Seton Hall University historian Edward Shapiro, author of *Crown Heights, Jews, and the 1991 Brooklyn Riot*, by far the definitive word on the subject, explained:[27]

> *The highlight of the week-long trial came when Nelson's attorney in his opening statement admitted that his client had stabbed Yankel Rosenbaum, but not because the victim was Jewish; rather, because Nelson was drunk from drinking beer and got caught up in the excitement of the moment. This strategy was ingenuous. If the jury accepted this contention, then Nelson could not be found guilty of violating Rosenbaum's civil rights because he was a Jew, the charge for which he was on trial. And because Nelson had already been acquitted for murder in the state trial in 1992, the principle of double jeopardy precluded him from being tried again for murder.*

This was a risky strategy. Nelson's lawyers, at both the 1992 and 1997 trials, already had denied that their client had stabbed Rosenbaum, despite Nelson's reported original confession. Now prosecutors could argue that the attorneys had lied on those occasions. Likewise, the defense knew it had to block introduction of all potential incriminating evidence from those trials. They were unsuccessful. Undermining their case further was the fact that they called forth no witnesses to testify about Nelson's allegedly inebriated state that night. In May, the jury reached its verdict, concluding that Nelson indeed had violated

Rosenbaum's civil rights, but that the case for his being directly responsible for the death was not proven beyond a reasonable doubt. In August of that year, Nelson received a 10-year sentence, but allowing for time served and good behavior, he was released from federal prison in Texas in June 2004 and transferred to a halfway house in New Jersey.

As for Charles Price, the other prime instigator of the riot, after being charged with incitement, Judge Trager in 1998 had handed down a sentence of 21 years and 10 months, the lengthy sentence owing to Price's extensive criminal record. As described earlier, he lucked out in January 2002, when his conviction, like that of Nelson, was thrown out by a federal appeals court. Price's attorneys, however, fearing the consequences of a new trial, decided to cop a plea. Price won a reduced sentence of 11 years and eight months, with time off for good behavior.

Al Sharpton, in a saner world, would have been arrested and prosecuted for incitement along with Price. But he was untouchable. He had the whole city scared. Mayor Dinkins, whom Sharpton previously had denounced as an "Uncle Tom" and "that nigger whore turning tricks in City Hall,"[28] wouldn't go near him, fearing mob reprisals and a loss of political capital. As it turned out, the Crown Heights riot undid his political capital anyway. He lost his 1993 re-election bid by a 51-48 percent margin to his Republican challenger, Rudy Giuliani, the same white man he had defeated four years earlier. The election of Giuliani, a no-nonsense former Manhattan federal prosecutor, was bad news for the Rev. But his rage, like that of his at-large supportive mobs, still burned. In 1995, this rage would fuel an event on his Harlem turf even more lethal than the Crown Heights riot. And as in Crown Heights, there would be an unmistakable undercurrent of anti-Semitism.

CHAPTER 11

FUNERAL PYRE AT FREDDY'S FASHION MART

Landlord-tenant disputes typically have had an extra edge when race comes into the picture. This is perhaps nowhere as true as in Harlem, which despite extensive white settlement ("gentrification") in recent years, remains a symbolic capital of black America. The deadly riot there in July 1964, which spread to Brooklyn and kicked off several consecutive "long hot summers" in the nation's cities, to an extent was an outgrowth of a black-organized rent strike.[1] The memories of those days would come back with a vengeance during the latter months of 1995, culminating in a mass murder at a Harlem clothing store, Freddy's Fashion Mart, on December 8 of that year. And contrary to his own choreographed denials, Al Sharpton had more than a little to do with this.

Freddy's Fashion Mart was located in the heart of Harlem, at 272 West 125th Street, across from the Apollo Theater. It was a successful business. The store's owner was a white Sephardic Jew, Fred Harari, who leased space from the landlord, a black Pentecostal church known as the United House of Prayer for All People. He also in turn subleased a portion of his space to The Record Shack, a longtime business headed by a black man, Sikhulu Shange. Sometime in 1995, Harari informed Shange that he wanted to expand his clothing store, and accordingly, would terminate the sublease agreement at the end of the year. Shange would have to leave. He refused. This was purely a business decision. Race had nothing to do with it. The Record Shack had been operating from that location for around 20 years. If Harari didn't want Shange around on account of his race, the record store wouldn't have been there in the first place. And this was Harlem – what sane white person was going to discriminate against blacks in Harlem? In any event, Fred Harari was not the landlord; he could terminate the sublease only with the approval of the church. Anyone with street smarts could size up the situation: The United House of Prayer for All People was using Harari to do its dirty work in case of a protest.

And a protest happened soon enough, courtesy of Al Sharpton. Word got back to him that a black business owner was about to be evicted by a white exploiter – in Harlem! The case was a natural for Sharpton. Reverend Al encouraged pickets of Freddy's, leaving day-to-day logistics in the hands of a neighborhood street vendor with a criminal record, Morris Powell, head of National Action Network's Buy Black Committee.[2] Many black picketers wanted a sequel to the Crown Heights riot, shouting phrases such as "Jew bastards" and "the blood-sucking Jews." Powell did nothing to discourage them and everything to encourage them. "This street will burn," he warned, adding, "A cracker is a cracker is a cracker."

The duo would make similar threats during appearances on black-owned radio stations WLIB and WWRL, where Al Sharpton's weekly show had been broadcast.[3] "We are going to see that this cracker suffers," Powell said into an open microphone on Sharpton's show on August 19, 1995. He added: "Reverend Sharpton is on it. We have made contact with these crackers. We don't expect a lot out of them. They haven't seen how we feel about anything yet. We are going to show them." Apparently, Powell had a thing for the Jews:

> *They think they gonna drive this man out of business, they gotta be out of their minds. We are not gonna stand by idly and let a Jewish person come in black Harlem and methodically drive black people out of business up and down 125th Street. If we stand for that, we'll stand for anything. Which we've been doing.*

Sharpton himself proved an adept rabble rouser. In a broadcast on WWRL on September 9, 1995, he menacingly intoned:

> *We will not stand by and allow them to move this brother, so that some white interloper can expand his business on 125ᵗʰ Street. And we're asking the Buy Black Committee to go down there, and I'm gonna go down there, and do what is necessary to let them know that we are not turnin' 125ᵗʰ Street back over to outsiders as it was done in the early part of this century.*

Several weeks later, on an October 21 WWRL broadcast, another black activist, Norman "Granddad" Reide, issued this threat to local Jews:

> *I am saying to the Jewish community, and specifically to Abraham Foxman, that you come out and utter a word, an accusatory remark against Reverend Sharpton, Jesse Jackson, Donna Wilson, Reverend Shields or Gary Byrd, we will boycott you. And nobody loves money any more than the Jewish people. Thank you.*

In the minds of such tyrants, individual property rights on even an elementary level must yield to raw tribalism. Those merchants not adhering to this directive can expect violent retaliation. Much as the loathsome Sonny Carson had stage-managed the anti-Korean grocer boycott in Brooklyn several years earlier, Powell, with aggressive encouragement from Sharpton, was enraged that a non-black could manage a successful enterprise in a black neighborhood. That local blacks may have been regular customers of Freddy's Fashion Mart apparently never occurred to them. Fred Harari, far from sucking the economic lifeblood from Harlem blacks, was helping to provide it.

The protests would continue well into the fall. Violence increasingly was in the air. Then, at warp speed, it happened. On December 7, one of the most virulent of the black protestors, Tracy "Shabazz" Ligon, forced his way into Freddy's and then proceeded to shout, 'I will be back to burn the Jew store down – burn, burn, burn."[4] Ligon, who had an extensive criminal record and often stayed at a nearby home-less shelter, was a part-time employee of the record store. Only the day before, he had been arrested by transit police for subway turnstile-jumping. The next day, December 8, the worst fears came to pass. Another demonstrator, a black-nationalist ex-con and part-time street peddler[5] named Roland J. Smith, aka Abubunde Mulocko, burst into the store with a loaded .38 revolver, ordering all black customers out. The handwriting was on the wall: White people, or at least non-blacks, were going to die. Smith/Mulocko then doused several clothing bins with paint thinner, lit the bins on fire and shot several people. He then turned the gun on himself. In all, eight persons, including the deranged Smith/Mulocko, died from gunshot wounds, smoke inhala-tion or both. And though nonblack customers and employees were the targets, one of the dead was a black security guard. Most, if not all, of the others were Hispanic. Aside from Smith/Mulocko, mercifully dead by his own hand, the departed were: Kareem Brunner, Olga Garcia, Angelina Marrero, Cynthia Martinez, Luz Ramos, Mayra Rentas and Garnette Ramautar.

Accounts of Sharpton's role in the Freddy's Fashion Mart massacre, even the most critical ones, typically end here. Yet there was a highly significant coda. Reverend Al knew he had a public relations night-mare on his hands, possibly even worse than the one in Crown Heights. In full damage control mode, Sharpton for years afterward denied any role. In his 2002 autobiography, *Al on America*, he explained:[6]

> *I wasn't even at the scene…when that guy burned down Freddy's. No one in the community connected me to the fire. They knew what happened. None of the family members of the victims of the fire implicated me. They sued Freddy and the city. They didn't sue me. Because they knew I had nothing to do with it. My only role was in fighting for justice in the same nonviolent manner I have my entire career.*

This spin almost defies belief. His claim is akin to imagining Josef Stalin saying he had nothing to do with any Soviet labor camp deaths because he wasn't personally at the camps. The undeniable reality is that Sharpton, far from being a misunderstood innocent, was an instigator. Through his Buy Black Committee and his radio program, he escalated tensions among people eager to have their own primitive hatreds validated. To publicly threaten an "interloper," whether in person or over the airwaves, constitutes an incitement, especially given the racial element. Incitement to riot is classified as a crime for a good reason: Words, and the way they are spoken, really can inflame. In the case of Freddy's Fashion Mart, the flames were literal as well as figurative. Innocent people died.

Though not citing him by name, Mayor Giuliani implied that Sharpton should be held accountable. "There has to be a full investigation of any others who might have complicity in bringing this tragedy about," said the mayor. "If others from the outside had not tried to use it to move their own agenda, it may very well be that this tragedy, or a tragedy of this dimension, never would have occurred."[7] Rather than ponder the possibility that the mayor was right, Sharpton instead called him out, exclaiming, "He (Giuliani) has played the race card every time he could."[8] One almost had to laugh – here was Reverend Al, of all people, calling out *someone else* for exploiting racial tension! Harlem Congressman Charles Rangel likewise appeared more concerned over the welfare of Sharpton than of the deceased persons and their families. To imply that Sharpton contributed to the massacre, Rangel insisted, "is just not fair, but more importantly could be jeopardizing his life."[9] The congressman apparently was blind to the fact that Sharpton not only had jeopardized innocent lives, he indirectly had helped take them.

Sharpton was never arrested for incitement related to the attack, but police investigators did question Shabazz Ligon about Sharpton and his lieutenant, Morris Powell, and their racially charged comments over the air. The lawyer for Sharpton and National Action Network, Michael Hardy, told Ligon not to answer these questions because they might raise potential conflicts of interest. Police also asked Ligon if his comment about "bloodsuckers" referred to Fred Harari. Hardy, speaking for Ligon, responded: "He (Ligon) said no. They asked him if he was talking about the clothing store and he said, 'Well, yes, I was talking about Freddy's.' But then I asked him if he would have used that term for any store in those circumstances and he said yes."[10]

Fred Harari proved a resilient fellow. Within a relatively short time, he renovated the store, renamed it Uptown Jeans and began operating again.[11] Al Sharpton's wingman, Morris Powell, didn't like this latest development. In response, he revived his street boycott. "How's it that these Jews are able to come back and do business around here, come back stronger, with two or three stores?" he fumed. Well, Mr. Powell, maybe it's because "these Jews" actually work for a living. There was a very real possibility for a second round of destruction and death at this point. Harari's lawyer, Robert Rimberg, stated in court papers: "Powell, if permitted to continue [the current protest], is setting the stage for another tragedy." To head this possibility off, Sharpton in late 1998 attempted to broker a deal between Harari and Powell. While word of a formal agreement was unavailable, peace in the end was achieved – and very likely with the aid of a monetary "contribution" to Sharpton from Harari.

Al Sharpton, confident he was off the hook, already had other projects in mind. Foremost among them: Take over Giuliani's job or at least discredit him professionally. Opportunities eventually would come on both counts.

CHAPTER 12

GIULIANI-ERA POLICE CONTROVERSIES: RUBBING WOUNDS RAW

From the moment Rudy Giuliani took office as New York City mayor on New Year's Day, 1994, Al Sharpton had it in for him. The new mayor had the temerity to defeat a black incumbent, David Dinkins, the previous November. Though Sharpton thought little of Dinkins, he viewed Giuliani as far worse, especially after Giuliani had made clear that Reverend Al's services weren't needed. In even more depressing news for Sharpton, Giuliani during the following several years had proven effective, especially when it came to crime. He understood, as his predecessor apparently had not, that for a city to be great, it had to be livable – and that nothing destroys livability more than crime and the pervasive fear of it.

It was a fact: New York's the criminal underclass was overwhelmingly black and Hispanic. Sharpton was one of many minority activists who saw "racism" lurking beneath the new administration's anti-crime initiatives. Indeed, he was so incensed that he ran for mayor as a Democrat in 1997. Announcing his candidacy that year on Martin Luther King Day, he conveyed his intent to undo the Giuliani legacy. He would frame the issue as The People versus Mayor Giuliani. In *Al on America*, published nearly a year after Giuliani had stepped down, Sharpton wrote: "There are those who will say that Giuliani brought back a quality of life to New York City. They will say that he was concerned with people and helped drive down crime to make their lives more comfortable. No, Rudy Giuliani used his policies to help make the city more business-friendly."[1] He also would declare: "So Giuliani doesn't like me? Good – I don't like him, either. He doesn't want to talk to me? Good – I don't want to talk to him either."[2]

Sharpton during the late Nineties was a man obsessed. Convinced the mayor was sanctioning police brutality against blacks under the guise of promoting public safety, he ached to find a smoking gun to discredit the mayor and enhance his own credibility. He would find it in three separate incidents occurring in August 1997, February 1999 and March 2000, whose victims, respectively, were Abner Louima, Amadou Diallo and Patrick Dorismond, each a first- or second-generation black immigrant.

In Abner Louima, a Haitian-born resident of Brooklyn, Sharpton had a tailor-made campaign issue: a palpable act of brutality by four white cops against a helpless black suspect. And the Rev milked it for all it was worth, implying that the "real" criminal in all this was Mayor Giuliani.

It was Friday night, August 8, 1997. Abner Louima, a 30-year-old security guard, married with one child, headed off with his brother and a cousin to Club Rendez-Vous in East Flatbush, a popular night spot among Haitian ethnics in Brooklyn.[3] The place had a bad reputation – and with good reason. Gunfire between patrons was common despite the metal detector at the front door. In the previous year alone, a bouncer, two doormen and a security dog had been shot. Once in a while, ex-members of the Tonton Macoutes, the feared secret police of once and future Haitian dictator Jean-Claude "Baby Doc" Duvalier, would start a rumble. Around 3 A.M. closing time, August 9, Louima and a few other men, while exiting the club, noticed two women in a violent catfight in the middle of the street surrounded by dozens of onlookers, any number of whom appeared ready to jump in. One woman was screaming at the other in Creole: "*Bouzin!! Kite neg moin!*" ("Slut!! Leave my man alone!"). In response, Louima and some other men tried to intercede.

Meanwhile, someone had called the cops. At least eight officers from the 70th Precinct arrived soon enough. The cops saw the situation and knew they had trouble on their hands. About 200 agitated people were in the middle of the street. This was not simply "a fight," but a potential full-scale riot. As officers of the law, they went about breaking up the melee anyway. In the course of their action, one of the cops, Officer Justin Volpe, was sucker-punched. He identified Abner Louima as the assailant. A fellow officer, Thomas Bruder, was a witness. "It is wild," he said. "I hear a commotion. I look over my left shoulder, and Volpe is in a fight with Abner Louima." Bruder insists Louima threw the sucker punch: "Absolutely. It was Louima." A witness standing next to Louima, Teddy Petion, a respiratory therapist, disputed this account. "It wasn't Abner who threw a punch at the cop," said Petion. "It happened so fast. Abner went in to break up a fight between two girls. He took out his security badge from his job...Abner and one of the officers began arguing, and Abner said, 'I'm going to get your badge number.'" It was at that point, said Petion, when Officer Thomas Wiese yelled, 'Let's get him!" and hit Louima on the head. Another Haitian – the one who reportedly (from Petion's standpoint) threw the punch at a cop – had made a run for it, leaving Louima at the mercy of police.

Whether or not this was a case of mistaken identity, Officers Volpe, Bruder and Wiese, along with Officer Charles Schwarz, put the collar on Louima. Had they followed basic procedure, not much would have come of the incident. Unfortunately, the arresting officers – most of all, Volpe, 25, himself the son of a cop – couldn't leave well enough alone. First, en route to the police station, one or more of them beat Louima with fists, nightsticks and hand-held radios. Upon arrival, they booked him for disorderly conduct, obstructing arrest and resisting arrest, then strip-searched him and put him in a holding cell. Then, in the ultimate indignity, they took him to a bathroom and cuffed his hands from behind his back, whereupon Officer Volpe repeatedly sodomized Louima with a broom handle, badly damaging his teeth and rectum. As an encore, Volpe walked through the station holding the bloody broom, boasting to a sergeant that he "took a man down tonight."

One day later, Louima was taken to the emergency room at Coney Island Hospital. A nurse, suspicious of the claim by escorting police officers that his extreme injuries were the result of "abnormal homosexual activities," called Louima's family and the NYPD Internal Affairs Bureau. When word got out of how the injuries actually occurred (Louima would be hospitalized for two months), Haitian and other civil rights groups were outraged. On August 29, an estimated 7,000 demonstrators, with Al Sharpton on the front line, marched on City Hall and the 70th Precinct Station House, chanting the familiar words, "No Justice, No Peace." Former Mayor Dinkins was also there. And once the legal and public-relations phases kicked in, any number of black public figures, including Johnnie Cochran, Don King, former Haitian President Jean-Bertrand Aristide and TV host Montel Williams, also made their presence known. All recognized an opportunity to put Mayor Giuliani, the NYPD and all of white American on trial. Cochran and other lawyers filed a civil damage suit against the City of New York for a reported $465 million, positioning themselves for a chunk of the proceeds. Brooklyn U.S. Attorney Zachary Carter announced he was pursuing civil rights prosecutions. *Vanity Fair* correspondent Marie Brenner recognized a feeding frenzy. "However grotesque the injuries suffered by Abner Louima," she wrote, "the incident soon turned into a more grotesque urban morality play illustrating New Yorkers' deftness at using someone else's tragedy for personal gain. From the moment Louima wound up battered and kneeling in a cell at the 7-0 (i.e., Precinct 70), he was destined to become the focus of a war of competing agendas from which he would eventually emerge as a new power in the city, if his medical condition allowed."[4]

Al Sharpton, mayoral candidate, saw a defining moment. And this brought him into contact with Sanford Rubenstein, a lawyer hired by the Louima family. Rubenstein was well-known as a personal injury attorney specializing in police brutality cases. In various occasions, he had extracted multimillion-dollar settlements from the City of New York. The pair became fast friends. Sharpton referred to him as "Brother Rubenstein"; Rubenstein returned the favor, calling him "Brother Sharpton." A partnership could be mutually advantageous. Rubenstein could get invaluable publicity given the high likelihood of Sharpton turning the Louima incident into a national crucible on race. And Sharpton, ever the politician, could get an image enhancement. Rubenstein and Sharpton, in fact, could be seen locking arms on the front line in that August 29 march.

For once, Reverend Al had a defensible campaign, in contrast to the reprehensible Tawana Brawley, Crown Heights and Freddy's Fashion Mart fiascos that won him so much public revulsion. Sharpton reveled in the afterglow of the rally, declaring it was a sign of his political strength. Growing public outrage over police brutality, he insisted, would carry him to victory in the September 9 Democratic primary against his opponents, Manhattan Borough President Ruth Messinger and Brooklyn City Councilman Sal Albanese. But he never hesitated to let anyone know within shouting distance the identity of his real opponent. Speaking at one of his weekly Saturday rallies at his Harlem office, Sharpton, sounding more than a little like Muhammad Ali, remarked, "I want to thank Sal and Ruth for getting me in shape. And then it's going to be me and Rudy, down to the main bout." Then, he directed a taunt at the incumbent mayor, "You've been running from me for the last four years." Anticipating victory in the primary, he continued: "But now it's me and you, Rudy, and I'm going to whip you all over town!"[5] The Rev came close to getting his wish. Messinger, following a vote recount, barely exceeded the 40 percent minimum threshold necessary to avoid a runoff; she would lose to Mayor Giuliani in the November general election by a dozen percentage points. Sharpton received 32 percent.

Sharpton, to the relief of sensible people everywhere, didn't get to be mayor. But he still had plenty of pull in mobilizing opposition to the NYPD. For a change, a sizable segment of the white public actually was with him. Federal prosecutors launched a civil rights case against the cops who worked over Abner Louima.[6] With Sharpton around, they had an extra incentive to win indictments. A victory was virtually inevitable. The only issue was how much of one. Over time, the results would be known. The prime culprit, Justin Volpe, already off the police force, admitted in court in May 1999 that he had rammed a broomstick up Abner Louima's rectum and then thrust it in his face. In December of that year he received a stiff 30-year sentence, with the earliest possible release date being August 3, 2025. Charles Schwarz, also gone from the NYPD, after having a previous conviction overturned, in 2002 pleaded guilty to perjury for falsely claiming that he had not taken Louima to the station house bathroom where the assault occurred. Officers Thomas Bruder and Thomas Wiese were convicted of obstruction of justice, but had their convictions overturned by a federal appeals court in 2002. A fifth officer, Michael Bellomo, was found not guilty of attempting to cover up the beating of Louima and another Haitian immigrant by Volpe earlier in the night. Sanford Rubenstein handled the civil case, winning $8.75 million in combined judgments in July 2001 against the City of New York and the local police union; Abner Louima received about $5.8 million of that.[7]

While the Louima case was working its way through the halls of justice, another and this time lethal case emerged. On the afternoon of February 5, 1999, Reverend Sharpton was sitting in his office when the representative of an African ethnic association arrived with a story that hadn't yet even hit the local papers. The previous night, the visitor recounted, police fired off dozens of shots at an unarmed 22-year-old black street vendor from the Republic of Guinea, Amadou Diallo. Close to half those bullets struck Diallo, killing him almost instantly. Officers on the scene mistakenly had believed Diallo had a gun and was about to shoot them. Sharpton concluded this was murder, not self-defense. Moreover, it was the inevitable result of Giuliani's racial profiling policy. Surely the cops wouldn't have engaged in such overkill had the suspect been white.

On the surface, Sharpton sounded plausible. The previous night, Amadou Diallo was coming home from work. Entering the vestibule of his apartment building in the South Bronx neighborhood of Soundview, he was accosted by four white plainclothes officers from the NYPD Special Street Crimes Unit. The police believed that he fit the description of a black serial rapist reportedly spotted in the neighborhood. They asked for identification. Diallo reached into his jacket to get his wallet. That's when the cops opened fire. They let off a combined 41 shots, 19 of which struck him. Diallo was killed instantly. Sharpton described the incident this way:[8]

> *It was a slaughter. Amadou Diallo would not have faced forty-one bullets even if he were standing before a firing squad!...(F)or many of us it underscored the lack of value placed on the lives of black men in Rudy Giuliani's New York City. It put the issue of racial profiling at the center of our consciousness, and it was a wake-up call to all of black America. Amadou Diallo's only crime that night was being black. It could have been any one of us, any one of our children.*

By the middle of the month, a grand jury began hearing evidence in the case. Sharpton wanted to help things along, organizing and leading large demonstrations in front of downtown police headquarters to demand that the four officers – Kenneth Boss, Sean Carroll, Edward McMellon and Richard Murphy – be indicted. Over the next several weeks, nearly 1,200 persons were arrested for disorderly conduct. Arrestees included Jesse Jackson, NAACP President Kweisi Mfume, Ossie Davis, Ruby Dee, Susan Sarandon, former Mayor David Dinkins, Congressman Charles Rangel, Chloe Breyer (daughter of U.S. Supreme Court Justice Stephen Breyer) and prominent clergy and labor leaders. On one occasion, former Mayor Ed Koch wanted to be arrested, but couldn't make it in time.

On March 31, 1999, the grand jury came back with indictments of all four officers. The accused pleaded not guilty in New York State Supreme Court in the Bronx. That December, a state appeals court ruled the trial should be moved to Albany, citing pretrial publicity. Sharpton and his allies anticipated convictions. But after a three-week trial in February 2000, a jury of seven white men, one white woman and four black women acquitted the officers on all charges. Almost a year later, in January 2001, the U.S. Justice Department announced it would not press civil-rights charges.

Al Sharpton, other civil rights leaders and major media (particularly the *New York Times*), were apoplectic over what they insisted was a gross miscarriage of justice. But was it? Aside from the fact that four of the jurors were black, evidence indicates this was an impartial jury who had concluded that the police had not committed murder.[9] The cops on the scene were there for one reason: to track down an armed rapist believed to be responsible for as many as 51 assaults, 10 in Soundview alone. Almost *any* suspicious-looking behavior by a black might well mark that person as a culprit.

The real story went like this. Four cops in an unmarked car were cruising in the neighborhood when they spotted a man nervously pacing in the doorway and peering into the windows of 1157 Wheeler Avenue, a small brick apartment building. This very well could be the rapist, they thought. Officers Carroll and McMellon got out of the car, identified themselves as police officers, and asked the man, Amadou Diallo, to stop. Diallo, however, refused to heed them. He continued through the poorly-lit vestibule and toward the inner door. Officers Carroll and McMellon at that point ordered Diallo to come out with his hands up. Turning away, he suddenly reached into the pocket of his baggy jacket and quickly pulled out what Carroll thought was a gun. "Gun!," Carroll shouted. "He's got a gun!" McMellon, believing his life was in danger, shot at Diallo three times before accidentally falling backward, falling off the steps, and breaking his tailbone. Carroll, seeing his partner down, understandably thought he'd just been shot. He opened fire at

Diallo. Bullets ricocheted into the street. Officers Boss and Murphy, thinking a full-scale firefight was underway, jumped out of the car and began shooting at Diallo who had been shot already, but wasn't prone. Two of the officers searched Diallo's body to retrieve his gun, but found instead only a wallet and a shattered pocket beeper.

It was a terrible case of mistaken identity, exacerbated by Amadou Diallo's status as an illegal immigrant. He'd recently entered the U.S. claiming political asylum; he told American authorities that he was orphaned by a massacre and tortured by police in Mauritania. In fact, his homeland was Guinea (a French-speaking West African nation not to be confused with either Equitorial Guinea or Guinea-Bissau), and his parents were well and alive. His reluctance to deal with New York cops was driven heavily, if not entirely, by his status as an illegal immigrant. New York City during the Koch years a decade earlier had declared itself a "sanctuary city," effectively imposing a gag rule on police asking about a suspect's immigration status. With a sensible immigration policy in place, in other words, Amadou Diallo likely still would be alive – though probably not in America.

Heather Mac Donald, writing in the Manhattan Institute quarterly, *City Journal*, put the incident in perspective:[10]

> *The killing of Amadou Diallo was an unmitigated tragedy, demanding close investigation into police training procedures, to see if any feasible safeguards could have prevented it. But nothing in the police department's recent history suggests that it as part of a pattern of excessive force. Nothing that is known of the case to date suggests that the shooting was anything but a tragic mistake; the officers acted in the good-faith, though horribly mistaken, belief that they were under deadly threat.*

Also missing from Sharpton's blinkered view that Giuliani had declared open season on blacks was the context of crime. Blacks, in New York and other major U.S. cities, were disproportionately perpetrators of violent criminal acts.[11] And under Giuliani, the city was safer – much safer – than under Dinkins.[12] In 1993, Dinkins' last year in office, there were more than 2,200 homicides, a figure that dropped to 633 in 1998, the last calendar year prior to the Diallo killing. The NYPD's Street Crime Unit's policy of seeking out and confiscating illegally-owned guns was perhaps a major reason; gun-related homicides plummeted by 75 percent. Also in decline was the use of deadly force by police. Police had killed 23 civilians in the line of duty in 1993, a figure that had fallen to 19 in 1998, despite the fact that arrests had risen from 266,000 to more than 400,000 during this period. Black residents, for the most part, had little quarrel with such trends. According to a Justice Department survey released in June 1999, 77 percent of New York City blacks were "satisfied" or "very satisfied" with local police.[13]

Sharpton's political stock would get a further boost, and Giuliani's another drop, in the middle of March 2000 with another allegation of excessive, and lethal, police force. The city was tense enough already. The four police officers charged in the Diallo shooting had been acquitted just three weeks earlier. The new case revolved around the death of an American-born black Haitian ethnic, Patrick Dorismond.[14] Dorismond, 26, a Brooklyn resident and a father of two, like Abner Louima, worked as a security guard. And like Louima, he liked to unwind at nightclubs – including those with a reputation for attracting a bad element.

It was about 12:30 A.M., March 16, 2000. Patrick Dorismond and a friend, Kevin Kaiser, also a security guard, were standing outside the Distinguished Wakamba Cocktail Lounge in midtown West Side Manhattan on Eighth Avenue between 37th and 38th Streets. This club was located near Dorismond's employer, the 34th Street Partnership. Suddenly, a man approached Dorismond and Kaiser, asking where he could buy some marijuana. "You got smoke?" the stranger asked. That stranger was a plainclothes NYPD undercover cop, Anderson Moran. The NYPD had been targeting the Wakamba as part of its anti-drug initiative, Operation Condor. The corner had a reputation as a hangout for drug-dealing members of the Bloods gang.

Unaware that this was a sting, Patrick Dorismond loudly responded that he was not a drug dealer. Then, he reacted in the worst possible way, said the cops, throwing a sucker punch at Detective Moran. Kaiser then jumped in and attacked Moran. Clearly in danger, Moran sent out a distress code signal to his backup "ghosts," Officers Anthony Vasquez and Julio Cruz, who quickly came to their partner's aid. At that point, the partners heard either Dorismond or Kaiser yelling, in reference to Moran, "Get his gun!" Vasquez then drew his weapon and identified himself as a police officer. But Dorismond, rather than pull back, attempted to grab Vasquez's 9mm pistol, inadvertently causing the weapon to fire. Unfortunately, the bullet went into Dorismond's chest. An ambulance arrived on the scene minutes later and took Dorismond to St. Clare's Hospital, where he was pronounced dead.

Dorismond's friend, Kevin Kaiser, provided an opposite account. He claimed none of the officers had identified themselves before or during the altercation. And far from being the aggressor, he said, Dorismond was the victim. It was Detective Moran who was "in their face" and threw a sucker punch. Vasquez's attorney, Philip Karasyk, flatly contradicted this account. "It's a tragic accidental shooting precipitated by the deceased lunging for the gun after Detective Vasquez identified himself," said Karasyk.[15] As for who threw the first punch, Police Commissioner Howard Safir said at a press conference that it was Dorismond. "Mr. Dorismond attacked the undercover officer," Safir asserted.[16]

So who was telling the truth? Given Patrick Dorismond's criminal history,[17] the police version of the story was plausible. Back in 1987, as a 13-year-old, Dorismond was arrested for robbery and assault. He was arrested again in 1993 for attempted robbery and assault. And in 1996, he was arrested for criminal possession of a weapon. As for the juvenile case, it was dropped and never went before a judge. The 1993 accusation involved Dorismond punching a friend who had brought him $5 worth of marijuana instead of the $15 for which he had paid; Dorismond pleaded guilty to a reduced charge of disorderly conduct. And in the

1996 case, Dorismond allegedly had threatened a motorist with a gun, screaming "Don't sign your death warrant!" Yet no gun was recovered, enabling him to luck out; he received a sentence of community service for fourth-degree weapons possession. None of this apparently had dissuaded Dorismond from pursuing his goal of becoming a New York City cop.[18]

In releasing Dorismond's criminal history to the public shortly after his death, the Giuliani administration had courted a second controversy because those records included his juvenile conviction, which had been sealed. Parallel to that, with the support of Mayor Giuliani, by now running for Daniel Patrick Moynihan's pending vacant U.S. Senate seat (due to a term limits law passed by voters in 1993, he was prohibited from seeking a third term as mayor),[19] police released a toxicology report showing Dorismond had marijuana in his system at the time of his death. These moves enraged the dead man's family, Haitians and blacks generally. "Another unarmed black man, it could have been my brother," said Ena Tucker, a co-worker of Dorismond.[20] Tensions ran high at Dorismond's funeral, attended by an estimated 3,000 persons. An explosive fight broke out, resulting in a reported 27 arrests and 23 injuries to police officers.[21]

Al Sharpton saw his moment. On March 29, 2000, he urged New York's congressional delegation to demand an investigation by Attorney General Janet Reno into the Giuliani administration's release of Patrick Dorismond's juvenile record; probe the circumstances that led to the release of Dorismond's records; and request that a federal judge appoint a special monitor to oversee the NYPD. In response, lawmakers said they would send a letter to Reno, asking her to speed up the ongoing U.S. Attorney's probe into potential police conduct in the suspect's death. They declined to act on the two other requests. "How can the Dorismond family expect to get due process when you have the chief executive of the city and chief law enforcement officer of the city already painting (a picture) that in some way the victim caused his own death?," Sharpton asked.[22] Several days earlier, Reverend Al had declared: "We will not stand by and let this family be castigated...We are calling on the federal government to come in this case to bring justice."[23]

The wheels of justice already were in motion. On March 17, just one day after the fatal shooting, the law firm of Johnnie Cochran, Al Sharpton's close ally, announced it would file a wrongful death suit against the City of New York and the three undercover officers. In May, the Dorismond family filed a $100 million civil suit against the City. Meanwhile, a state grand jury convened to decide whether to criminally indict Officer Vasquez for the death of Patrick Dorismond. Separate from that, a City grand jury met for that purpose. The criminal cases, much to Sharpton's chagrin, didn't pan out. On March 25, 2000, only a little over a week after the death, District Attorney Robert Morgenthau announced that the grand jury had refused to indict Officer Vasquez, concluding the shooting was accidental. "What the grand jury found is that on the basis of the evidence, nobody could be charged with a crime," said Morgenthau.[24] Four months later, on July 27, the City grand jury came to the same conclusion. Reverend Sharpton joined Dorismond's parents and sister at an emotionally charged news conference, calling upon the U.S. Justice Department to take over the case. Nothing, however, came of this effort. The wrongful death suit, at least, bore fruit. In March 2003, the City of New York announced a settlement with the Dorismond family for $2.25 million.

Taken together, Sharpton's campaigns to treat the Louima, Diallo and Dorismond cases as police brutality run amok seemed motivated in large measure by a personal dislike of Rudy Giuliani and, more broadly, his administration's success in promoting public safety. Reverend Al dressed up extraordinary exceptions as the everyday norm in order to more effectively peddle the view that Giuliani was a political gargoyle who enabled racism and ran cover for a rogue NYPD. Sharpton's campaigns exhibited little or no understanding of the high stress that police face when making arrests, even "routine" ones. Yet in any number of ways, the campaigns had succeeded. They made him look like a concerned civil libertarian, if only on the surface. They expanded his base of support on the streets. And they undermined Mayor Giuliani's popularity to the point of convincing him in May 2000 to withdraw from the U.S. Senate race in New York whose eventual winner was First Lady Hillary Clinton.[25]

Let it be said that the widespread bitterness against certain police officers in the Louima, Diallo and Dorismond cases, up to a point, was justified. Any society with a respect for liberty must hold police accountable in evidence-gathering, arrest and detention and other procedures. But that doesn't alter the fact that Sharpton exploited these cases to ramp up his own political stature and black resentment. And his indignation was selective. If a bad cop was black, somehow this wasn't an issue. During the late Nineties, for example, dozens of members of the Los Angeles Police Department's anti-gang unit, known as the Rampart Division, were responsible for numerous shootings, beatings, thefts, robberies and false frame-ups. Many of those cops were black, as was then-LAPD Police Chief Bernard Parks, who in fact had been suspected in covering up a number of these felonies. Lowering police hiring standards to achieve more racial/ethnic diversity on the force was a very plausible reason for this "Rampart" scandal.[26] The City of Los Angeles wound up settling more than 140 civil suits for a combined $125 million. For some reason, Sharpton did not see fit to comment on any of this. One only can imagine the consequences had Sharpton won that 1997 New York mayoral race.

CHAPTER 13

HAVING IT HIS WAY:
THE BURGER KING AFFAIR

Al Sharpton for decades has seen Jesse Jackson as a mentor. That admiration has led him to emulate Jackson's practice of coaxing corporations into donating funds to him and other persons ostensibly fighting for black interests. Use high-pressure brinksmanship, Jackson counseled, and management will capitulate.[1] In 2000, Reverend Al made his debut as a business shakedown artist. His target: Burger King. The Miami-based fast food corporation, he asserted, had double-crossed a Detroit-area black franchisee, La-Van Hawkins, who had grown very wealthy in the restaurant business. Hawkins sued the company, which in turn countersued. Sharpton, meanwhile, launched a boycott.

To understand why Sharpton backed La-Van Hawkins, it would be useful to take an extended look at just who Hawkins is. If nothing else, this campaign was a first. Up until that time, all of Sharpton's clients had been a motley mix of the criminal and the merely sleazy. As a youth, Hawkins had a criminal past himself, but to his credit, he put that phase of his life way behind him to become one of the country's most successful restaurateurs. Born in Chicago in 1960, he grew up in that city's now-demolished Cabrini-Green public housing project, notorious during its existence as a haven for drugs, violence and gangs. During teen years, he belonged to a gang and had an expensive drug habit. Certain family events, however, caused him to leave high school and find work at a local McDonald's. As cliché would have it, he "turned his life around," channeling his aggression into productive work. He quickly worked his way up to general manager of the restaurant chain's busy Water Tower outlet in downtown Chicago. By the end of the Seventies, he had gone to work for Kentucky Fried Chicken, rising to the rank of regional vice president. In 1986, still only in his mid-20s, he left KFC to become a partner in an investment group headed by Texas oilman T. Boone Pickens. The group built 15 Bojangles restaurants in Baltimore, Philadelphia and Washington, D.C., and then sold them to the company. Hawkins used the profits to purchase Checkers restaurant franchises. By 1990, the year he turned 30, he opened his first Checkers outlet in Evergreen Park near Chicago. By 1995, he owned nearly 50 of them across the U.S., generating a combined $65 million in revenues annually. That later year he also founded his own management company, Inner City Foods Corporation, to develop Checkers franchises.

Hawkins was just getting started. In 1995 he also founded the Baltimore-based Urban City Foods, which would develop and operate Burger King restaurants located in areas designated under Clinton-era legislation as Empowerment Zones and Enterprise Communities. Soon enough, in 1996, Burger King and Hawkins announced plans to open as many as 225 outlets over a five-year period, focusing on drive-thru service. By September 1997, 25 outlets, mainly in Chicago, were up and running. These units, Hawkins claimed, averaged sales of almost $2 million, almost double that of traditional sit-down Burger Kings. In 1998, Hawkins combined his operations under a new Detroit-based enterprise, Hawkins Food Group LLC.

From the start, Hawkins, a man of expensive tastes and an expansive waistline, had been a champion of black economic self-empowerment. With his motto, "teach, reach and motivate," he told *Nation's Restaurant News*, "My No. 1 goal is to use the Checkers brand to provide economic empowerment in the black community and to make as many black millionaires, regional vice presidents, and managers as I can." He promoted from within and paid well. He also used some of his personal wealth to support black political candidates. This combination of business success and racial identity politics made him attractive to Al Sharpton. Their bond became realized when the Hawkins-Burger King partnership deteriorated in 2000.

La-Van Hawkins owned 28 Burger Kings. Unfortunately, to get there he borrowed heavily from the company. And he was way behind on his loans. An impatient Burger King decided to pull out. A highly agitated Hawkins responded by enlisting black attorneys Johnnie Cochran and Willie Gary, who promptly sued Burger King in April 2000 for $1.9 billion, alleging breach of contract and racial discrimination. For public relations ammo, the lawyers invited Al Sharpton aboard. Reverend Al proved a willing and able partner. And his help would come in handy because only several days after Hawkins filed suit, Burger King countersued, alleging Hawkins had failed to repay more than $8 million in outstanding loans.

Several months later, in September 2000, Al Sharpton announced he would go to Wall Street to announce a five-day countdown to a nationwide boycott of Burger King if the company did not agree to discuss the possibility of reversing its revocation of the franchise agreement; hire a minority-owned investment firm to handle a proposed initial stock offering; and hire a minority-owned advertising agency. "Burger King is pulling a whopper over the black community," Sharpton told the Associated Press in a telephone interview. "This is part of a pattern of racism."[2] He also indicated his intention to picket selected Burger Kings in New York City. The Rev's spokeswoman, Rachel Noerdlinger, said that New York was chosen as the target because of its relative absence of black-owned outlets.

The last thing the company wanted was bad publicity from Al Sharpton. Three months earlier, in June, British beer and spirits conglomerate Diageo PLC, then the parent company of Burger King, had announced plans for a stock offering. It was clear that the Reverend Al and La-Van Hawkins were timing their boycott for maximum effect. In September, Sharpton and Burger King provisional CEO Colin Storm, who had come over from Diageo's Guinness Brewing Division, met for two hours at Burger King headquarters. The encounter was cordial enough to put the boycott on hold.

The good will, such as it was, would be short-lived. In a testy letter to Storm in October, Sharpton accused the company of failing to follow through on research to document minority purchasing levels. Storm wrote back to Sharpton, effectively telling him to take a hike: "We believe we have addressed the diversity issues you have raised. We can only conclude your actions are solely an attempt to pressure Burger King Corp. into making a settlement with Mr. Hawkins that has no commercial or legal basis." Storm added that a boycott would have an adverse impact on the very blacks whose interests Sharpton had professed to champion. A boycott, noted Storm, "could have great economic consequences on all stakeholders of Burger King, including our minority franchisees and our minority vendors."[3] Minority franchisees themselves made the same point. Through their trade group, the Minority Franchise Association, they issued the following statement:[4]

> *There are 1,173 minority-owned Burger King Corporation restaurants nationwide – 15 percent of the 7,380 franchise-owned Burger King stores in the United States. The Minority Franchise Association of Burger King Corporation is a 26-year-old national organization made up of 75 minority franchisees. As a group, we are united in our opposition to the national boycott of Burger King Restaurants initiated by La-Van Hawkins and his companies along with the Reverend Al Sharpton.*

In their haste to humble a "racist" corporation, then, Sharpton, Hawkins, Cochran and Gary apparently overlooked the fact that black and other minority group franchisees, like their white counterparts, had to make a living – and that a boycott was the last thing these franchisees needed.

Burger King made for an odd target for a racially-based lawsuit. If anything, it had been bending in every direction to become an industry leader in "diversity." In its response to Sharpton, the company noted the following: the number of its black suppliers had more than doubled in recent years; it had 32 minority vendors; nearly 1,200 of its 7,830 U.S. restaurants were minority-owned; Burger King had a 17-year relationship with UniWorld Group, a black-owned advertising agency; and it was actively seeking black investment firms to oversee its IPO.[5] That Sharpton would single out Burger King for a race-based boycott was in line with a longstanding pattern of picking an apparently compliant target. Burger King resisted, surely a healthy sign. Management on some level sensed that appeasing shakedown artists is futile and, at best, buys time until the next shakedown.

Burger King won its court battles. In December 2000, U.S. District Judge Marianne Battani ruled from her bench in Ann Arbor, Mich., that La-Van Hawkins and Burger King had signed a "clear and unambiguous" agreement in July 1999 barring him from suing the company for any problems that arose prior to that time.[6] Hawkins, she concluded, had no standing to sue. That same month, the New York State Supreme Court ruled that Hawkins and two of his companies had to pay $8.4 million to a Burger King affiliate to repay 21 delinquent loans. Sharpton responded with typical belligerence, especially toward the federal court ruling. "We will nonviolently come in and take over," he said. "I'm prepared to go to jail before I allow them to practice – without any sense of outrage or any sense of recourse – discrimination based on a technicality." Perhaps Reverend Al failed to understand that enforceable contracts necessarily are based on "technicalities." Perhaps he also failed to understand that forcibly "taking over" someone else's property is anything but nonviolent.

Though the boycott fizzled and the lawsuits failed, La-Van Hawkins wound up doing very well. True, he didn't win anything close to $1.9 billion. But that sum was a classic lawyer's opening offer. The actual settlement came soon enough. In January 2001 Burger King agreed to buy back 23 of Hawkins' restaurants for a reported sum of roughly $30 million.[7] For someone who couldn't, or more plausibly wouldn't, pay his debts, it was a hefty payday.

Al Sharpton, having gotten his feet wet in the field of corporate brinks-manship, ironically enough, triggered a rift between him and one of his role models, Jesse Jackson. As it turned out, Jackson sided with Burger King on this one, cutting a separate deal with Burger King CEO Colin Storm on the premise that by working with rather than against the company, he could improve opportunities for blacks. He also had another, albeit less altruistic and publicized motive: Burger King had been bankrolling his Rainbow/PUSH organization for nearly 20 years. The corporation estimated at the time that its cumulative donations to Jackson amounted to about $500,000, though Jackson put the figure at only $125,000.[8]

Whatever Jackson's actual motives, Sharpton saw betrayal. He wrote in *Al on America*:[9]

> *Our split became public when a young man named La-Van Hawkins came to me looking for help. He was promised 225 Burger King franchises. He built half of them and it got backed up, and there was some litigation that ended with Burger King pulling the deal.*
>
> *Burger King said Mr. Hawkins had done some things that they didn't agree with. And I said, "But you made a commitment to the black community to build these stores. Even if you don't do it with Mr. Hawkins, you can fulfill your commitment with somebody else."*
>
> *They said no. And I led a boycott of Burger King in New York. Jesse publicly disagreed with the boycott, and that's when we started having public disagreements.*
>
> *I couldn't believe that he, who taught me in my youth about fighting these corporations and making them accountable, would publicly come out against my doing the very thing he'd taught me how to do.*

Sharpton and Jackson at this point were barely, if at all, on speaking terms. Their feud was akin to the sporadic war over the years between

East Coast and West Coast rappers. Sharpton always had been far friendlier with black nationalists than Jackson had been anyway. He managed to coax several of them, including Louis Farrakhan, to support Hawkins. Eventually, Sharpton and Jackson reconciled. They may have their spats, the pair reckoned, but in the end, what united them – the need for shakedowns – outweighed any strategic disagreements emerging in the pursuit of that end.

La-Van Hawkins' career, meanwhile, would take an interesting trajectory after the January 2001 settlement. He already had cash to burn from the proceeds of sale of the nearly 90 Detroit-area Pizza Huts he'd bought in 1998 through a new company, Wolverine Pizza LLC, not to mention the proceeds from the Burger King settlement. He eventually sold his interest in the Pizza Huts for more than $95 million. A colorful self-promoter who liked letting the good times roll, Hawkins placed posters of himself inside his restaurants so that customers would recognize his portly presence. He owned large homes in the Detroit and Atlanta areas, owned a private jet, had a personal chef, and drove a Bentley and other luxury cars. He was living large, literally and figuratively. His Hawkins Food Group was bringing in more than $200 million in annual sales. In 2002, he opened a restaurant in downtown Detroit, Sweet Georgia Brown, part of an upscale marketing strategy.

Increasingly, Hawkins developed an interest in politics – the wrong kind. The FBI recently had launched a probe into allegations of widespread corruption in Philadelphia under the administration of black Mayor John F. Street. The prime target was a Street friend and fundraiser, Ron White. Hawkins was indicted on fraud and perjury charges in June 2004. He would be convicted in 2007 and sentenced to 33 months in prison and fined $25,000. About a dozen people in all were ensnared in various "play for pay" scandals, though Mayor Street was not among them. White would die of natural causes before going on trial.

The Philadelphia case managed to give Hawkins unwanted exposure of his pattern of stiffing creditors. He owed more than $70,000 to a Georgia attorney, $393,000 to a Detroit design firm, $82,000 to a Detroit radio station, and $49,000 to a phone service provider.[10] Burger King apparently was in good company. Hawkins also had a blind spot for public-sector creditors. In a separate federal case in Detroit, Hawkins pleaded guilty in April 2009 to one count of tax fraud, part of a nine-count indictment. Federal investigators had concluded that Hawkins during 2001-03 had deducted $5.3 million from Pizza Hut employee paychecks for income-withholding and F.I.C.A. (i.e., Social Security and a portion of Medicare) contributions, but did not forward the money to the government. In July 2009 he was given a 10-month prison sentence, to be served concurrently with his Philadelphia sentence, and ordered to make $5.7 million in restitution.[11] He wound up serving 18 months.

Once out of prison, Hawkins found himself on the receiving end of new legal problems in the form of a civil suit filed in November 2011 by a Chicago husband-wife couple, Darnell Johnson and Tonya Van Dyke. Hawkins had promised to provide the pair with $20 million in backing for a planned expansion of their restaurant, Chicago Home of Chicken & Waffles. The couple charged that Hawkins not only reneged on the deal, but also used their name and a key recipe without authorization at one of his own restaurants.[12] They asked the court to set a damage award for two counts of breach of contract, and sought $21 million for other charges. In another lawsuit, an Ohio-based business services company, Cadlerock Joint Venture LP, in June 2012 accused Hawkins of defaulting on $5.85 million in promissory notes to JPMorgan Chase Bank.

In spite of all this, La-Van Hawkins remains very much active. He owns a number of popular restaurants in Chicago with local restaurateur Jerry "Magic Man" Kleiner. And he's back in Detroit, planning a new venture. He's a street-smart, ambitious businessman who knows how to cut a deal and bounce back from adversity. In a number of ways, Hawkins is a genuine role model for troubled young black males. Yet at the same time it is highly difficult to look past his profligacy, avoidance of creditors, and public corruption. And his lawsuit against Burger King, aided by Al Sharpton, gave all the appearance of an extortion attempt.

Reverend Al already was looking ahead to another business opportunity. It would appear in the form of a celebrity far more renowned than La-Van Hawkins.

CHAPTER 14

MICHAEL JACKSON AGONISTES

By 2002, Michael Jackson, the King of Pop, had a problem: He wasn't selling records – not like he used to anyway. It had been two decades since the release of *Thriller*, the highest-selling album of all time. The singer, normally projecting a cool persona, had heated up for war at a press conference on July 6, at Al Sharpton's headquarters in Harlem. He was there to proclaim his partnership with the Reverend in fighting what he felt was rampant racism in the record industry.

This brouhaha had a very specific context. Jackson was convinced that Sony Music Entertainment, parent of Columbia/Epic/CBS Records, was refusing to promote his newest album, *Invincible*, because he was black. Never mind that Jackson's innumerable surgical alterations by now had made him look whiter than most whites. Never mind either that Sony had spent at least $30 million and possibly as much as $40 million[1] producing the album and another $25 million promoting it. Michael Jackson believed himself to be a victim of racial injustice. And Al Sharpton was the man to see to get something done about that.

At heart, this was a battle over money. The Japanese-owned Sony, which had bought CBS Records back in 1988, recently had loaned Jackson $200 million against future earnings. It was a staggering sum by any measure. And it was a mark of Sony's confidence in Jackson to deliver revenues. Quite obviously, the company had every incentive in the world to promote Jackson's recordings. But why did Jackson need the money, having already made so much of it during his career? A major reason, if not *the* reason, was his pathological incapacity for distinguishing between whim and need, whether in professional or personal life. The man just couldn't control his spending urges.[2] The situation wasn't helped by a January 1994 out-of-court settlement in which Jackson agreed to pay a reported $22 million to the family of a boy he allegedly molested at his Neverland ranch near Santa Barbara, California.[3] *Invincible*, released in the fall of 2001, already had sold some six million copies worldwide. Though most musical acts would kill for that kind of sales volume, it wasn't nearly enough to pay off the advance.

Jackson pointed his finger at Sony, and more specifically, Tommy Mottola, head of Sony Music Entertainment, parent company of Columbia/CBS Records. During June, the King of Pop launched a worldwide blitz to highlight his break with Sony. He attended a protest in front of Sony of London on June 15, later attending a fan club event at the Equinox nightclub where he spoke for the first time about his issues with Sony, calling Mottola a "devil."

Jackson's choreographed broadside had the support of family and some friends. And he was prepared for battle. Just prior to the release of *Invincible*, Jackson had informed Tommy Mottola that he was not going to renew his contract with Sony. In retaliation, Mottola indefinitely postponed single releases, video shoots, promotions and advances. While it's possible that Mottola, a product of the tough streets of the Bronx, came off as vindictive, that hardly was evidence of "racism." Aside from Jackson's lack of evidence, Mottola previously had been married to American superstar pop singer Mariah Carey, she partly of black descent, and now was wedded to Mexican pop singer-actress Thalia. And race aside, vindictiveness is par for the course in the record industry.

What people may have been unaware of was the increased attraction of Jackson to Al Sharpton. On June 5, only a month before the press conference, he announced that he had joined National Action Network. And on the big day, July 6, before a packed house at NAN headquarters in Harlem, the King of Pop vented:[4]

The recording companies really, really do conspire against the artists. They steal, they cheat, they do everything they can, especially [against] black artists...People from James Brown to Sammy Davis Jr., some of the real pioneers that inspired me to be an entertainer, these artists are always on tour, because if they stop touring, they would go hungry. If you fight for me, you're fighting for all black people, dead or alive.

Jackson made sure that people knew the real villain was Tommy Mottola. Among other things, Mottola was "mean," "racist" and "devilish." To emphasize his final point, Jackson, in the manner of a third-grader, held a photo of Mottola with devil's horns superimposed over it and called Mottola "very, very, very devilish."

After Michael Jackson concluded his speech, he declared, "Let's march on Sony today!" He rented a tour bus to bring Sharpton and other supporters down to Sony's U.S. corporate headquarters on Madison Avenue in midtown Manhattan. Though the offices were closed – this was a Saturday – Jackson, who seemingly had every major media outlet in the country tagging along, knew that didn't matter. When the entourage arrived at the building, Jackson would lead a familiar chant: "No Justice, No Peace."[5]

Oddly, Al Sharpton was skeptical of Jackson's claim about Mottola's racism. Two days later, on July 8, Sharpton and two record producers, Cory Rooney and Steve Stoute, came to Mottola's defense. Reverend Al put it this way: "I have known Tommy for 15 or 20 years, and never once have I known him to say or do anything that would be considered racist. In fact, he's always been supportive of the black music industry. He was the first record executive to step up and offer to help us with respect to corporate accountability when it comes to black music issues."[6]

In the Rev's eyes, Tommy Mottola was off the hook but other industry honchos were not. Appearing live on CNN that evening, Sharpton had this to say about Michael Jackson and the recording industry:[7]

Well, I think that Michael has said very clearly that he's concerned about how artists are treated in general and about the fact that there seems to be a particular problem in the music industry when it comes to race. I mean when you look at the fact that out of four major record companies today you've never had a black president of either company, you can't find black businesses that have real long-term contracts. Artists are charged with millions of dollars in promotions, yet they can't guide where they go.

So in this national summit tomorrow that Michael will be a part of, you have people like the child of Otis Blackwell, who wrote all of Elvis Presley's hits and never got the credit or the money. This is a historic problem that needs to be dealt with, and I think that Michael Jackson, being the largest record seller of all time, adds a lot of weight to the concern.

But Sharpton may have had a money motive of his own. He recently had formed a coalition with Johnnie Cochran, who had represented Jackson in that 1993-94 child molestation suit (this was just before his criminal defense of O.J. Simpson), to investigate record industry exploitation of black artists. While Sharpton did not see Mottola as a racist, he clearly believed otherwise about the record industry as a whole. By making bad publicity for the industry, there loomed the possibility of scoring moral points on behalf of black artists, producers and other industry people, and as a bonus, generating industry donations to National Action Network. Coincidentally or not, Sony Music was a sponsor of the 2012 NAN convention in Washington, D.C.

The Michael Jackson affair made a lot of noise, but failed to generate either a legal battle or a boycott from hell. Jackson's contract with Sony officially ended in 2002, though Jackson clearly had directed his animus more at Mottola than at Sony.[8] *Invincible* went on to sell roughly 13 million copies worldwide, nowhere near the territory of *Thriller* (70 million) or its follow-up, *Bad* (36 million), but enough at least temporarily to keep creditors from banging on his door.[9] Jackson again would prove himself a high-risk client a couple years later when Santa Barbara County prosecutors charged him with criminal child molestation. After a trial that dominated headlines during the early months of 2005, a jury found him not guilty on all charges.[10] Jackson, eager to avoid the spotlight – and income taxes – temporarily resettled in Bahrain, though his financial troubles would worsen.[11] In 2008 he reportedly converted to Islam and changed his first name to "Mikaeel."[12]

Whatever Michael Jackson's true spiritual leanings were, they would not be expressed on earth for much longer. On June 25, 2009, he unexpectedly died at a rented home in Los Angeles on the eve of a major tour. Fans the world over mourned. Al Sharpton was among the intimates and admirers delivering eulogies at the July 7 public memorial service at the Staples Center in Los Angeles. The cause of death, as reported by the Los Angeles County Coroner's Office, was "acute Propofol intoxication" accompanied by the presence of Valium, Lorazepam and Ephedrine. The office later would rule the death a homicide. Jackson's personal physician, Dr. Conrad Murray, would be charged with involuntary manslaughter in February 2010 and convicted by a jury in November 2011. He received the maximum four-year sentence, though he served just two years.

Michael Jackson was gone. So was his lawyer, Johnnie Cochran, who died of a brain tumor in March 2005. Tommy Mottola was fired as head of Sony Music in January 2003 following his music division's heavy losses over the previous six months and his increasingly strained relationship with Sony Corporation Chairman Howard Stringer. He bounced back quickly, signing a five-year, $40 million deal with Universal Music Group to reboot Casablanca Records, purchased from PolyGram several years earlier.[13] As for Al Sharpton, all he did was run for president of the United States. After a brief show of statesmanlike behavior, he would return to true form. The world was his stage.

CHAPTER 15

THE TROUBLES IN JENA, LOUISIANA

Jena, Louisiana doesn't appear at first glance to be a place that would generate intense national attention over racial injustice. Even during the Jim Crow era, there had been no documented hangings of blacks in this community of about 3,000 persons, located in LaSalle Parish. Local relations between whites and blacks had been for the most part amicable over the past decade. Yet for several months, beginning in September 2006, civil-rights leaders and their allies focused their rage on the town as though it were some lingering stone-age backwater coming back to haunt the whole country. The catalyst was the growing tension and violence between white and black high school students. Yet more accurately, the violence was a one-way street: It was being perpetrated by blacks against whites. That many blacks throughout the country perceived the situation to be the opposite owed largely to Al Sharpton.

As the standard script had it, there was a large outdoor shade tree on the Jena High School campus where whites congregated, but blacks were discouraged from approaching. On August 30, 2006, with a new school year underway, a black student nervously asked if he was allowed to sit there. The principal gave his approval. A trio of whites, bent on scaring blacks away, soon hung a pair of nooses from the tree that were discovered the following morning. The culprits were caught, but received only a suspension. Local blacks expressed outrage at this slap on the wrist in the face of KKK-style terror. Tensions at the school mounted palpably over the next few months, culminating in a black-white schoolyard fight.

Yet the six blacks involved in the scuffle were charged with attempted murder rather than suspended. Blacks and their supporters, outraged over this apparent double standard, demanded the "Jena 6" be freed. On September 20, 2007, Al Sharpton, Jesse Jackson and other public figures led roughly 20,000 marchers in a rally through the streets of Jena. Until the Jena 6 get justice, they proclaimed, no black anywhere in America is safe.

This, in a nutshell, was the story Al Sharpton and other "civil-rights" leaders spun nonstop to gullible audiences. Blacks, they said, are in peril not only in Jena, but throughout the nation. Here is how Sharpton explained the situation in a post-rally interview:[1]

> *You think we brought thousands to Jena. You wait 'til we go to D.C. and bring the whole country, because there's Jenas all over America. There's Jenas in New York. There's Jenas in Atlanta. There's Jenas in Florida. There's Jenas all over Texas.*

He would follow this nonsense up with testimony before a subcommittee of the House Judiciary Committee on October 16:[2]

> *What I would beseech this committee to look into the fact that Jena is all over this country. It's hangman nooses at Columbia University in New York. It's even a hangman noose at the site of 9/11. It's in North Carolina. It's in California. All kinds of reports.*
>
> *And what has been most troubling is the silence of the federal government…What has happened in Jena and what has happened all over this country while we're watching nooses on the news every night, while we're watching hate crimes.*

This denunciation, and others like it, bore no relation to reality. Honest sources, especially *Jena Times* reporter-assistant editor Craig

Franklin,[3] knew the real story, citing facts that Sharpton and his allies conveniently left out.

There was never any "whites-only" tree on the Jena High School campus. The tree in question had been planted in 1986 and only recently had grown tall enough to provide shade. The school administration had put tables under it to facilitate socializing. Anyone, white or black, was allowed to sit there. Yes, students at Jena, like at many other multi-racial high schools, tended to self-segregate on the basis of race. But this had nothing to do with official policy. The idea that Jena High School administrators were promoting "segregation" is as absurd as saying that schools all across the nation have established "white lunch tables" because blacks and whites generally prefer eating among themselves at tables of their choosing. Moreover, the black student who asked if he could sit at the "white" tree intended it as a joke, one of several such questions asked at a boys-only orientation assembly.

The students who hung the nooses were unaware of the potential racial connotations of their act. During the early morning hours of August 31, two black nylon nooses were discovered hanging from the tree. They were not even proper nooses, but crudely tied loops. Proper or not, the school administration soon took down them down, so soon, in fact, that almost no students even saw them. The administration eventually learned the identities of the pranksters. The three youths responsible, all white, explained they recently had seen the "Lonesome Dove" TV mini-series which at one point depicted Texas Rangers hanging several (white) cattle rustlers. The nooses were hung in school colors aimed at a rival school football team with a Western-themed nickname.[4] None of the students had any idea that their act could be perceived as symbols of lynching. "They didn't have a clue what nooses mean to blacks," noted Franklin. *The ropes were nothing more than a prank.*

The students who hung the nooses were punished – and severely. Given that no wrongdoing occurred, no punishment should have been meted out. But unfortunately the school administration *did* mete out

discipline, and of a harshness far exceeding the "crime." The perpetrators, if that is the right word, had to attend an off-campus disciplinary
program for nine days, serve two weeks of in-school suspension and several Saturday detentions, subject themselves to a school discipline court,
pass a psychological evaluation to determine that they were not threats
to others, and undergo monitoring under a family-crisis intervention
program. If that were not enough, local police, the FBI and federal
prosecutors each grilled them. It was "political correctness" at its most
repellent.

Why did the administration go to this extreme? School Superinten-
dent Roy Breithaupt explained:[5]

> *Even though we'd determined their true motivation had nothing
> to do with racial hate, we had to acknowledge that to the black
> community it would be perceived in that manner. Therefore,
> severe action was taken regarding the students and the hanging
> of the nooses.*

The admission was breathtaking in its fecklessness. Here was the
white head of a local school system stating that it is better to damage the
lives of innocent whites than risk being falsely charged with "racism" by
potentially violent blacks. Making the discipline all the more inexplicable was that the investigation, by state law, had to be kept entirely confidential. In other words, had the students not been punished, nobody
would have been the wiser.

**Tension over the nooses likely would not have occurred had the
results of the investigation been made public.** On September 6, 2006, a
white student was hit in the head from behind and was treated at a local
emergency room after witnessing a nasty fight between a white girl and
a black girl. Police were assigned to the school on September 7. The
next day, a student reportedly had brought a gun to school. The school
authorities kept students in classes for three hours while police searched
students and school grounds. Had the results of the noose probe been

made public, tensions would not likely have mounted. As it was, for nearly three months thereafter, no racial incidents occurred either on or off campus.

Blacks inflicted violence against whites, not the other way around. By early December 2006, the noose incident seemed almost moot. A pair of off-campus fights between black students and white townspeople – neither instigated by the latter – raised tensions anew. Then, on December 4, an on-campus incident took the conflict to a new level. A black player on the high school football team, Mychal Bell, walked up to a white student named Justin Barker, who was not one of the three accused noose-hangers, and sucker-punched him to the ground. Suddenly, at least five other black youths, and as many as ten, started kicking him. According to court documents, Barker probably was unconscious before he hit the ground, where attackers brutally stomped him. When Assistant Principal Gawan Burgess arrived at the scene, he genuinely thought Barker was dead. He was rushed to the hospital and underwent emergency surgery, running up a bill of $5,467. LaSalle Parish District Attorney Reed Walters was properly outraged over the details. This was no "fight" or "rumble" between evenly-matched parties. This was a vicious, unprovoked attack that came close to a killing. He charged six of the attackers with attempted murder.

The original charges against the six black offenders, as opposed to the three white "offenders," were entirely justified. The charged black offenders – Mychal Bell, Robert Bailey, Carwin Jones, Bryant Purvis, Jesse Ray Beard and Theo Shaw – in short order came to be known as the "Jena 6." And they had plenty of supporters, all denouncing what they saw as a miscarriage of justice. To them, it was a travesty that half a dozen blacks were indicted for attempted murder in a schoolyard "fight," while three "racist" whites weren't being charged for hanging nooses. They especially were exercised that District Attorney Walters decided to try the first defendant, Mychal Bell, as an adult. Yet in fact, he had every reason to do so. Bell, only 16 at the time of the assault, had been on probation for an unrelated assault and battery he'd committed on Christmas Day 2005. And since that incident, he had been found guilty under the juvenile system of three more crimes – two assaults and a property offense. In mid 2007, on the eve of his trial for the beating of Mr. Barker, the prosecution reduced the charges to aggravated second-degree battery and conspiracy. On June 28, 2007, after less than three hours of deliberation, a jury of five women and one man found Bell guilty. A student testified at the trial that just before Bell attacked Barker she heard a black say, "There's that white motherfucker that was running his mouth."

Evidence apparently didn't matter. To his supporters, Bell was a victim, not a victimizer. Suddenly, the world spotlight was on Jena. Here was proof of the permanence of the Old South. Critics denounced the verdict because the jury was all-white. But in point of fact none of the blacks summoned for jury duty that day showed up. The big guns of black radicalism now came to town. Al Sharpton showed up on August 5 with a message: "You cannot have some boys assault and charged with nothing, some boys hanging nooses and finish the school year, and other boys charged with attempted murder and conspiracy. That's two levels of justice, and two levels of justice is an injustice." A little over a month later, on September 10, Jesse Jackson arrived in Jena, demanding that Bell's conviction be tossed out and that the charges against the remaining five defendants be reduced to misdemeanors. He warned that in absence of such action, the town could expect a "major demonstration." Clearly, the animosity between Sharpton and Jackson during the La-Van Hawkins affair was behind them.

Politicians also were getting in their licks. Senator Hillary Clinton, D-N.Y., told the NAACP, "This case reminds us that the scales of justice are seriously out of balance when it comes to charging, sentencing, and punishing African-Americans." Senator Christopher Dodd, D-Conn., said the verdict proved that this nation still is afflicted with "de facto segregation." The Congressional Black Caucus called the events in Jena "an unbelievable example" of "separate and unequal justice." The media weighed in, too. A *New York Times* editorial opined, "It's impossible to examine the case of the so-called Jena Six without concluding that these black teens have been the victims of a miscarriage of justice, with a clearly racial double standard at work."[6]

The pressure must have gotten to Louisiana State Judge J. P. Mauffray, Jr. On September 14, he vacated Mychal Bell's conviction as an adult and ordered a retrial in juvenile court. District Attorney Walters, however, was made of sterner stuff and vowed to try all of the defendants on adult felony charges.[7] On September 20, the date of Mychal Bell's original sentencing, an estimated 20,000 persons, virtually all black and heavily bused in from elsewhere, came to Jena for a day of protest. Moral indignation ruled the day.

The six defendants now were celebrity victims. Two of them, Carwin Jones and Bryant Purvis, took the stage on October 13 at the Black Entertainment Awards ceremony in Atlanta to present rapper Kanye West with the Video of the Year award for his hit single "Stronger." The show's host, black comedian Katt Williams, declared: "By no means are we condoning a six-on-one beatdown...But the injustice perpetrated on these young men is straight criminal."[8] Actually, what was "straight criminal" was the fact that six or more people nearly beat Justin Barker to death. Bell pleaded guilty in December 2007 to a juvenile charge of second-degree battery and was sentenced to 18 months in jail. A year and a half later, in June 2009, each of the remaining five defendants pleaded no contest to misdemeanor battery, thus managing to avoid jail time. As part of the plea bargain, they agreed to pay restitution to Barker to settle a civil suit that he and his parents had filed on November 29, 2007.[9]

The Jena Six, for the most part, continued in their criminal ways. Mychal Bell was the worst of the bunch, but not the only perpetrator. For one thing, the accused blacks and their respective families embezzled from the "defense fund" that the NAACP had set up for them. The fund generated anywhere from $250,000 to $400,000 (accounts vary) in contributions before lawyers took up the case *pro bono*. What happened to all that money? Much of it went toward enriching car dealers. Mychal Bell's mother purchased a Jaguar, while Robert Bailey's mother took delivery of a BMW. Robert Bailey, in a supreme moment of audacity, posted Internet photos of himself and another defendant virtually swimming in $100 bills. Though this surely constituted embezzlement, no prosecutions occurred.

It wasn't as if the defendants, and Bell's parents, had forsaken conventional crime:[10]

- Bryant Purvis was arrested in February 2008 for an assault causing bodily injury against a fellow high school student in Texas, where he since had moved.

- Carwin Jones was arrested in LaSalle Parish in May 2008 for misdemeanor battery. The charge very easily could have been a felony. He allegedly struck a man from behind as several people, including Jones, had approached the man. His friends were carrying baseball bats. Jones claimed he was not at fault since the incident was triggered by a fight the previous day in which was not involved.

- Jesse Ray Beard was arrested, and then convicted, for battery and vandalism. He received a suspended sentence and was placed under house arrest. He subsequently enrolled in the Canterbury School in Connecticut, with half of the nearly $40,000 annual tuition paid out of the Jena Six defense fund.

- Mychal Bell, having since moved to Monroe, Louisiana, was stopped in Oklahoma while on a weekend pass for speeding and not having proper vehicle insurance. By being out of Monroe, he was violating the terms of the pass. Given the behavior of Bell's parents, it wasn't too hard to see why Bell turned out the way he did. After the Louisiana High School Athletic Association had turned down his request for an extra year of eligibility on the Jena football team, his father, Marcus Jones, blamed his son's attorney, Carol Powell-Lexing. After the hearing, Jones allegedly spat at Ms. Powell-Lexing and pushed her to the floor. In a separate incident, Bell's mother, Melissa Bell, was arrested on October 11, 2008 on two counts of aggravated battery for hitting two women with a shovel. Were that not enough, Mychal Bell, that December shot himself in the chest days after his arrest on a shoplifting charge.[11] The wound was not life-threatening.

One defendant, Theo Shaw, hasn't broken the law, but may wind up doing worse. Of course, he would be armed with good intentions. At age 17, after his arrest, Shaw thumbed through a law book while in jail, looking for a loophole that would lower his bail and facilitate his release. He eventually got a reduction, from $130,000 to $90,000. The experience was an epiphany: He saw a law career ahead. By 2012, following his graduation from the University of Louisiana at Monroe, he could be found working as a community advocate for the New Orleans office of the Southern Poverty Law Center (SPLC), a Montgomery, Ala.-based nonprofit group with a yen for recklessly applying the label of "hate group."[12] "I would ultimately like to be a trial attorney," Shaw remarked. "This could be my ego, but I really think I could be an awesome trial attorney as far as being able to advocate on behalf of other people – being able to tell their story to a jury in a compelling way."[13] Another defendant, Jesse Ray Beard, also has benefited from Southern Poverty Law Center largesse. It was an SPLC board member, Alan Howard, who became Beard's legal guardian and enrolled him in that Connecticut boarding school. After graduating, Beard enrolled at Hofstra University.[14] As the old saying goes, "You can't make this up."

Granted, even the worst of us generally deserve a second chance. But what is appalling here is the notion that these thugs were dealt a bad deal. Reality check: They nearly beat an innocent person to death, not the other way around. It is a testament to both the mendacity and

effectiveness of "civil-rights" leaders like Al Sharpton that they succeeded in convincing much of the public that group assault and battery
isn't nearly as bad as innocently throwing some nylon nooses over a tree
branch – and that speaking out in opposition to such a claim constitutes racism. Of course, when whites do express freedom of speech on
a racial issue, even in jest, Sharpton may be all over them. A prominent
white radio talk show host would learn the possibilities.

CHAPTER 16

HOLY WAR ON DON IMUS

Of all prominent radio personalities in America, Don Imus ranks among the most witty, iconoclastic and combative. Born in 1940, he's been on the airwaves for decades, and is an author and philanthropist as well. His daily talk show, "Imus in the Morning," has been nationally syndicated since 1993. To a large extent, his popularity stems from his willingness to offend canons of good taste, often in the form of racial and ethnic comments. In his "shock jock" profession, giving offense is assumed, though with the ever-present risk of going too far. The main purpose of comedy in any medium, including radio, is getting audiences to laugh at life's foibles and absurdities. It's not the evening news. Most people, even common targets of barbed humor, accept that.

In the spring of 2007, Imus went too far – at least as Al Sharpton saw things. Reverend Al pounced, and gave Imus a choice: publicly grovel or lose his career. At the time Imus' show had been syndicated by the CBS Radio Network and simulcast by MSNBC-TV. That arrangement would not last long.

It was Wednesday, April 4, 2007, and Imus, along with his executive producer, Bernard McGuirk, were on the air discussing the previous night's NCAA Division I Women's Basketball championship game in which the University of Tennessee had defeated Rutgers University. Imus, referring to visible tattoos on several Rutgers players, called the women "rough girls." McGuirk amplified the remark, calling the women "hardcore hoes." Imus then described the players as "nappy-headed hoes." McGuirk then pointed out that the two teams looked like "the

Jigaboos versus the Wannabees," a reference to the 1988 Spike Lee movie, *School Daze,* based largely on the (black) director's own student years at Morehouse College in Atlanta.

This banter was crude – and accurate. Dark-skinned and light-skinned blacks at Morehouse, as at other black colleges, really did live in separate social circles. And as life imitated art, a fight broke out on the set between the two factions of actors; Lee, recognizing a golden moment, ordered cameras to roll. The problem, quite obviously, was that Imus and McGuirk had violated an unwritten rule barring whites from saying "offensive" things that blacks routinely say to and about each other, and often even less tactfully. The transcript, released to the press that evening by the George Soros-funded Left-leaning watchdog group, Media Matters for America (MMA), reveals a poor choice of words, yet nothing genuinely sinister:

Imus: That's some rough girls from Rutgers. Man, they got tattoos and...
McGuirk: Some hard-core hoes.
Imus: That's some nappy-headed hoes. I'm gonna tell you that now, man, that's some – woo. And the girls from Tennessee, they all look cute, you know, so, like – kinda like – I don't know.
McGuirk: A Spike Lee thing.
Imus: Yeah.
McGuirk: The Jigaboos vs. the Wannabees – that movie he had.

This brief stretch of dialogue was no "hate crime." Indeed, it was a good deal tamer than the lyrics found on many black hip-hop records.[1] Notwithstanding, several listeners called to vent their anger. Thanks to MMA, word of Imus and his producer's exchange spread quickly. Imus, taken aback, first dismissed the conversation as "some idiot comment meant to be amusing." When the brouhaha didn't die, he issued a formal apology:[2]

158

*I want to take a moment to apologize for an insensitive and
ill-conceived remark we made the other morning regarding the
Rutgers women's basketball team, which lost to Tennessee in the
NCAA championship game on Tuesday. It was completely inappropriate and we can understand why people were offended.
Our characterization was thoughtless and stupid, and we are
sorry.*

Imus' enemies, predictably, were unimpressed. Indeed, they saw
this as a signal to close in for the kill. Al Sharpton, Jesse Jackson, the
National Association of Black Journalists and other activists demanded
that CBS and MSNBC-TV drop Imus' show. The Rutgers women's basketball team leaped into the feeding frenzy, holding a news conference
to express "our team's great hurt, anger and disgust toward the words
of Mr. Don Imus," with Coach C. Vivian Stringer practically beatifying
her players.[3] Executives at NBC, petrified of bad publicity and a possible
boycott, refused to stand by Imus. "We take this matter very seriously,"
said Allison Gollust, NBC's senior vice president for news communications. "We find the comments to be deplorable, and we are continuing to review the situation." Apparently, it was a short review. By the
close of Friday, April 6, the network announced a two-week suspension
of MSNBC simulcasts.

Imus' future in broadcasting was now in jeopardy. He decided upon
emergency damage control: Appear live on Sharpton's radio show,
"Keepin' It Real." It was a mark of Sharpton's power that Imus came to
him. On April 9, the pair had a lengthy on-air exchange. And while
Imus did not grovel, this was still Sharpton's turf. There was little Imus
could do to come out on top. With censorious bombast, Sharpton told
his guest on the air: "I'm going to say what you said was racist. I'm going to say what you said was abominable. I'm going to say you should be
fired for saying it." Imus retorted, "That's fine," whereupon Sharpton
called for a commercial break.[4]

Shock jock Don Imus on Sharpton's radio show in wake of Rutgers controversy. (AP/Wide World)

The networks were more scared than ever. Eight companies – American Express, Bigelow Tea, General Motors, GlaxoSmithKline, PetMed Express, Procter & Gamble, Sprint Nextel, and Staples – by now had pulled ads from Imus' show. On April 11, NBC capitulated. Its news division president, Steve Capus, announced that MSNBC no longer would simulcast "Imus in the Morning," effective immediately. Seeing that the coast was clear, CBS Radio the next day canceled its syndication agreement. CBS President Les Moonves rationalized the move as changing "a culture that permits a certain level of objectionable expression that hurts and demeans a wide range of people."[5] Moonves' choice of words might have been related to his private meeting with Al Sharpton and Jesse Jackson shortly before the announcement.[6]

Thankfully, it was not the end of Imus' career. In early May 2007, Imus filed a wrongful termination suit against CBS for the remaining $40 million on his five-year contract. He was on strong legal ground. The contract contained a clause acknowledging CBS had hired and supported Imus on the basis of his "irreverent" and "controversial" stances.

Unfortunately, irreverence and controversy had limits when Sharpton and Jackson set them. Imus and CBS settled that August. On November 1, 2007, following negotiations, Citadel Broadcasting announced it had agreed to a multiyear contract with Imus. The new "Imus in the Morning" program would be syndicated nationally by ABC Radio Networks and would operate out of the Citadel-owned WABC in New York City. A couple weeks later, the *New York Times* reported that Imus and the video cable network RFD-TV had come to terms on a simulcast agreement.[7] That December 3, he returned to the airwaves.

Al Sharpton wasn't happy about this, but he made clear that his antennae would be out. "We'll monitor him," he said. "I'm not saying I'm going to throw a banquet for him and say welcome home. He has the right to make a living, but because he has such a consistent pattern with this we are going to monitor him to make sure he doesn't do it again."[8] Once more, the Reverend was true to a consistent pattern of despots everywhere: Free speech for me, but not for thee.

CHAPTER 17

SEAN BELL AND FRIENDS: REBELS WITHOUT A CASE

Al Sharpton's career often gets a boost in credibility, however undeserved, when denouncing excessive police force against a black suspect. That was the case in the wake of a fatal November 2006 police shooting in Queens, N.Y., which Sharpton parlayed into a massive campaign. The Reverend Al employed his typically selective use of facts to mobilize black opinion against law enforcement following the death of Sean Bell and the wounding of two of his friends, Joseph Guzman and Trent Benefield, at Bell's bachelor party. His anger would burn even hotter when all three police officers were found not guilty a year and a half later.

Sean Bell seemed a 23-year-old man with a future. The part-time electrician from Queens was looking forward to marrying his girlfriend, Nicole Paultre, with whom he had two daughters. The wedding would not happen. The wee morning hours of November 25, 2006 would be his last.

It was the evening of November 24. Bell, Guzman, 31, and Benefield, 23, wanted to celebrate Bell's last night as a single man at Club Kalua, a strip joint in the Jamaica section of Queens. Upon their arrival they met up with some friends. The place had a rough reputation. Undercover police officers had been investigating the club for weeks in response to complaints by patrons and local residents about on-premises guns, drug sales and prostitution. Police recently had made eight arrests. They were out in force that night, too.

According to sources at the scene, the trouble began inside. Guzman had been involved in an argument over the services of a prostitute.[1] Five cops observed a man put a stripper's hand on his belt to reassure her that he would protect her from an aggressive customer. The altercation then spilled to the sidewalk. The cops witnessed a heated exchange between Bell's friends and a pimp. Apparently, one of the pimp's hookers agreed to have sex, but with no more than two members of the eight-member Bell entourage. During the altercation, the pimp kept his hand inside his jacket, as if he were holding a gun. Bell then reportedly said, in reference to the pimp, "Let's f**k him up." His companion, Joseph Guzman, responded, "Yo, go get my gun." Officer Gescard Isnora, himself black, reported this exchange over his cell phone to other cops.

Fearing that things could get out of control, Isnora went to his unmarked car to get his service revolver. When he returned to the scene, Bell, Guzman and Benefield had gotten into their car and appeared ready to drive away. Believing the trio were about to commit a drive-by shooting against the pimp, Detective Isnora, standing on the passenger side of the vehicle, moved toward the car to question the occupants. He identified himself as a police officer, displayed his badge, and told the driver, Bell, to stop. Bell responded by driving forward, striking both Isnora and a police minivan. He then backed up and slammed into the minivan once more. At this point, Isnora, by his own account, saw Guzman reach for his waistband. Perceiving a deadly threat, he opened fire. Four other undercover detectives reflexively began shooting as well, killing Bell and wounding Guzman and Benefield. In all, the cops fired off a combined 50 shots, 26 of them striking the three young men inside the car. A search of the car afterward turned up no gun. Benefield would be released from the hospital on December 5; the more critically wounded Guzman was released the following January 25.

Of the five officers who fired their weapons (a sixth officer was on the scene, but had not opened fire), two were white, two were black, and the other was a black-Hispanic mix. On that basis alone, it was hard to make a case for this being a racially motivated killing. But the victims were a black and Hispanic mix – there were no whites. So it wasn't that surprising that Al Sharpton entered the picture. Within days, he and Jesse Jackson led elected officials, clergy, community members and victims' relatives on a weekend walk to the site of the shootings. He actually sounded conciliatory. "We appeal to people: Don't do anything disruptive or in any way contrary to the memory of Sean Bell," Sharpton said to the crowd. "We do not want the world to see him as anything other than what he was. He was not violent. He was not a thug. He was not in the street. Don't use your anger to distort who he was."[2] But then, without any objection from Sharpton, Jesse Jackson announced: "This is a symbol, not an aberration. Our criminal justice system has broken down for black Americans and the young black males."[3] Soon enough, the Bell family designated Sharpton as their "adviser."

Protests continued into the following week. Public officials, though reluctant to condemn the shootings as racially motivated, were less than supportive of the police officers. Police Commissioner Ray Kelly put all five officers on paid administrative leave and stripped them of their weapons. "It sounds to me like excessive force was used," said Mayor Michael Bloomberg, calling the fact of 50 shots fired "inexplicable" and "unacceptable."[4] Governor George Pataki likewise stated, "Obviously, 50 bullets fired into or at an unarmed individual in New York is excessive force, but the appropriate response to that is something that I think the investigation of the mayor and the police commissioner will reveal."[5]

But the three young men lionized by Reverend Sharpton had excesses of their own. The late Sean Bell had been arrested three times, twice for drug dealing and once for a firearms possession; in each case, he was released on his own recognizance.[6] Only three months before his death, he'd sold crack cocaine to an undercover cop. Even more damaging, the *New York Daily News* quoted an unnamed drug dealer from Queens who alleged he had been shot by Bell on July 13, 2006 over a drug turf dispute, an account police sources called credible.[7] The other two shooting victims were cut from the same cloth. Joseph Guzman had been arrested nine times, at least once for firearms possession and armed robbery.

Trent Benefield had three prior arrests at the time of the shootings, at least one of them for illegal firearms possession. Following his release from the hospital, he resumed his lawbreaking. In December 2006, he was picked up at a Harlem gambling raid. And in September 2007, he was arrested for slugging his girlfriend in the face; the couple already had a child together.[8]

Benefield in particular had acquired an unusual benefactor: Al Sharpton. In his statement to the police following the latter incident, he indicated that he didn't have to work because he gets all his money from National Action Network. "Every month they give me whatever I need," he said. Apparently, his needs reached $3,000 a month. One of his lawyers, Sharpton ally Sanford Rubenstein, confirmed that Benefield was being supported by a special NAN fund.[9] The criminal case, meanwhile, had taken center stage during 2007 and the early months of 2008. Sharpton and other activists were calling for a special prosecutor. Governor Eliot Spitzer, who would resign from office in March 2008, did not see a need for it. Attorney General Andrew Cuomo promised to keep an eye on the proceedings. The Queens District Attorney's Office interviewed over 100 witnesses and presented more than 500 exhibits to a grand jury. On March 16, the grand jury indicted three of the five undercover officers – Gescard Isnora, Marc Cooper (also black) and Michael Oliver. They pleaded not guilty at their arraignment three days later and were released on bail on their own recognizance. They also chose to submit themselves to a bench rather than jury trial. After hearing testimony from about 50 witnesses, State Supreme Court Justice Arthur J. Cooperman on April 25, 2008 issued his ruling: not guilty on all counts. Black demonstrators outside the courthouse seemed ready to go to war. Sharpton told them to stay calm. It was a delay tactic. He had an alternative plan: the coordinated city shutdown described in Chapter One.

The main reason for the not-guilty verdict was that Guzman and Benefield proved to be their worst enemies on the witness stand. Guzman, who'd already done five years in prison, was downright combative. At one point during cross-examination by Detective Isnora's lawyer, Anthony Ricco, Guzman replied: "You know what needs to happen? This (he makes a shooting gesture) needs to happen to your family." Guzman also had a faulty memory, describing, for example, Isnora's black gun as silver.[10] Benefield also undermined the prosecution's credibility.[11] He didn't claim to have seen Isnora because as Ricco put it, "he doesn't know what he looks like." In response to a question about his physical condition that fateful night after drinking three Long Island iced teas and smoking marijuana, Benefield responded that he was "intoxicated, not drunk." Benefield swore Bell never drove his Nissan Altima forward and then in reverse, yet on an audiotape recorded 90 minutes after the shooting, Benefield told police that Bell did precisely that. "I wasn't telling the truth," said Benefield of his original statement. Benefield swore in court he never drank any Hennessy brandy that night, yet on the audiotape he told the cops he was the last to leave the nightclub because he had to "finish my Hennessy." None of the accused officers took the witness stand in their own defense, preferring to allow Judge Cooperman to hear transcripts of their grand jury testimony.

Meanwhile, parallel to the criminal case was a civil one. Aided by Sanford Rubenstein and another Sharpton lawyer, Michael Hardy, family and friends of Sean Bell filed a $50 million wrongful death suit against the City of New York in July 2007. After three years of negotiations, the City in July 2010 settled with the plaintiffs for $7.15 million.[12] It was an impressive score for an act of vehicular assault. The success of the Sharpton bunch found its opposite in the misfortunes of the accused.[13] An NYPD administrative trial in the fall of 2011 ruled that Gescard Isnora, an 11-year veteran on the force, had acted improperly and would not be eligible to collect his pension. Detectives Cooper and Oliver were forced to resign, but at least could collect their pensions. Lt. Gary Napoli, though not having fired any shots, also was forced to resign, though with his pension eligibility intact. Another officer, Detective Paul Headley, already had left the force. Officer Michael Carey was exonerated at the administrative hearing, the only cop in the incident to go unscathed.

The Sean Bell criminal case has remained a burr in Sharpton's saddle. He thought he had surefire criminal convictions. Yet there was only one reason why the accused police officers were exonerated: The evidence for a conviction wasn't even remotely convincing. Sharpton will never be convinced of that. For him and his allies, evidence is secondary to the need to sustain the narrative of black suffering and redemption. The Queens shootings merely were another chapter in his campaign to attach racial grievance to incidents not warranting it. And despite his inexplicable newfound respectability as a pragmatic healing force in the Age of Obama, Sharpton, by now an MSNBC anchorman, hasn't forgotten how to take it to the streets to manufacture the appearance of racial injustice. A fatal incident in Florida in February 2012 would give him the opportunity to show how much he still remembered.

CHAPTER 18

VILIFYING GEORGE ZIMMERMAN, SANCTIFYING TRAYVON MARTIN

Sanford, Florida is a long way from New York City. A fast-growing city of about 50,000 located in the central part of the state, a little north of Orlando, it doesn't seem like a place that would attract one of Al Sharpton's blinkered moral crusades. But in fact Sanford was the site of an incident that unleashed on a national scale the demagoguery underlying so much of today's civil rights activism. The case attracted the attention of news organizations, members of Congress, President Barack Obama, Attorney General Eric Holder, and virtually every radical in the country, black or otherwise, determined to see America as irredeemably racist. It also led to an utterly unjustified state prosecution that very nearly destroyed the life of an innocent man.

It was about 7 P.M., February 26, 2012, a rainy evening in Sanford. George Zimmerman, a 28-year-old white man serving as a neighborhood watch anti-crime volunteer, shot to death a seemingly harmless black child, Trayvon Martin; he and his father had been staying with the father's girlfriend. Zimmerman, patrolling the area in his pickup truck, spotted Martin walking from a convenience store toward the residential development where his father's girlfriend lived. Trayvon Martin, on the basis of his hooded sweatshirt, looked suspicious. Zimmerman parked his vehicle, got out, and confronted Martin. Righteously angry that he was being targeted because of his race, he resisted Zimmerman's strong-arm tactics. The two got into a scuffle. Suddenly, without justification, Zimmerman shot Martin to death. Based on a police call from

Zimmerman's cell phone, police arrived on the scene. Despite this being a case of murder, the police decided against charging Zimmerman. This was a cover-up.

Thus went the official "civil rights" version of the story. If nothing else, it made for entertaining moral theater. Here, said civil rights activists, was proof of the permanence of white racism in America – a black child walking down the street, armed only with a smile, a bag of Skittles and a bottle of iced tea, cruelly profiled and gunned down by a retrograde redneck upset by his suspicious (i.e., black) appearance. This, after all, was Florida, deep in the heart of Dixie, where such things are to be expected. Justice demanded that heads roll for this hate crime and cover-up.

Over the next several weeks, a crescendo would grow demanding that George Zimmerman, and indeed all of white America, be put on trial. Early in March, a little over a week after the shooting, Trayvon Martin's parents, relatives and attorney held a press conference to call attention to the case. On March 14, the parents created a petition on the radical website Change.org calling for Zimmerman's arrest. In a little over a week, the petition would gather about 1.5 million signatures. The parents were blitzed with media inquiries – more than 400 in one day alone. On March 22, Sanford Police Chief Billy Lee, under intense state and local pressure, announced he would temporarily step down. That same day, the parents met with officials from the U.S. Justice Department. Florida Republican Governor Rick Scott and his attorney general, Pam Biondi, announced the appointment of State's Attorney Angela Corey as special prosecutor, despite the latter's well-earned reputation for professional misconduct.[1] The next day, March 23, President Obama, eager to "get to the bottom of exactly what happened," publicly weighed in with the immortal words: "You know, if I had a son, he'd look like Trayvon."

It was a situation tailor-made for the president's friend and ally, Al Sharpton, who in fact already was on the case. On March 22, the day before Obama's statement, Reverend Al, having come down from New

York, gave an incendiary speech before an estimated 8,000 persons in Sanford's Fort Mellon Park. Standing with Martin's parents, he told the cheering crowd: "Twenty-six days ago, this young man Trayvon Martin…went to the store for his brother. He came back and lost his life. Trayvon represents a reckless disregard for our lives." Sharpton added: "Enough is enough. Zimmerman should have been arrested that night. You cannot (claim to) defend yourself against a pack of Skittles and iced tea."[2] After the parents spoke, Sharpton urged the crowd to donate funds to advance Trayvon Martin's cause. After displaying a check for $2,500, Sharpton announced that black television personality Judge Greg Mathis had pledged $10,000. Several elected Florida officials also spoke, most significantly, Rep. Corrine Brown, D-Fla., who yelled: "I want an arrest. I want a trial." She then asked the crowd: "What do you want?" The crowd responded: "We want an arrest."[3]

The following month Sharpton turned up the heat further. He brought Trayvon Martin's parents onstage on the opening day of National Action Network's annual conference, which in 2012 was held in Washington, D.C. For the record, Attorney General Eric Holder was the keynote speaker. He assured the overwhelmingly black audience that he would do everything possible to file federal charges.

The political climate thus had made the arrest and prosecution of George Zimmerman inevitable. Even on the Right, few people were willing to come to Zimmerman's defense, lest they be tagged a "racist" or accused of complicity in a hate crime. As fate would have it (and perhaps it was no coincidence at all), on the same day Martin's parents took the stage with Sharpton, George Zimmerman was arrested in Florida on a state second-degree murder charge. The "civil rights" faithful rejoiced. Racism at last was getting its just deserts.

There was one problem with the official story: It was a total misrepresentation. It either yanked facts from context or omitted them altogether so as to avoid the inevitable conclusion that George Zimmerman acted in self-defense. Indeed, were he not armed that evening it would have been him, and not Trayvon Martin, who would lay dead. The real story – the version Al Sharpton and his audience either ignored or called a "smear" – fully exonerated Zimmerman.[4]

The parents of Trayvon Martin, Tracy Martin, second from left, and Sybrina Fulton, fourth from left, talk to Sharpton, as they watch a April 2012 news conference announcing charges against George Zimmerman. (AP Photo/Evan Vucci, Pool, File)

George Zimmerman lived with his wife in a modest townhome complex in Sanford known as The Retreat at Twin Lakes. During his off-work hours he volunteered as a patrol captain in a neighborhood crime prevention program. Given the surge in burglaries and other crimes there, there was good reason for the program. From January 1, 2011 through February 26, 2012 – the night of the shooting – the development had been the site of more than 400 police calls.[5] Zimmerman, in other words, perceived a crime problem *because there really was a crime problem.* Moreover, far from being a racially-charged renegade lone wolf, he was well-liked by black as well as white residents. Zimmerman had been named head of the community watch council in September 2011. From the start, he and other council members worked closely with local police. Yes, Zimmerman was armed. But he had been licensed to carry a firearm by the State of Florida since November 2009. The notion that he was a mentally unstable "vigilante," out for personal glory and contemptuous of law, is ludicrous.

The crime problem would get very real for Zimmerman during the early evening hours of February 26, 2012. It was just after 7 P.M. Zimmerman, driving his truck toward a neighborhood convenience store, encountered a male teenaged pedestrian who looked suspicious. His name was Trayvon Martin, a high school student from Miami-Dade County. He and his father, Tracy Martin, were up in Sanford to stay for a while with his father's girlfriend, also a resident of The Retreat at Twin Lakes. Far from being a "child," as his sympathizers to this day insist on describing him (often displaying an absurdly dated photo), Trayvon Martin was at least six feet tall, a good four inches taller than Zimmerman. He was in Sanford because he was on a 10-day school suspension – and not his first suspension. He also was wearing a hooded sweatshirt, commonly known as a "hoodie." Criminals often wear this article of clothing for the purpose of concealing their identity during a crime. As this was central Florida, it was hard to believe that the motive for wearing such apparel was "cold weather." Maybe this teen wasn't about to commit a crime, Zimmerman thought, but he certainly looked more suspicious than the average person. It wouldn't hurt to observe and report.

At 7:09 P.M., Zimmerman called a non-emergency police number to report a suspicious person on the premises. He told the dispatcher: "We've had some break-ins in my neighborhood, and there is a real suspicious guy," adding, "This guy looks like he is up to no good or he is on drugs or something." The individual, noted Zimmerman, had his hand in his waistband and was walking around looking at various homes. About two minutes into the call, he told the police dispatcher,

"He's running," to which the dispatcher responded, "Which way is he running?" At that point, there was a noise on the tape suggestive of a vehicle door chime, an indication Zimmerman had gotten out and followed the suspect on foot. But the suspect was fast, and he ran between townhouse clusters rather than along a sidewalk. Zimmerman soon lost sight of him. The dispatcher asked if he was following him. Zimmerman replied that he was. The police response: "We don't need you to do that." Contrary to common belief, the dispatcher wasn't ordering him not to follow, but simply telling him that such action wouldn't be necessary. Zimmerman in no way was "stalking" the suspect or taking the law into his own hands. Notwithstanding, he consented to the request. He did, however, ask for police to arrive. The call ended at about 7:15 P.M.

Zimmerman went back to his truck. It was at this time that Trayvon Martin, seemingly out of nowhere, aggressively confronted Zimmerman and menacingly asked, "What's your problem, homie?" Zimmerman replied, no doubt with a high degree of fear, that he didn't have a problem. He then reached for his cell phone. Martin responded, "You do now," and charged at Zimmerman, decking him with a sucker punch. Having just committed a crime, Martin proceeded to amplify it, pinning a prone Zimmerman and slamming his head onto the pavement. When Zimmerman yelled in anguish, Martin told him to shut up and slammed his head again. And to emphasize his point, Martin allegedly told Zimmerman, "You're gonna die now." Zimmerman had every reason to take the assailant at his word. But he also had the means to save his life. Zimmerman pulled out a handgun from his pocket, and after a brief struggle, fired one shot at close range, hitting Martin in the chest. "You got me," Martin said, falling backward. By 7:30 P.M., he would be dead.

Police shortly arrived on the scene in response to a number of "911" calls, and took Zimmerman in for questioning. Following the interrogation, they decided against arresting him. Sanford Police Chief Billy Lee had concluded there was no evidence to dispute Zimmerman's assertion that he had acted in self-defense. What Sharpton and other civil rights paladins ignored is that Zimmerman was badly hurt. Sanford Police Officer Timothy Smith asserted: "While I was in such close contact with Zimmerman, I could observe that his back appeared to be wet and covered in grass, as if he had been lying on the ground. Zimmerman was also bleeding from the nose and back of his head...While the SPD was attending to Zimmerman, I overheard him state, 'I was yelling for someone to help me, but no one would help me.'"[6] Moreover, the official medical report revealed that Zimmerman had suffered a broken nose and head lacerations a result of Trayvon Martin's attack.[7]

None of this apparently mattered to the people baying for Zimmerman's blood. The Congressional Black Caucus was primed for action.[8] Rep. Bobby Rush, D-Ill., wearing a gray hoodie and a pair of sunglasses, spoke on the House floor to demand a full federal investigation. "Racial profiling has got to stop," he said. "Just because someone wears a hoodie does not make them a hoodlum." He then was escorted off the floor by the House sergeant-at-arms for inappropriate dress. Rep. Hank Johnson, D-Ga., called the shooting an "execution." Rep. Maxine Waters, D-Calif., proclaimed on CNN, "I, personally, really truly believe this is a hate crime." On the same show, Rep. Emanuel Cleaver, D-Mo., stated: "The issue is the low esteem in which black life is held, particularly black males."

Outside Congress even more strident voices could be heard.[9] Jesse Jackson, whose capacity for mindless exaggeration is seemingly limitless, was true to form. He declared in an interview with the *Los Angeles Times*: "Targeting, arresting and convicting blacks, and ultimately killing us, is big business." Nation of Islam leader Louis Farrakhan, sent this ominous Twitter message to followers: "Where there is no justice, there will be no peace. Soon the law of retaliation may very well be applied." The New Black Panther Party was even more direct: It offered a $10,000 bounty for killing Zimmerman.

Lost amid this poisonous climate was the salient fact that even if there was reason to arrest Zimmerman – and there wasn't – he was entitled to a presumption of innocence. The whole idea of the criminal justice system is to quell seething passions, not cater to them. Public officials have a responsibility to ensure that an orderly procedure exists through which evidence can be introduced and explained. One does not assume a defendant's guilt; one must prove it beyond a reasonable doubt. Unfortunately, in the minds of Reverend Al and his troops, racial loyalty trumps rule of law.

Special Prosecutor Angela Corey and her staff, aware of the difficulty of securing a conviction based on actual evidence, opted to play to the media-driven image of Trayvon Martin as a benign black victim of a malicious white stalker. At the trial, which began on June 10, 2013, the prosecution team was aggressive but ineffective. Long on insinuations of racial motive, they could not come up with a convincing case to convict Zimmerman. A little over a month later, on a Saturday night, July 13, the all-female, six-member jury, following 15 hours of deliberation over two days, came back with its verdict: Not guilty of second-degree murder or manslaughter.[10] The prosecution's case not only failed to rise to the standard of "beyond a reasonable doubt," it failed to rise at all. Its star witness – if she could be called that – was a 19-year-old acquaintance of Trayvon Martin named Rachel Jeantel, whose testimony was uncooperative, ungrammatical, surly and self-contradictory. That the case even went to trial was a travesty. Harvard law professor and appellate lawyer Alan Dershowitz, long one of the sharpest legal minds in the country, was unsparing in his denunciation of the prosecution:[11]

> She (Angela Corey) submitted an affidavit that was, if not perjurious, completely misleading. She violated all kinds of rules of the profession, and her conduct bordered on criminal conduct. She, by the way, has a horrible reputation in Florida. She's known for overcharging. She's known for being highly political. And in this case, of course she overcharged. Halfway through the trial she realized she wasn't going to get a second-degree murder verdict, so she asked for a compromised verdict,

for manslaughter. And then, she went further and said that she was going to charge him with child abuse and felony murder. That was such a stretch that it goes beyond anything profession- ally responsible. She was among the most irresponsible prosecu- tors I've seen in 50 years of litigating cases. Believe me, I've seen good prosecutors and bad prosecutors, but rarely have I seen one as bad as this prosecutor, Angela Corey.

Opponents of the verdict, markedly less versed in the law, respond- ed with canned outrage. They sent a multitude of death threats to Zimmerman and immediate family members, which forced them at least temporarily to leave their home. Some took to the streets. In Los Angeles and Oakland, black mobs rioted and smashed property. And Al Sharpton took the lead. Calling the verdict "an atrocity," he vowed in Washington, D.C. that he would lead a "Justice for Trayvon" day in 100 cities on Saturday, July 20 to demand, for starters, that federal civil rights charges be filed against Zimmerman. "People all over the coun- try will gather to show that we are not having a two- or three-day anger fit. This is a social movement for justice." But the combined protests did not produce even hundreds of thousands of demonstrators, much less the promised millions. In Chicago, even with Jesse Jackson as the featured speaker, only about 6,000 protestors showed up. In New York, only several thousand showed up in Harlem outside NAN headquarters despite the fact that the rally featured Sharpton and reigning hip-hop/ pop power couple Jay Z and Beyonce. In most cities, the rallies attracted at most several hundred protestors. And the attendees were overwhelm- ingly black, undercutting the notion that the "Justice for Trayvon" move- ment was a multiracial "rainbow."

Sharpton's close ally, Attorney General Eric Holder, had begun the groundwork for a criminal probe well before the trial. This was not sur- prising given his lengthy track record, especially in his current position, of subordinating rule of law to radical, racially-driven politics.[12] So far the case appears shelved. But Holder hasn't given up on his search for a smoking gun. And though the case resulted in a "not guilty" verdict, it set a dangerous precedent. Very few whites, even those with the money to hire a top-flight lawyer, would want to go through what George Zimmerman managed to endure. Apparently, that's not a concern of Al Sharpton, always attuned to the next "atrocity" against blacks.

CHAPTER 19

RACIAL DEATH BY POLICE CHOKEHOLD?

The current mayor of New York City, Bill de Blasio, is cut from a very different cloth than his Republican predecessors, Rudy Giuliani and Michael Bloomberg. Giuliani, an ex-federal prosecutor, was a centrist law-and-order Republican. Bloomberg, a billionaire businessman, was a liberal, but tough on crime as well. By contrast, de Blasio is an unreconstructed far-Left Democrat whose rhetoric has leaned more toward excusing criminals than punishing them. And small world – his black wife, Chirlane McCray, brought former Al Sharpton aide Rachel Noerdlinger aboard as her chief of staff. Lately, Sharpton has emerged as an equal opportunity accuser. But this may not be a good sign.

It was July 17, 2014, about a half-year into Mayor de Blasio's tenure. Several NYPD cops in Staten Island asked a large black male, Eric Garner, to stop selling untaxed loose cigarettes. He was a familiar sight. But this time, rather than comply, Garner indicated, and defiantly, that he would not cooperate. "I'm tired of it," he declared. "This stops today. I didn't do nothing. Every time you see me, you want to harass me, you want to stop me." An amateur cell phone video revealed him to be placing his hands on his hips, daring police to come and get him – which they did. Several police officers quickly closed in and arrested Garner. And they did so with perhaps more zeal than the situation warranted. The video captured one of the officers, Daniel Pantaleo, inflicting what appeared to be a neck chokehold to subdue Garner, 43, a married father of six. The NYPD had banned this procedure in 1993. The officer then pressed Garner's head onto the pavement. In addition, Garner reportedly several times had said, "I can't breathe," before losing consciousness. Contrary to widespread rumor, he was not killed during the arrest. Garner suffered a cardiac arrest in the ambulance taking him to Richmond University Medical Center (in Staten Island), where he was pronounced dead about an hour later.

It was a terrible outcome. Nobody cheered it, no more the police than anyone else. But was it a crime? The evidence here is less than conclusive.

On the surface, there was a strong case for an indictment. The New York City Medical Examiner's Office ruled the death a homicide, stating Garner died from "the compression of his chest and prone positioning during physical restraint by police."[1] The City also suspended four emergency workers without pay after witnesses reported they did not administer CPR or oxygen to the motionless Garner. Staten Island District Attorney Daniel Donovan called for, and got, a criminal grand jury. The potential prime exhibit was the video. It showed Officer Pantaleo, age 29, an eight-year NYPD veteran, applying what appeared to be a chokehold – and with a minimum of resistance, if any, from the suspect. Even Police Commissioner William Bratton, who had returned in January 2014 to the job he had held during 1994-96 (under Mayor Giuliani), admitted, however cautiously, that excessive force likely had been used. "As defined in the department's patrol guide, this would appear to have been a chokehold," he said at a news conference on July 18, the day after Garner's death. Referring to the police rulebook, he noted that a chokehold includes "any pressure to the throat or windpipe which may prevent or hinder breathing or reduce intake of air." While not illegal, a chokehold violates official police procedure and thus is subject to administrative discipline.

Al Sharpton, a man of surfaces but not much depth, saw a campaign. Predictably, he chose to focus on the possibility of a race-based violation of civil rights than a race-neutral violation of due process of law. It would not take long to rumble. Though Officer Pantaleo was stripped of his gun and badge and put on desk duty, and his partner was reassigned, Sharpton on August 23 led thousands of marchers across Staten Island to protest the "racist" killing. Many demonstrators, seeing a parallel between this case and that of the shooting death of another black "gentle giant," Michael Brown, in the St. Louis suburb of Ferguson two weeks earlier (see next chapter), chanted, "Hands up, don't shoot! Hands up, don't shoot" – an allusion to the unsubstantiated claim that a Ferguson cop had shot Brown while the latter was peaceably surrendering. Another frequent chant was: "No justice, no peace. No racist police."[2]

Sharpton and his minions may carp all they wish, but the evidence is nonexistent that Eric Garner was targeted for arrest, and then death, because he was black. Moreover, the evidence is less than clear that the cops even had committed a crime. Consider the following.

Eric Garner's death was very much a function of his precarious physical condition. At 6'3", 350 lbs., the obese Garner had heart disease, diabetes, sleep apnea and asthma, medical problems which even the City Medical Examiner's Office admitted had contributed toward his death.[3] Garner's friends stated that his asthma was so severe that he had to quit his job as a horticulturalist for the City Parks Department; he wheezed whenever he talked and could not walk even a block without having to rest.[4]

Garner had a lengthy criminal history. Since 1980, he had been arrested by NYPD cops more than 30 times for a variety of offenses, including assault and grand larceny. Indeed, at the time of his death, he was out on bail for illegally selling cigarettes, driving without a license, marijuana possession and false impersonation.[5] Selling loose cigarettes bought out of state, which was his offense during his fatal encounter, is a common hustle to avoid tobacco sales taxes. Granted, from a libertarian standpoint, there is a valid case for leaving cigarettes (and other "sinful" products) entirely untaxed – and cigarette taxes in New York are exceptionally onerous.[6] But the larger point here is that Garner had a long, demonstrated history of contempt for the law.

Garner had resisted arrest that day in Staten Island. For all that the video supposedly implicates police, it also implicates Garner. It reveals him swatting the arms of a white cop attempting to take him into custody, telling the officer, "Don't touch me!" Like it or not, using force to disobey a police directive is a bad move for anyone, regardless of race. Former New York City Police Commissioner Bernard Kerik[7] puts it this way: "You cannot resist arrest. If Eric Garner did not resist arrest, the outcome of this case would have been very different. He wouldn't be dead today."[8]

Officer Daniel Pantaleo might not have used a chokehold after all. Police union officials and Pantaleo's lawyer, Stuart London, argue that Pantaleo did *not* use a chokehold, but rather an allowable takedown move. Patrick Lynch, president of the New York City Patrolmen's Benevolent Association, remarked: "It was clear that the officer's intention was to do nothing more than take Mr. Garner into custody as instructed, and that he used the takedown technique that he learned in the academy when Mr. Garner refused."[9] The lawyer, Stuart London, emphatically agrees. "There was no pressure ever applied to his throat or neck area," he said.[10]

A chokehold, though justifiably barred by the NYPD, rarely is fatal. Between 2009 and mid-2014, the NYPD Civilian Complaint Review Board received 1,128 chokehold allegations.[11] It would a stretch to assert that any more than a small fraction of these cases involved the death of a suspect. Indeed, it is highly likely that none of these incidents were fatal.

The person who filmed the arrest has some legal issues of his own. The amateur filmmaker is one Ramsey Orta, 22, a resident of Staten Island. About two weeks after Garner's death, NYPD officers arrested Orta and charged him with two counts of criminal possession of a stolen .25-caliber Norton semiautomatic handgun that he allegedly had attempted to place in the waistband of a teenaged girl on the sidewalk of a Staten Island street with a reputation for drug-dealing.[12] Despite his tender age, Orta already had racked up an impressive adult criminal record – convictions for two felonies and six misdemeanors. Yet he is "100 percent sure" the cops framed him. "They searched me, they didn't find nothing," said Orta. "They searched the girl, they found the gun on her. Then all of a sudden, they're telling me to turn around."[13] The girl, Alba Lekaj, 17, also was arrested and charged with gun possession and marijuana possession. Her mother, understandably, is less than supportive of this claim. "He (Orta) not only had a gun," she said, "but he put my daughter in trouble, so it's a very, very bad thing."[14] Orta's criminal history *is* relevant here, for it raises the possibility that he shot only that footage which he thought would incriminate the cops.

The lead police officer on the scene herself was black. That would be Sgt. Kizzy Adoni. She had testified before the grand jury: "His (Garner's) condition did not seem serious and he did not appear to get worse" as he lay on the sidewalk and afterward. At no time does the video recording show Adoni ordering Officer Pantaleo to stop applying what appeared to be a chokehold. She, like other officers at the scene, was given immunity for testifying; i.e., they would not have been charged with a crime even if Pantaleo were accused of one. Adoni's words, and the fact of her being black, severely undercut race as a motive for Officer Pantaleo's actions, banned or not.[15]

Al Sharpton, ever dismissive of facts, swooped in to become the "adviser" to Eric Garner's family. Legal action soon materialized. On October 7, the family, led by Garner's mother, Gwen Carr, announced their intention to file a $75 million civil suit against the City of New York, the NYPD and several officers involved in the episode.[16] On the criminal front, a state grand jury convened in late September to review evidence to determine if criminal charges should be filed against Officer Pantaleo. Parallel to that, Reverend Al and the family began pressuring the U.S. Justice Department to conduct its own investigation. Indeed, toward that end, they already had met with an unnamed U.S. Attorney in New York in late August.[17] On October 2, with Sharpton and the Garner family in Washington, D.C. for a news conference, the word came down: Attorney General Eric Holder planned to resign. Whoever would be in charge of an eventual investigation – Holder or his successor – federal action would be required one way or another, averred Sharpton. "If you have the federal government that does not depend on local police, you have a more objective and fair investigation," he said. "It protects everyone."[18] Such words could not be more misguided. There is every reason to believe that Eric Holder, with his long and clear pattern of subordinating rule of law to radical politics,[19] would leave Daniel Pantaleo, all other arresting officers on the scene, and possibly the entire NYPD, *unprotected* from the arbitrary exercise of federal authority.

By contrast, a state investigation seemed an unbiased and thorough approach. The Staten Island District Attorney's office and the NYPD from the start have been fully aware that any grand jury would scrutinize every aspect of the case, especially adherence to official police procedures. Police Chief Bratton has stated on several occasions during his tenure that he is committed to removing abusive police officers from the force. Neither he nor any other public official has implied that Officer Pantaleo, if indicted, charged and found guilty, should avoid punishment. Police everywhere should be accountable to the public. But an investigation must proceed on the need to protect individual civil liberties, not on the opportunities to use the race of a particular victim as a pretext for a trophy hunt for racial bias. And it can't be held hostage to the possibility of mob rule. Reverend Al, itching for federal action, sees the Eric Garner case as a racial trophy hunt.

The state grand jury, however, did not see conclusive evidence of a crime, racially motivated or otherwise. On December 3, 2014, jurors announced its decision: It would not indict NYPD Officer Daniel Pantaleo. In delivering its vote of "no true bill," members concluded there was insufficient basis for a prosecution. In a prepared statement, Staten Island District Attorney Daniel Donovan offered condolences to Garner's family and friends: "Clearly this matter was of special concern in that an unarmed citizen of our County had died in police custody...All 23 members of this community who comprised the Grand Jury in this matter dutifully fulfilled that commitment by attending each and every one of the sessions that began on September 29, 2014, and concluded on December 3, 2014."[20] Far from racing to conclusions, the grand jury heard testimony from at least 38 persons, including 22 civilians who had seen part or all of the interaction between Garner and the NYPD cops.[21]

Reverend Al Sharpton saw a whitewash. With Eric Garner's widow and mother standing next to him, he held a news conference that evening at National Action Network headquarters in Harlem.[22] Rev. Sharpton announced he was organizing a March on Washington, set for Saturday, December 13. "We have no choice but to keep on fighting because it could be your child next," he stated. Disingenuously holding out an olive branch, he added: "We will continue? We must continue. All of our protests, we will not have violence, or inflict pain on others." Eric Garner's widow, Esaw Garner, soon stepped up to the microphone. She announced: "This fight ain't over. It's just begun. I'm determined to get justice for my husband. He should be here celebrating Christmas with his children and his grandchildren."

Sharpton's chief protector-enabler at the Justice Department, Attorney General Eric Holder, announced at that very time that was opening a civil rights probe into Garner's death. "Our prosecutors," he said, "will conduct an independent, thorough, fair and expeditious investigation."[23] Given the quickness of his response to the grand jury decision, to say nothing of his pattern of anti-white tendencies in pursuing cases, the claim should be taken with a grain of salt. As Holder is set to resign shortly, he is unlikely to complete the task. But his putative successor, Loretta Lynch, U.S. Attorney for the Eastern District of New York, would provide an enthusiastic follow-through. And why wouldn't anyone believe as much? First, Lynch, like Holder, is black. Second, she has a radical egalitarian view of racial issues.[24] Third, her jurisdiction covers Staten Island, where the Garner incident occurred, in addition to Brooklyn, Queens and Long Island's Nassau and Suffolk Counties. As she wants the job of attorney general, she can't afford to appear half-hearted about prosecuting a high-profile case such as this on her own turf. And fourth, if approved by the Senate, Lynch would owe her job in large measure to Al Sharpton, whose role in vetting candidates was well-known even before the announcement of her nomination on November 7.[25] To ignore Reverend Al here would be, shall one say, getting off to a bad start.

Meanwhile, out in the streets, demonstrators in a number of U.S. cities protested the grand jury decision, and not necessarily legally, for several days and nights. In New York City, Denver, Philadelphia, Washington, D.C. and elsewhere they have been jamming public spaces, at times blocking traffic. If the Washington, D.C. event of December 13 happens, they can march to their heart's content. The high degree of public tension should keep Al Sharpton busy on this case. Yet this may wind up as a sidebar item compared to another fatal incident, and its ongoing aftermath, that occurred in August in the St. Louis area. Sharpton has seen fit to visit the area more than once to exacerbate conflict. From all evidence, he's done a pretty good job.

CHAPTER 20

ST. LOUIS FUSE

As the Sean Bell case amply demonstrated, Al Sharpton can alternate between the roles of Good Cop and Bad Cop in the aftermath of a crime with racial implications. As a Good Cop, he claims to be a calming influence, imploring his black audiences to "stay cool" and "remain nonviolent" until all facts are known. As a Bad Cop, he reverts to his default setting of incitement. This behavior has been evident in the seemingly never-ending aftermath of the shooting death by a white police officer of an 18-year-old black male, Michael Brown Jr., around noon on Saturday, August 9, 2014 in the St. Louis suburb of Ferguson, Mo.[1]

A St. Louis County grand jury, after hearing extensive testimony and combing through voluminous written and photographic evidence, announced over three months later, on November 24, that it would not indict the police officer in question, Darren Wilson, for murder, voluntary manslaughter or involuntary manslaughter. It was the right decision. At best, the eyewitness evidence against Wilson was extremely contradictory;[2] at worst, it was utterly unconvincing. Yet dozens of blacks in Ferguson rioted almost as soon as the news came out that Monday evening. They torched businesses, threw rocks and bottles at police, smashed windows, looted stores, and fired off dozens of gunshots. Police responded with pepper spray and tear gas. By the following morning, the "protestors" had set fire to at least 20 local businesses and a row of cars at a dealership. More than 60 people were arrested, about half of them on felony charges. In other cities, including Atlanta and New York, rioters blocked traffic arteries.[3] Additional rioting occurred in

Ferguson on Tuesday night, with more than 40 persons arrested. And over the Thanksgiving weekend, protestors in the Washington, D.C. and other metro areas blocked traffic.

Anti-white activists are convinced this was a case of police murder. Unable to secure an indictment from a state jury, they are demanding nothing less than a full-scale federal intervention. Reverend Al Sharpton, predictably, is prominent among these people. Reacting to the news of the grand jury decision, he remarked at a news conference at National Action Network headquarters: "It was expected, but still an absolute blow to those of us that wanted to see a fair and open trial." He also vowed to "continue to organize and mobilize" around the country to "escalate a federal indictment."[4] One can be certain that Sharpton would be less adamant had the cop been black.

The rioting following the grand jury's refusal to indict, like the roughly two weeks of sporadic street protests and riots in Ferguson in August following Brown's death, were attempts to hold the criminal justice system hostage. A careful and deliberate review of the evidence indicated that Officer Darren Wilson was not the aggressor. To the contrary, he had engaged in the most elementary self-defense. In other words, had Wilson not fired his weapon, in all likelihood the funeral would have been his own. Sharpton's campaign to cast Michael Brown as an "unarmed" martyr for civil rights is as fraudulent as the campaign he mounted in Florida to prosecute George Zimmerman, the alleged "murderer" of Trayvon Martin. Moreover, his presence in the St. Louis area in August may have extended the rioting during that time for several days.

Al Sharpton from the start has been engaged in shuttle diplomacy in this case. He arrived in St. Louis for a news conference a few days after the shooting of Brown and stayed for well over a week. He returned in late-October, mid-November and again the day after the grand jury announcement. For the Rev, these were homecoming events of a sort. Back on July 12, 1999, he was among hundreds of persons who blocked Monday morning rush hour traffic on Interstate 70 north of downtown

St. Louis – he had participated at the invitation of local civil rights leaders for the purpose of boosting minority contracting and hiring for local highway construction projects. The demonstrations, which led to well over 100 arrests, led to an agreement between the State of Missouri, a minority contractor called MO-KAN, and various construction firms to establish a new job training center. Sharpton eventually was fined $600, and, in a rare show of compliance, paid up.[5]

The Rev's stated purpose for coming to St. Louis in 2014 was to obtain justice for the deceased Michael Brown and his grieving family. The way he and other mourners have spun the story, this was yet another case of a racially-rigged system of law and order depriving blacks of their inalienable rights. This account of things is superficial at best. A retracing of events will show why. While there were many conflicting versions of events during grand jury testimony, the following storyline stands by far as the most credible.[6]

It was Saturday, August 9, around noon in Ferguson, Missouri, a modest middle-class north side St. Louis suburban community of about 20,000. Officer Darren Wilson was driving his SUV police cruiser slowly through a residential neighborhood on Canfield Drive when he noticed two young black men, Michael Brown and a friend, Dorian Johnson, walking in the middle of the street. He ordered the pair to move to the sidewalk. The directive might not have been issued in a "pretty please" voice, but it was reasonable all the same. There was no reason to interpret it as abusive or racially motivated. Walking in the middle of a street is potentially dangerous for pedestrians and motorists alike. It is the job of law enforcement officers in any community to promote the general public safety as well as to investigate and apprehend specific reported crimes. Officer Wilson was well within his authority to tell the pair to move to the sidewalk. What he didn't know is that the exercise of that authority would produce a crime scene.

According to the official police report, Michael Brown did not take kindly to this directive. Rather than comply, he flew into a rage while Officer Wilson was sitting inside his police SUV vehicle with his window

189

open, sucker-punching Wilson at least twice. Officer Wilson, properly panicked, pushed Brown away with his left hand and then pulled his Sig Sauer P229 service revolver from his holster. "Stop or I will shoot," Wilson yelled. Having raised his weapon, Brown attempted to grab it and responded, "You're too much of a pussy to shoot me." Wilson soon pulled the trigger twice from inside the SUV, but that the pistol failed to fire. Wilson fired his gun twice again, with one of the shots striking Brown on the hand. Brown and his friend then ran away. It was obvious that Brown's intent was to kill the officer. Wilson, by the way, never previously had used his service pistol in the line of duty.

Wilson at that point got out of his car. In response, still in a pique of rage, Brown suddenly wheeled around and charged at Officer Wilson at top speed. Rightly fearing for his life, Wilson pulled out his pistol and shot Brown multiple times. The initial hits failed to stop Brown's charge. It was then that Wilson fired the kill shot. While this was not known at the time, Brown only minutes earlier had ripped off merchandise at a nearby convenience store and physically assaulted a clerk who tried to get him to pay. The assault, captured on a hidden store camera, subsequently was released by police.

Some eyewitnesses told a completely different story. One witness, Philip Walker, said he was on the porch of an apartment complex overlooking the scene when he heard gunfire and saw an officer with Michael Brown on the street. Brown, Walker told the Associated Press, "was giving up in the sense of raising his arms and being subdued." The officer "had his gun raised and started shooting the individual in the chest multiple times" and then, with Brown lying on the pavement wounded, stood over him and shot him. Walker, however, admitted that he did not see the circumstances that led to the first shot. Brown's friend, Dorian Johnson, told KMOV-TV in St. Louis that the pair were walking home in the middle of the street from a convenience store when a police officer, from inside his squad car, told the pair to move to the sidewalk. After Johnson and Brown ignored the directive, the officer got out of his car and fired his gun. "We wasn't causing harm to nobody," Johnson remarked. "We had no weapons on us at all," he said, but the officer fired a shot anyway, causing the pair to flee. "He shot again," said Johnson, "and once my friend felt that shot, he turned around and put his hands in the air, and he started to get down. But the officer still approached with his weapon drawn and fired several more shots."

These latter versions of the story diverged so widely from the police version that it was impossible to reconcile them. And a good many blacks, joined by some whites, chose to believe the anti-police account of things. News of the killing spread throughout the community and then the St. Louis area. Crowds gathered in the streets of Ferguson for a prolonged series of protests. Their protests lasted some two weeks. While the daytime demonstrations were more or less peaceful, the nighttime demonstrations were not. Certain elements of the overwhelmingly black crowd rioted, on occasion smashing windows of small businesses, breaking into the premises and looting merchandise. In at least two instances, they set fires to stores. St. Louis County Police SWAT teams arrived on the scene, firing tear gas canisters at crowds assembled at a gas station that served as an impromptu staging ground. More than 150 persons were arrested, many of them from out of state.

Reverend Al Sharpton arrived in St. Louis to hold a press conference on Tuesday, August 12, three days after the shooting. The rioting was well underway. Sharpton was too smart to openly agitate the crowds, knowing his newfound reputation as a "pragmatic" healer would be in jeopardy. President Obama and Missouri Democratic Governor Jay Nixon each issued statements denouncing the rioting and the allegedly excessive use of police force. Sharpton called for peace in the streets. At the news conference, with Michael Brown's family members in attendance, he described Brown as a "gentle giant." To become violent in the wake of his death, he emphasized, would be to betray his good name. He and others then spoke at a local church before an overflow audience.

Sharpton speaks in Ferguson, Missouri on Friday, Oct. 31, 2014. Brown's
mother, Lesley McSpadden, right, and father Michael Brown, Sr. listen.
(AP Photo/St. Louis Post-Dispatch, Christian Gooden)

Sharpton's true intentions for being in town became clearer in a speech at Greater St. Marks Family Church in St. Louis the following Sunday morning, August 17. He declared: "Michael Brown is gone. You can run whatever video you want. He is not on trial. America is on trial!"[7] He inveighed against the Web posting of Brown assaulting a convenience store clerk: "I have never in all my years seen something as offensive and insulting as a police chief releasing a tape of a young man trying to smear him before we even have his funeral."[8] Apparently, it hadn't occurred to Sharpton that the tape almost beyond a reasonable doubt revealed Brown to be a thug. The Rev's real problem, as anyone could grasp, is that once revealed, the display of the video likely would undermine public sympathy for Brown. Sharpton also threw in a disingenuous dose of moral equivalence: "Looting is wrong. We condemn the looters. But when will law enforcement condemn police who shoot and kill our young people? We got to be honest on both sides of this discussion."[9] And at Michael Brown's funeral service on August 25, Sharpton declared before an overflow crowd in the thousands: "America, it's time to deal with policing. We are not the haters. We're the healers." His eulogy also included these decidedly non-healing words: "Michael Brown's blood is crying out for justice. Those police that are wrong need to be dealt with."

Even more revealing were Sharpton's remarks in an ambush interview conducted by a prominent conservative St. Louis blogger, Adam Sharp, on August 12. Though aligned with the local Tea Party, Sharp tried to outflank Sharpton from the Left. Alluding to the phrase "Snitches Get Stitches," spray-painted on a Quik Trip convenience store that had been looted and torched two days earlier, here is how things went down:[10]

> **Sharp:** Since you are a federal snitch, sir, do you fear for your life?
> **Sharpton:** I'm not a snitch, but today I want to tell the feds about a cop that needs to go to jail.
> **Sharp:** Are you in fear for your life being a federal informant and...
> **Sharpton:** I want to inform on this policeman today.
> **Sharp:** Are you here to snitch on the rioters?...Are you here to work with your FBI partners?

Sharpton did not respond to this question. Beyond this point, the interview broke down. It is hard to deny this "journalist" was an obnoxious and presumptuous bully, content to repeat an absurd accusation until he coaxed a "gotcha" response. That said, he deserves credit for having teased out Sharpton's motive for being in town. Three days later, on August 15, with local blacks likewise demanding the officer's identity, Ferguson police, reluctantly, released his name. The cop, Darren

Wilson, a six-year veteran on the force with no record of disciplinary action against him, took an indefinite leave of absence after the release of his name. And after the release of the grand jury report, he resigned from the force shortly thereafter. Wilson understood he would be a marked man.

Even before Wilson's name had been released to the public, Michael Brown's mother, Lesley McSpadden, had called for his death. Anyone wondering why Brown turned out the way he did would do well to examine the mother's approach to conflict resolution. On October 18, 2014, over two months after her son's death, McSpadden was a central figure in a family-related mob assault and robbery occurring on a restaurant parking lot just blocks from the shooting.[11] According to the Ferguson police report, which had been suppressed for a couple weeks until its release, several people, including Michael Brown's paternal grandfather, Pearlie Gordon, were selling 'Justice for Mike' merchandise on the parking lot of Red's BBQ, when around 1:20 P.M., several cars pulled up. About 20 to 30 people then jumped out and rushed the budding entrepreneurs. One of those assailants, according to at least eyewitness, was Lesley McSpadden, who shouted an epithet. The report stated that Gordon was "repeatedly struck in the back of the head by an unknown subject" and "knocked to the ground." It then stated that McSpadden "then ran up and punched (Gordon)." Police arrived in less than four minutes. One person, a cousin of Michael Brown named Tony Petty, was taken to a local hospital. Some of the assailants ran away with $1,500 in merchandise and a suitcase containing $400 in cash. Keep in mind that Al Sharpton is this woman's "adviser." Keep in mind as well that McSpadden and Michael Brown's father, Michael Brown, Sr., were guest speakers at a November 12-13, 2014 United Nations human rights conference in Geneva, Switzerland.[12]

The Obama administration might not be calling for Officer Darren Wilson's death, but it is doing everything it can to create a pretext for throwing him in prison. Moreover, it wants to chasten local enforcement agencies around the country, all the better to make it legally painful for cops to defend themselves against a violent attacker if the attacker is black. Attorney General Eric Holder, eager for a smoking gun that would expose a hidden racial motive on the part of police, has been giving it his all. He arrived in the St. Louis area nine days after the fatal encounter for an opportunity to express his views on the case.[13] At a speech at Florissant Valley Community College, Holder waxed autobiographical, recalling instances of police "harassment" growing up in Washington, D.C. that amounted to nothing more than requests based on reasonable suspicions. He also was in the process of pulling out the stops at the Justice Department. He told the *St. Louis Post-Dispatch* that he had assigned 40 FBI agents to the case, a show of manpower that did not even include prosecutors at the U.S. Attorney's Office in St. Louis. He also noted that agents have interviewed hundreds of people. That's a whole lot of muscle, even allowing for the incendiary climate fanned by his good friend, Al Sharpton.

On September 4, Holder made it official: The Justice Department would launch an investigation into whether local Ferguson police officers have engaged in patterns of excessive behavior.[14] The review would examine racial profiling, stops, searches, frisking and handling of mass demonstrations (i.e., riots). Holder appeared bent on finding something that will stick to his target, no matter how long it takes. Rather than show the slightest degree of support for law enforcement, the attorney general decided, on the basis of one apparently justified case of police self-defense, that the Ferguson police department, and very likely many other departments across the country, are incubators of race hatred. As *Weekly Standard* senior editor-writer Christopher Caldwell observed: "The government has always been on the wide of those seeking to restore public order. Now Obama and Holder have placed the government on the side of the uprising – or at least on the side of those who would restore order on the terms demanded by the uprising."[15]

Lawyers for Michael Brown's family, Benjamin Crump and Daryl Parks, have made little secret of where they stand. Crump and Parks, both black, previously had represented the family of Trayvon Martin.

At an August 17 rally in Ferguson, Crump declared: "We know that this was an execution." And five area residents have filed a $40 million civil suit against the Ferguson Police Department for various violations of their rights. Protestors also have kept up the pressure. Their leaders know that as long as they can make the news, the Justice Department will have every incentive to "discover" evidence that will incriminate Officer Wilson and his department. On Wednesday, September 10, about a month after the shooting, St. Louis-area protestors reprised their tactic of 15 years earlier, attempting to shut down Interstate 70. Spokespersons for the black mob stated that the purpose of their action was to force the appointment of a special prosecutor in place of St. Louis County Prosecutor Robert McCullough. This effort did not succeed. Police prevented protestors from entering the highway.[16]

Al Sharpton and his allies in high and low places should save their strength. The material facts of this case overwhelmingly point to one conclusion: Michael Brown brutally attacked Officer Darren Wilson without warning or provocation, and Wilson, by killing Brown, was saving his own life. There is no basis for believing that this was a police murder. Like the "murder" of Trayvon Martin, a criminal prosecution would have been incapable of meeting the bar of "beyond a reasonable doubt." Even before the official grand jury report was released, several realities, much of it based on eyewitness accounts, had supported this conclusion.

Michael Brown had established himself as a criminal even before his encounter with Wilson. Brown's defenders are peddling the line that he had "no prior criminal record." This claim, even if true, is highly disingenuous. Its sole purpose is to establish Brown's innocence, and hence, Wilson's guilt. About 10 minutes prior to the police encounter, hidden video footage showed a young black male bearing an identical likeness to Brown stealing merchandise from a nearby convenience store. The merchandise in question turned out to be about $50 worth of cigars. This act, at the very least, qualifies as petty larceny. The camera also showed that on his way out of the store, Brown shoved and terrorized a diminutive store clerk attempting to get him to pay. *These are crimes.* It is significant that none of Brown's manifold defenders have come forward to assert that the person terrorizing the clerk was someone else. As for Michael Brown's apparent lack of a criminal record, he likely did have one – as a juvenile. While juvenile crime laws vary from state to state, as a general rule, most crimes committed by minors, save for truly heinous ones, are shielded from public view and/or expunged from the record once the minor becomes an adult. Given that Brown had turned 18 only months prior to his death, he had virtually no time to amass any adult convictions. And even if Brown was clean until the day of his death, there is a first time for every criminal.

Officer Wilson did not behave in any way that justified a violent response by Brown. Wilson was driving his patrol car slowly through a Ferguson neighborhood when he encountered Brown and a companion, Dorian Johnson, jaywalking in the middle of the street. Wilson then told the pair to move to the sidewalk. This was a reasonable request. There is no reason to assume that Officer Wilson's request had anything to do with the race of the pedestrians. Even if it had, there is something elementary here. When a police officer issues a directive of any sort toward a civilian, the civilian has an obligation to comply unless he can explain why he can't. Brown and Johnson failed to comply with the directive not because they couldn't, but because they *wouldn't*. Brown in particular took offense. For him, obeying a request by a white cop somehow constituted a symbolic surrender to the enemy. Brown apparently perceived the request as something "done" to him and thus as something requiring instant revenge.

Michael Brown assaulted Wilson, not the other way around. Newspaper and Web articles sympathetic to Brown routinely have referred to him as "unarmed." Yet the use of that word is misleading. Each year in this country, countless crimes are committed without the benefit of a gun, knife, blunt object or other weapon. Hands and feet can be lethal to an intended victim, especially when the assailant is large. And at a reported 6'4," 292 lbs., Brown was as large as a typical NFL lineman.

Sharpton's description of him as a "gentle giant" was right about the "giant" part – and dead wrong about the "gentle" part. Brown, rather than comply with a simple request, allegedly charged at Officer Wilson, who sitting in his SUV with his window open. Brown cold-cocked him with at least one sucker punch, and likely two, which, according to initial reports, had created an orbital blowout fracture of one of Wilson's eye sockets.[17] Then, Brown reportedly reached into the vehicle and tried to steal Officer Wilson's service revolver, with the clear intent of killing him. Fortunately, Wilson, though injured, was still conscious and possessed of his faculties. He was able to wrestle Brown away from the car's interior, protect his gun and fire off a couple shots.

Officer Wilson had very good reason to use his weapon after that. Self-anointed "anti-racist activists," apparently unfamiliar with the nature of police work, are enraged that Wilson used his gun against Michael Brown, and worse, fired off six rounds that hit him. They also insist that Brown was shot while surrendering and that at least one of the shots hit Brown from the back. This, they have insisted, constitutes a police murder. The facts suggest something else. Remember, Brown already had: 1) sucker-punched Wilson; and 2) attempted to steal Wilson's service revolver with the obvious motive of killing him. Having just committed two felonies against a cop, plus acts of larceny and assault at a convenience store shortly before, he wasn't finished. Brown walked away from Officer Wilson's vehicle, at which point Wilson got out of his car. It was at that point, noted numerous eyewitnesses, that Brown wheeled around and bum-rushed Wilson at top speed. Wilson knew he had to act within the next few seconds or his life would be in jeopardy. He pulled out his gun and shot Brown, hitting him repeatedly but failing to slow the attack until he fired off the final shot. *St. Louis Post-Dispatch* crime reporter Christine Byers sent this tweet: "Police sources tell me more than a dozen witnesses have corroborated the cop's version of events." Michael Brown's defenders counter that she recanted her tweet the next day, yet the recantation itself may have the result of pressure from newspaper management.[18] Despite the ritual guerrilla theater taunt by demonstrators – "Hands up, don't shoot" – the evidence that Officer Wilson had fired shots at the back of a stationary Brown raising his arms in surrender is unconvincing, if not an outright lie.

A local autopsy showed that all six bullets hit Brown from the front. Two anonymous sources from the St. Louis County Medical Examiner's Office, under fear of reprisal, stated on August 18 that Brown had six gunshot wounds, and that every bullet struck the front of his body. In addition, they said, Brown had marijuana in his system. County Medical Examiner Mary Case released the results to state prosecutors late on August 15. She was very transparent. "I welcome anyone who wants to do additional autopsies," she remarked. "Michael (forensic pathologist Michael Baden) is someone I know… I'm not upset at all."[19] In all, as of late August there had been three autopsies including one performed by the Pentagon on orders from Attorney General Holder. None had indicated any shots hitting Brown from the back.

Police were justified in not quickly removing Michael Brown's corpse from the street. Much of the denunciation of the Ferguson police department has centered upon the supposed injustice of white cops not quickly removing Brown's body until several hours after his death. Yet this moral indignation is highly misplaced. First of all, the corpse was part of a crime scene. Law enforcement officers on the scene of a dead body, as a matter of standard practice, seal off the area, establish a police line, and gather material evidence. Police left Brown's corpse on the street for a good reason. Had they removed it prematurely, they would have run the risk of tainting the evidence and blowing the case. Second, if there was a delay in the removal of Brown's body, it wasn't the doing of the cops, but of a growing and violent black mob. Here is a word-for-word explanation from the funeral director as to why it took so long to remove Brown's body:[20]

> *It was not a safe situation…The police could not control the crowd. There was times where we feared for our lives…There was gunshots while we were there…It took so long because we*

*could not do our job. It was unsafe for us to be there. [A cop told
the Whitakers]: 'Stay in your vehicles. You guys do not have
vests. The best thing for you to do is to kind of get down and let
us get control of the situation.'*

Any suggestion that police willfully delayed the removal of Michael
Brown in order to give themselves time to fabricate evidence is ludicrous. But then, in any war – race wars, included – truth is typically the
first casualty.

**The potential star witness for the prosecution, Dorian Johnson,
was unreliable.** The standard account of events given by Michael
Brown's mourners is that without provocation, Officer Wilson grabbed
Brown's neck, tried to choke him, and then fired several shots from the
back at Brown, who was walking away. The main source of this information, however, is Brown's companion that day, Dorian Johnson. And as it
turns out, Johnson, age 22 at the time of the shooting, had some serious
credibility problems of his own. First, hidden video footage inside the
convenience store from which Brown had stolen merchandise suggests
that Johnson did more than accompany Brown; he aided and abetted
the theft. Second, Johnson had a few skeletons in his closet. An investigative report by KMIZ, the ABC television affiliate in the Columbia-
Jefferson City, Mo. area, revealed that Johnson had an outstanding local
warrant for his arrest for a theft dating back to June 2011. Johnson also
had been charged with giving police false information in connection
with the incident. Were that not enough, he may have admitted that
Brown was the assailant after all. According to a news story broken 10
days after the shooting by radio station KFNS-FM 100.7, aka "the Viper,"
in St. Louis, Johnson recanted his original story, which he had given as
an exclusive to MSNBC – the same network, perhaps no coincidence,
where Al Sharpton has been giving six o'clock news and commentary
since August 2011. The radio station even posted the news of the recantation on its Facebook page.

Officer Wilson's own testimony, which was not released until after the grand jury announcement, should demolish any lingering illusions about Michael Brown's benevolence. Wilson testified to the grand jury[21] that on that fateful August 9 encounter, Brown reacted to his request to move to the sidewalk with a shocking and sudden rage. His face, said Wilson, looked "like a demon."[22] Wilson stated that when Brown reached into his police vehicle and tried to take his gun, the suspect was so physically overpowering that he (Wilson) "felt like a 5-year-old holding onto Hulk Hogan." And then, after Brown ran away from Wilson, Brown suddenly stopped, turned to face Wilson, and far from raising his hands in a gesture of surrender, made "a grunting, like aggravated sound." Brown then clenched his left hand into a fist, tucked his right hand under his shirt toward his waistband, and began charging at the officer. It was only at that point, testified Wilson, that he used his service revolver to subdue Brown.[23]

Even just *one* of these considerations would have warranted a dismissal of the case. But taken together, they made any indictment preposterous. The St. Louis County grand jury – which consisted of nine whites and three blacks – deliberated at length. It met for 25 separate days over a three-month period, hearing a combined 70 hours of testimony from about 60 witnesses. The grand jury also pored through forensics reports, police radio logs, medical documents and FBI tapes of bystanders. County Prosecutor Robert McCullough asserted that the jury considered "absolutely everything" that could be considered testimony or evidence in the case.[24] A minimum of nine of the 12 grand jurors were necessary to bring forth an indictment. Presumably possessed of rational minds, none of the jurors should have voted in favor of an indictment on any charge. As for the evidence being racial "biased," at least six black witnesses provided anonymous testimony backing up Officer Wilson's account.[25] Moreover, the accounts offered by witnesses who were hostile to police were so contradictory as to be useless. The grand jury had no choice but *not* to indict.[26]

The state's case against Officer Darren Wilson, for all intents and purposes, is over – not that it ever should have been brought forth in the first place. And while the U.S. Justice Department civil rights investigation continues, it is highly unlikely to result in an indictment. The standard for a successful prosecution is higher for federal than for state cases. Under federal law, prosecutors would have to show not only that Officer Wilson had intended to deprive Michael Brown of his civil rights, but that Brown didn't pose any immediate threat. In effect, the Justice Department would have to prove that any reasonable police officer, faced with a similar situation, would not have resorted to firing his weapon.[27] Given the evidence, clearing that bar is almost inconceivable.

Al Sharpton and other "civil rights" activists, of course, are determined to get a conviction of Officer Wilson, and beyond that, the stiffest possible sentence. But it's precisely such people who underscore the need for a high bar for federal action. Even under Sharpton-enabling Attorney General Eric Holder or his heiress-apparent, Loretta Lynch, winning a conviction would be virtually impossible – as it should be. As for rioting, it will accomplish nothing, save for eroding what little sympathy Michael Brown's family has left with the reasoning portion of the public.[28]

Even before the grand jury announcement, Sharpton was in his Good Cop mode. In anticipation of the moment, he returned to the St. Louis area in mid-November to announce that he would stand alongside protestors, emphasizing that any demonstrations should be nonviolent. His assurances as to the latter were something short of comforting. At one point, he offered: "If there is not justice for this family, then we have not achieved the goals of this movement."[29] In other words, anything short of a felony indictment against Officer Wilson would be an injustice. Maybe that's one reason why there were riots – and not just in Ferguson. Potential rioters, their minds shaped by racial politicians and news media covering for them, perceived an injustice and then rioted.

After the violence, Sharpton assumed the role of full-time Bad Cop in a 50-minute speech before a highly enthusiastic congregation at a St.

Louis church. With Michael Brown's biological parents, Michael Brown Sr. and Lesley McSpadden, sitting in the front row, Reverend Al delivered his usual high-testosterone menace disguised as moral-theological protest. "You won the first round, Mr. Prosecutor, but don't cut your gloves off, because the fight is not over," he thundered. "Justice will come to Ferguson!" He added: "God is going to use Michael to lead this nation to deal with police accountability."[30] To its great credit, the St. Louis County grand jury saw things differently. But it's highly unlikely that Sharpton, or the rioters he inspired, will come to recognize as much. For them, there are no black criminals if the intended victim is white.

CHAPTER 21

WHERE'S THE MONEY?

Part II of this book, in reasonably chronological order, thus far has summarized Al Sharpton's varied projects to foment mass direct action. But there is one more piece of the puzzle: his management, or rather mismanagement, of funds that have made these projects possible. Throughout his career, in fact, Sharpton has exhibited a recurring pattern of questionable and likely fraudulent practices in controlling the finances of National Action Network and any number of for-profit ventures. Equally disturbing, with a few minor exceptions, he has avoided legal consequences.

That Sharpton has generated donations from high places is indisputable. His three-day 60th birthday celebration in October 2014, underneath the hoopla, was a fundraiser that signified his ability to attract high-level donors. At his honorary dinner at Manhattan's Four Seasons restaurant, he declared, "I've been able to reach from the streets to the suites."[1] Few would argue the point. According to tax filings for 2011 and 2012 (the most recent years available), National Action Network generated more than $4 million in revenues for each year.[2] Yet Sharpton, more than ever, appears mired in debt, in both a personal and organizational context. Moreover, there is every reason to believe his financial woes have involved an illegal commingling of funds.

The root of the Sharpton's money problems is attitude. He appears to harbor a belief that since his life's calling is promoting social justice, his balance sheet integrity is at best of passing importance. This attitude is manifest in evading taxes, ignoring creditors, and hiding or falsifying income. The Center for Public Integrity, a Washington, D.C.-based non-partisan investigative journalism project, for example, described Mr. Sharpton this way in the 2004 edition of its *The Buying of the President* monograph series:[3]

> *Sharpton has built, with the aid of a core of wealthy contributors, a small empire of tax-exempt and for-profit companies and mingles their finances to confuse creditors and tax collectors alike. When called to account, he conflates his personal travails with his civil rights crusading, turning his own questionable practices into a vehicle for self-promotion and raising his political clout.*

Sharpton has heard the same music elsewhere. An audit of National Action Network by the Manhattan-based accounting firm of KBL, conducted in April 2010 and covering NAN financial records for 2008, concluded: "The organization [NAN] has suffered recurring decreases in net assets – and has been dependent upon advances from related parties and the nonpayment of payroll tax obligations – to maintain continuity." KBL added: "These circumstances create substantial doubt about the organization's ability to continue."[4] Financial disarray has continued to plague the group. But as long as Reverend Al is confident he can avoid the consequences, he will have little incentive to turn things around.

Accusations of mismanagement, including outright theft, go well back. Some 25 years ago, Sharpton was accused of looting about $250,000 from NAN's precursor nonprofit group, National Youth Movement. In July 1990, a trial jury, after deliberating for less than six hours, acquitted Sharpton of 67 counts of fraud and larceny charges brought forth by the New York State Attorney General's Office.[5] Yet the Rev was far less innocent than the verdict had indicated. Sharpton's attorney, Alton Maddox, called no witnesses to the stand during the entire trial. The prosecution, by contrast, called more than 80 witnesses. Not even the best defense in the world could have yielded a not-guilty verdict under those circumstances unless one considers the real possibility that any number of jurors had racially-motivated nullification on their mind. Maddox, suspended from practicing law not long after as a result of his refusal to address allegations of misconduct in the Tawana Brawley case, would claim without evidence that Attorney General Robert Abrams was trying to get back at him and Sharpton for having defended Brawley.

Sharpton's run for the presidency during 2003-04 was loaded with fundraising practices shady enough to prompt an FBI criminal probe.[6] The investigation was based on allegations by National Legal and Policy Center as part of a February 2, 2004 complaint NLPC had filed with the Federal Election Commission (FEC) over extensive political travels Sharpton took during 2002-03. These trips were not reported, as required, in FEC filings. NLPC also had alleged that National Action Network might have underwritten these expenses with large undisclosed gifts from unnamed donors, which would have been illegal.

Sharpton's presidential campaign, in fact, had invited scrutiny of his ongoing relationship with his favorite restaurateur, La-Van Hawkins. It seemed that Hawkins, along with a local attorney and Democratic Party fundraiser, Ronald White, had a phone conversation during which Hawkins expressed alarm that Sharpton's campaign fundraising might get people close to them into trouble. Hawkins told White that Sharpton had reported to the FEC only around $50,000 of the more than $140,000 they'd raised during the previous quarter for the campaign. "He's a train wreck – a plane crash waiting to happen," Hawkins said of Sharpton. It wasn't just talk. FBI investigators secretly had videotaped Sharpton pocketing campaign donations from Hawkins and White in a New York City hotel room – and then asking for $25,000 more.[7]

Sharpton had a habit of not complying with the law during that campaign. He failed to report in-kind contributions from a spare-no-expenses Atlanta fundraising event hosted by Hawkins in early 2003. *Ebony* magazine reported that Sharpton received free transportation to the event in the Hawkins Food & Entertainment Group private jet, along with Hawkins' personal chef. The article noted: "Hawkins worked the crowd, at times talking business and world politics with guests, at other times, seeming to 'shake down' guests for donations."[8] All told, campaign expenditures for visits to at least 100 cities did not show up in FEC filings.

In 2005, Sharpton denies 'pocketing campaign donations' during 2004 campaign. (AP/Wide World)

The NLPC complaint also cited a "consulting fee" of $25,000 paid by a Hawkins-owned company directly to Sharpton. Records of this transaction and other income and honoraria "disappeared" in a fire. According to the complaint:[9]

> *While Al Sharpton has been described in many ways, 'business consultant' is not the term that typically is used. This payment by an individual who subsequently became a major donor and then some to Sharpton's campaign is all the more questionable*

given the statement by the Sharpton campaign that records for
some of his 'consulting' work were destroyed in a fire which also
destroyed other records about honoraria and income earned by
Sharpton.

This wasn't the first time that a mysterious "fire" had destroyed Sharpton's records following a promise on his part to make National Action Network records public. Sharpton alleged the same thing happened back in 1997.[10] The Federal Election Commission had a problem in the wake of the more recent assertion. In May 2004, about two months after he had dropped out of the race, the FEC ruled that his campaign had to return $100,000 in federal matching funds and forgo another $79,709 for which he purportedly had qualified. In January 2004, the FEC already had fined Sharpton $5,500 as a result of an NLPC complaint, filed on April 18, 2003, over his failure to file a statement of candidacy and financial disclosure reports on time.

A criminal investigation happened, though at deliberate speed. In the early morning hours of December 12, 2007, teams of federal agents handed as many as 10 Sharpton employees and associates subpoenas to appear in front of a Brooklyn grand jury reportedly investigating various financial improprieties occurring during 2001-07, including his presidential campaign. "It was like a sting or a raid," said Carl Redding, Sharpton's chief of staff for much of the Nineties. "They converged on everybody."[11] As for La-Van Hawkins, he was convicted in May 2005 of perjury and wire fraud connected to the Philadelphia influence-peddling scandal; as mentioned earlier, he received a 33-month prison sentence. His associate, Ronald White, also was indicted in that case, but died of cancer beforehand.[12]

The story did not end there. In 2009, Sharpton acknowledged using campaign funds from prohibited sources. His campaign committee paid a $208,000 fine to the Federal Election Commission as part of a conciliation agreement. But he may still owe private creditors.[13] The conciliation agreement read: "The committee incurred $509,188 in campaign-related expenses on Sharpton's American Express card, but had made payments...totaling only $121,996. Thus, $387,192 was paid to Sharpton's American Express account expenses from other sources, including $107,615 in 'impermissible' donations from National Action Network. Overall, his campaign owed $925,713 in total debt, including back pay to 16 staffers and services provided by UPS."[14]

If Sharpton has a blind spot for campaign finance law, his adherence to tax law may be even less scrupulous. The man just doesn't like paying taxes. Granted, none of us do. But in Sharpton's case, he simply doesn't pay. Long ago, he had legal problems in this area. Charged in 1989 with three counts of $35,000 worth of state tax fraud, he eventually pleaded guilty in 1993 to a misdemeanor charge of failing to file a tax return for the year 1986. In return for the plea, prosecutors agreed to drop two felony charges. Though Sharpton would have to pay the back tax bill and a $5,000 fine, he avoided jail time.[15]

Having lucked out, he became emboldened. In May 2008, the Associated Press reported that Sharpton and his business entities owed nearly $1.5 million in back taxes and associated penalties.[16] The IRS in 2007 had obtained a $931,397 lien against him for unpaid personal income taxes, while the City of New York sought $365,558 and the State of New York sought $175,962 from his for-profit company, Reverend Al Communications Inc., which eventually was dissolved in July 2009.[17] Sharpton characterized the actions as nothing more than attacks on him and his beliefs. "Whatever retaliation they do on me, we never stop...that is why they try to intimidate us," he said.[18] Yet in July 2008 he worked out a reported deal with federal prosecutors in Brooklyn that would cut his overall tax bill and keep him out of prison. According to the *New York Post*, Sharpton agreed to pay back $1 million, including $500,000 upfront from the $1.8 million or more in back federal taxes going back to 2002.[19] These numbers did not include the $884,669 that the New York State Department of Taxation and Finance says he owed.

These troubles steadily have followed Sharpton since. In late 2011, the *New York Post* reported that National Action Network, Bo-Spanky

Consulting Inc., Sharpton Media LLC and Rev-Al Communications, were a combined $5.3 million in the red.[20] Of the $1.6 million in NAN debt, about $883,000 was attributable to unpaid federal payroll taxes, interest and penalties. Another $200,000 or more consisted of loans owed to Bo-Spanky and Sharpton Media. Then-NAN Executive Director Tamika Mallory stated that the group's board of directors had voted to resolve its tax issues. In addition to institutional debt, Sharpton personally owed the IRS around $2.6 million and the State of New York roughly another $900,000. He insisted at the time that he had worked out an installment plan to pay off taxes in each case.

The numbers change from year to year, but the song remains the same. In July 2013, MSN Money reported that National Action Network owed $871,688 in unpaid IRS and state filings, including penalties and interest.[21] And its overall deficit was in excess of $1 million. NAN's recurring tax problems could wind up being the downfall of that organization. Daniel Borokoff, head of the nonprofit monitoring group CharityWatch, explained the situation at the time: "He (Sharpton) could really get into a lot of trouble. It's a red flag that the group may go under."[22]

Given even more recent evidence, it is Sharpton himself who might go under. In August 2014, the *New York Post* concluded that he and his organizations had owed a combined $4.7 million in outstanding taxes and liens by the end of 2012.[23] Of this figure, around $3.4 million represented personal income taxes – around $2.6 million to the federal government and $806,875 to the State of New York. The nonprofit National Action Network owed $813,576 in federal taxes, while Rev-Al Communications and Bo-Spanky owed a respective $447,826 and $18.21 to the State of New York. Sharpton responded to the numbers by claiming that he is in the process of paying down this debt, the size of which, he insisted, was exaggerated. "It's significantly less," he said. "It's nowhere near the millions of dollars. We have totally lived up to our agreement with them." His creditors, perhaps clearing their throats, have heard such assertions before.

If Al Sharpton has few qualms about stiffing taxpayers, at least he is consistent: He stiffs businesses as well. In August 2003, during Reverend Al's presidential campaign, a black-owned Manhattan travel agency, Alpha International Travel, filed suit against Sharpton and National Action Network.[24] Sharpton during May 1, 2001-August 3, 2002 – before the campaign began – allegedly used phony credit card information to rack up a $193,131.97 tab in "airline tickets and hotel services." The suit read: "When Sharpton provided this false and misleading information...[he] knew that the information was false and that [Alpha] would rely upon such false information." Sharpton and his lawyer, Sanford Rubenstein, hotly disputed the accusation and claimed Alpha had fraudulently attempted to bill Sharpton personally and that the credit card number in question wasn't in existence at the time. But Alpha President Colin Hall dismissed this charge as nonsense. "They have everything and they've had it for months," adding that he got the credit card number from Sharpton personally. The KBL audit of National Action Network finances in 2008 had indicated that Alpha had accused NAN of failing to pay an outstanding debt of $50,000, a case which the NAN reportedly settled.

Sharpton likes fine hotel accommodations. Unfortunately, he's less than keen on paying for them. In 2009, the Peabody Hotel in Memphis filed suit in Shelby County Circuit Court against NAN for failure to pay about $70,000 for various services, plus more than $17,000 in attorney's fees and miscellaneous costs, related to the nonprofit group's April 2008 convention at that historic venue.[25] Sharpton eventually settled the case for $106,981.[26] He also has a special disdain for paying rent. Around 2002, National Action Network was evicted from its Empire State Building office due to six months of nonpayment of rent.[27]

Old habits have continued to die hard. Around mid-2011 he signed a sublease agreement with the Reston, Va.-based Conference of Minority Transportation Officials (COMTO) to set up a NAN office at the conference's Washington, D.C. suite.[28] COMTO had just moved its Washington operations to a building across the street. And it had put out the word to the nonprofit world that it had vacant space for rent. Sharpton, a regular White House visitor, jumped at the offer. The arrangement didn't take long to go bad. In November 2012 COMTO President Julie Cunningham (now deceased) indicated, with the sublease shortly set to expire, that NAN was seven months behind on its payments. The amount in arrears, including late fees, was more than $28,000. COMTO over several months had written polite reminders to Sharpton about his increasingly overdue rent, each time to no avail. COMTO Chairman Robert Henry Prince Jr. summarized the situation: "We were pleased that another group of similar status was coming in. We didn't know they wouldn't be honoring their rental agreement." Eventually, on the verge of eviction, Sharpton's top aide and media consultant, Rachel Noerdlinger, came to the rescue. While denying allegations that National Action Network was behind on the rent, she wrote out a $16,950 check for back rent and another $10,550 as a security deposit to cover a new lease. Sharpton had a similar delinquent rent problem with the management of the building that houses NAN's Phoenix chapter. He had racked up $5,500 in back rent before finally paying it off.[29]

It would be hard for the Rev to plead poverty in all this. According to IRS Form 990, which nonprofit organizations are required to file, National Action Network in 2011 and 2012 took in more than $4 million a year. Presumably, that's enough to retain a competent Certified Public Accountant. The problem is not a lack of competence or funds. It's a lack of good will. Al Sharpton, by his actions, has conveyed a belief that paying bills is optional. He'll pay, but only when absolutely forced to. This attitude by now should have given his donors second thoughts about cutting him additional checks. But since the checks keep coming, his rise to respectability continues.

PART III

TRIUMPH

CHAPTER 22

A PRESIDENTIAL CAMPAIGN...
AND ANOTHER

"All truth passes through three stages," observed the 19th-century German philosopher Arthur Schopenhauer. "First, it is ridiculed. Second, it is violently opposed. Third, it is accepted as being self-evident." This dictum may be said to apply to perceptions as well as truths. During the Eighties and Nineties, the perception that Al Sharpton was presidential material would have provoked riotous laughter. During 2003 and the first couple months of 2004, when Sharpton really did run for U.S. president, it was merely opposed. And although he did not come even close to winning the Democratic Party nomination, much more importantly, he achieved Stage Three: a respectability that otherwise might never have happened.

Perhaps Sharpton thought he was going to win the nomination and election, but victory wasn't the main point. Winning public respect was. In that, his campaign was a tremendous moral and public relations success. And though indirectly, it cleared the way for Barack Obama's presidential victory in 2008, an event that has elevated Sharpton's reputation beyond all expectations – perhaps even his own.

The Rev first mulled over the idea of running for president following accusations, unsubstantiated, that the Republican Party systematically "disenfranchised" black voters in the 2000 election and thus stole the election for George W. Bush. In May 2001, Sharpton indicated that he would be available as a presidential candidate for the Democratic Party.[1] The Rev's stock as a moral conscience, at least among his admirers, had

217

risen early that month when he was arrested in Vieques, Puerto Rico, along with dozens of other protestors, for trespassing on U.S. government property; they had gathered to protest Navy practice bombings at the site. Sharpton received a 90-day jail sentence. During his incarceration at the Metropolitan Detention Center in Brooklyn, N.Y., he went on a hunger strike, triggering many visits from sympathetic visitors. Who knew that America had its own Gandhi hiding in plain sight?

The terrorist attacks on September 11 of that year proved to be another clarifying moment. Sharpton, of course, didn't celebrate the attacks. But like a growing number of people on the Left and the Right, he argued that had we addressed more pressing national priorities at home rather than stick our collective noses in the Muslim world, the blowback of 9/11 would not have happened. During the course of 2002, Sharpton came to believe his hour had arrived: He was meant to lead the nation. On January 5, 2003, he declared his candidacy for the Democratic Party nomination for president. Later that month, he filed papers with the Federal Election Commission establishing a presidential exploratory committee.

Nobody expected him to win. And, in fact, he didn't come close. He carried no state primaries or caucuses. In the balloting at the 2004 Democratic convention in Boston late that July, he won no delegates. But to focus on his defeat misses the much larger issue. Sharpton saw his campaign as laying the infrastructure for a seismic shift in public opinion, a shift that might produce a president – even better, a black president – who shared his views, in turn raising the possibility of him becoming a shadow cabinet member. This, needless to say, *did* happen.

Sharpton always has been a street politician. But he was an experienced politician in the official sense as well. He had run for U.S. senator in 1992 and 1994, and, more credibly, New York City mayor in 1997. In the latter case, he picked up a huge black vote in the Democratic primary, so large in fact that he came very close to forcing a runoff with the leading party vote-getter, Manhattan Borough

President Ruth Messinger.[2] And he now was positioned to be a party kingmaker for presidential candidates seeking the black vote in New York. In 2000, Bill Bradley and the eventual nominee, Al Gore, practically genuflected before him at his Harlem headquarters. They knew who "the man" was.

But Reverend Al himself running for president – wasn't that a fantasy, a case of overreach? Sharpton came to believe it wasn't. Jesse Jackson, after all, had run in 1984 and again in 1988, wowing convention delegates with his oratory each time. The party took Jackson seriously then. There was no reason why it couldn't take Sharpton seriously now. Personal one-upmanship, however, was not Sharpton's main motive for seeking the presidency. He really believed that he was the natural leader of a progressive victory coalition.

Sharpton made his intent clear in his book, *Al on America*, which functioned as a presidential campaign tract as well as an autobiography. Published in October 2002, the book revealed Sharpton as driven by idealism. He saw a country that had gotten off-track, in foreign as well as domestic policy, and believed he was the person best-suited to put things back on track. Though an outlier, he wrote like a standard-issue Democratic Party politician. In the Introduction, he appeared supremely confident:[3]

> *In this new millennium, in this new America, it's time for new leadership – leadership that focuses on building alliances and intelligence. We've spent too much time training and flexing our military muscle. That is obsolete in a terrorist world. There must be more alliances and intelligence and less tanks and bombs.*
> *It's time for a leader who understands that our greatest strength is our differences. And being united – not just presenting a united front – is our greatest weapon. The next leader for this country must be able to look at all America and see her for what she will become and then work tirelessly to see her become it.*
> *I am that leader.*

Sharpton, an unreconstructed advocate for income, wealth and power redistribution, had little but disdain for Democratic Party moderates, as he explained in Chapter One, "Mr. President":[4]

> *People, especially many black people, got duped by Clinton. There are some who even refer to him jokingly as the first black president. Why? Because he could blow a horn and get along with blacks? I don't think Clinton's policies matched his social image.*
>
> *Where Clinton and the DLC (Democratic Leadership Council) succeeded in moving the party right of center, they failed in delivering policies that moved people right of poverty. I am running to deliver policies that will give people not just hope of sharing America's wealth, but policies that will make the working class partners in that wealth. My movement is the next generation of the Rainbow Coalition. We are poised to take back the party from the people who took it from us.*
>
> *I am running to take out the DLC, which I call the Democratic Leisure Class, because that's who it serves – the leisure class and the wealthy. They are pro-deregulation of business. They are openly anti-affirmative-action and pro-death penalty. In many ways they are no different from the Republicans. I see them as elephants in donkey's clothes. You cannot fit a donkey's jacket on an elephant's behind, and that's what they have been trying to do.*

Sharpton left no doubt that he was a man of the hard Left – the "Democratic wing of the Democratic Party," as former Vermont Governor Howard Dean frequently quipped during his own presidential campaign. And he spoke the language of his people, the blacks, arguably the most crucial bloc within the party along with organized labor. The Rev may not have been a first-stringer, but he was a player all the same.

When he ran for President in 2004, Sharpton received the support
of 2% of Democratic primary voters. (AP/Wide World)

As his campaign achieved liftoff, Sharpton encountered skeptics
in the press. Yet he proved adroit at dissembling any suggestion that
he was a racial politician. Appearing on the CNN political talk show,
"Crossfire," he was asked by conservative panelist Robert Novak if he felt
that mainstream Democrats, fearful of him, might run a more benign
black candidate to siphon away support. Here is how the dialogue went:[5]

Novak: *Reverend Sharpton, now, I don't think it's any sur-
prise to you to know that the people who run your party, the
Democratic Party, are scared to death of you running and mess-
ing up their game. Do you think they have instigated another
African-American, former Senator Carol Moseley-Braun of
Illinois, to run against you as part of a conspiracy?*

Sharpton: *Well, I mean, first of all, we have filed the exploratory papers. We'll officially start in the spring. I think that the clear objective of my race is to give a voice to a lot of issues and people that I think are the majority of Americans. I think that there may be all kinds of schemes. They are totally immaterial to me. First of all, I'm not running an African-American campaign. We're running a broad-based campaign that includes African-Americans and Latinos and gays and lesbians and laborers and others. So if they have a conspiracy, as you call it, on the African-American side, it won't help them, because our campaign will be much broader than that. And I think that if that's the case, they're playing a divisive race card, not me.*

Thus, Sharpton managed to deflect a charge, while affirming the supposedly universal appeal of his campaign. It was fancy footwork.

As a campaigner, Sharpton was a mix of street preacher and would-be statesman. For the first few months, the campaign was haphazard and disorganized. He would rectify the situation somewhat in April 2003, when he brought aboard Frank Watkins, a longtime Jesse Jackson aide, as his campaign manager. A much more unexpected source of help came from Roger Stone, a longtime Republican Party consultant with a well-earned reputation for mastery of the darker aspects of campaigning. For whatever reason, Stone decided to give a boost to Sharpton. Not only did Stone give advice to Reverend Al, he also reportedly put together his application for federal matching funds, raised funds in battleground states, and arranged for loans to the National Action Network.[6]

Sharpton's base, such as it was, wasn't large. Still, he had hardcore support among blacks. And that translated into his winning about 2 percent of the more than 16 million votes cast in the primaries. Much of that support came *after* his formal March 15 withdrawal from the race. He did especially well in Michigan (7 percent), New York (8 percent), South Carolina (10 percent) and the District of Columbia (20 percent).

With or without Roger Stone, this wasn't Sharpton's nomination to win. The hour belonged to John Kerry. By mid-March 2004, not that long into the primary season, the junior senator from Massachusetts already had left his upstart main opponent, Howard Dean, in the dust. Sharpton read the tea leaves. After dropping out of the race, he threw his support behind Senator Kerry. In turn, Kerry rewarded Sharpton by giving him a prime-time speaking slot at the national party convention in Boston and an opportunity to make stump speeches.[7] He knew that Sharpton's show of support, though not crucial, was hardly negligible. And when the climactic moment of team unity came following the acceptance speeches, Reverend Al stood at the stage podium, facing the cheering convention crowd with other party bigwigs – presidential nominee John Kerry, vice-presidential running mate John Edwards, former presidents Bill Clinton and Jimmy Carter, former vice-president Al Gore, and Democratic National Committee Chairman Howard Dean. Nobody was going to snub Reverend Al.

Al Sharpton hasn't run for president again. Then again, he hasn't needed to. He had showed he could function in the Democratic Party mainstream while affecting a statesmanlike appearance. It was a mark of how far leftward the party had moved since the early Seventies that Sharpton's positions were barely distinguishable from those of the other candidates. Sharpton's image – and image is everything in politics – was becoming one of a sensible progressive, not a loud, embarrassing, overweight reprobate. The party faithful no longer had to cringe at the thought of sharing a podium or even a few drinks with him.

The most potent effect of Sharpton's 2004 campaign, however, was its boost in stature of the Democratic convention keynote speaker, Barack Obama. A Harvard Law graduate and a candidate for U.S. senator from Illinois, Obama, born in 1961, impressed party leaders and major media alike with his easygoing one-on-one conversational style, uplifting speech rhetoric, and (especially) biracial ancestry. Here was a man, said the oracles of official opinion, whose very existence symbolized our nation's potential to Come Together. Unlike the still-risky Al

Sharpton, Obama seemed not at all divisive. In fact, he was the ultimate "best black." Obama was…*perfect*!

Obama would go on in the general election that year to wallop the Republican Party's version of the "best black," Alan Keyes, a stridently didactic religious conservative who hastily had been recruited by GOP leaders to replace the original nominee, Jack Ryan, the target of Chicago media bent on getting the skinny on Ryan's divorce of five years earlier. The press mavens got their victory in court.[8] And Keyes, who never had even lived in Illinois, lost to Obama by 70 percent to 27 percent in November.

When Obama took over the U.S. Senate seat vacated by retiring Republican incumbent Peter Fitzgerald, he already had his eyes on bigger game. The years 2005-07 witnessed a growing media-assisted Obama mystique. Here was a young renaissance man, a virtual unknown prior to the summer of 2004, who now might become our first black president. A lot of people came to believe this – and more to the point, *wanted* to believe this. Sharpton was one of them. He saw the future as belonging to Senator Obama, especially given the deepening dive in President Bush's popularity. He and his National Action Network, with growing corporate support, now could do more than sponsor annual confabs to celebrate blackness and Diversity. They could help choose the next president.

Sharpton wasted no time in preparing for 2008. He invited Barack Obama, along with Hillary Clinton and John Edwards, to speak at the 2007 National Action Network annual convention in New York City. Each expressed admiration for their host. Senator Clinton was forthright in her adulation: "I have enjoyed a long and positive relationship with Reverend Al Sharpton and National Action Network, and I don't ever remember saying "no" to them and I intend to remain their partner in civil rights as I clean the dirt from under the carpet in the oval office when I am elected president.[9] Senator Obama had this to say: "Reverend Sharpton is a voice for the voiceless, and a voice for the dispossessed. What National Action Network has done is so important to change America, and it must be changed from the bottom up.[10] And Edwards, who had been a Democratic senator from North Carolina and the 2004 party vice-presidential nominee, remarked: "I will work with National Action Network to fight poverty and seek justice for those marginalized in our society."[11] Later, on the eve of the Iowa caucuses, Obama, Clinton and Edwards, and/or their high-ranking campaign managers, called Sharpton to ask for an endorsement.[12]

Sharpton endorsed Barack Obama early in the game. Sometime in late 2007, several weeks before the Iowa caucuses, he decided that Obama deserved his support over the presumptive front-runner, Senator Hillary Clinton, D-N.Y. Sharpton recalled in his most recent book, *The Rejected Stone*, how he and Obama shared a soul food dinner at Sharpton's favorite Harlem haunt, Sylvia's Restaurant, and then made haste to a nearby private cigar club, the Grand Havana Room. Here came a moment for which even Obama was not prepared:[13]

Sharpton: I met today with President Clinton.
Obama: Yeah, yeah, I know you have to work with policy on her (Hillary). All I ask is, if you can't support me, try not to hurt me.
Sharpton: Nah, I think I'm going to support you.
Obama: (pleasantly shocked) Huh? I never asked you to do that.
Sharpton: No, you didn't. In my own way, I'm going to go out there and support you. I don't even know if you can win. Probably, to-night, I don't think you can win. But it won't be because I was in the way. I won't do to you what a lot of folks did to me.

Thus, a political friendship was born. Whatever impact Sharpton's endorsement had on black voters, it had to be favorable for Obama. The latter's long primary victory streak was driven in some measure by Sharpton's thumbs-up. With the Wisconsin primary as the catalyst, Obama surged past Mrs. Clinton in the delegate count. By May, he had established an insurmountable lead.

Because the vast majority of blacks vote Democrat, in theory, Republicans should feel immune to pressure to "reach out" to the black vote. Surely, there was no chance of the GOP nominating some-one like Obama. Al Sharpton, who always has burned with resentment toward whites of either party who didn't march to his tune, called on black voters in 2007 to punish any GOP candidate not showing up at presidential debate forums hosted by the National Urban League and the NAACP. "We can only assume you weren't courting us," he remarked.[14]

Yet perhaps out of fear of the wrath from the "civil rights" establishment – GOP top guns *have* courted Sharpton. And Sharpton has reciprocated. Way back in 1986, Sen. Al D'Amato, R-N.Y., sought and got an endorsement from Sharpton. At the time, he was in a re-election battle with his Democratic challenger, Mark Green, a Naderite Left-populist. D'Amato wound up handily winning by 57 percent to 41 percent, but his endorsement from the Rev, though anything but a freebie,[15] couldn't have hurt his chances. Much later, there was the aforementioned assistance from Roger Stone during the Sharpton's run for the presidency during 2003-04.

That latter campaign established a pattern of "reaching across the aisle." On February 12, 2008, President George W. Bush welcomed Sharpton and other black leaders to the White House as part of the ad-ministration's Black History Month celebration. Alluding to the recent events in Jena, Louisiana, Bush cautioned his audience: "The noose is not a symbol of prairie justice, but of gross injustice. Displaying one is not a harmless prank. Lynching is not a word to be mentioned in jest." Bush made no mention of the beating administered by at least a half-dozen black high school students in Jena of an innocent white class-mate or the fact that the controversy over the nooses was completely con-trived. Sharpton expressed approval of the president's remarks.[16] He also was getting Strange New Respect among public figures supposedly further to the Right than the milquetoast Bush. In the years after the 2004 campaign, he wound up befriending Fox News Channel talk show hosts Bill O'Reilly and Sean Hannity, Republican National Chairman Michael Steele, and former Georgia Republican Congressman and House Speaker Newt Gingrich.

Former House Speaker Newt Gingrich looks on as Sharpton speaks to reporters outside the White House, in May 2009, following their meeting with President Obama to discuss education reform. (AP Photo/Charles Dharapak)

Sharpton's partnership with Gingrich has been especially visible. In 2009, the pair, along with Obama Education Secretary Arne Duncan, went on a nationwide tour to promote education reform. In one video segment, Gingrich told Sharpton: "I really appreciate the leadership Reverend Sharpton is showing all across America." And in October 2011, Gingrich, a presidential candidate since May of that year, wished Sharpton a happy birthday in language suggestive of a Hallmark greeting card: "I had such a great time going around America with you...I will never forget it for the rest of my life. You were tremendous on those trips...I watched you speak up with courage and toughness on behalf of children in a way that all my life I will remember, and I will honor you for the way you were willing to take on interests on behalf of children."[17]

Examining the 2004 and 2008 presidential campaigns, it would be hard to avoid concluding that Sharpton had come out a winner each time. He had gotten his message out to the nation. He had used the opportunity to hone his networking, coalition-building and media outreach skills, an image refurbishment largely attributable to his 2004 campaign press secretary, Rachel Noerdlinger,[18] who since had become senior vice president of communications at National Action Network, and much more recently, chief of staff to Chirlane McCray, wife of current New York City Mayor Bill de Blasio.[19] And he had ensured, by virtue of his early endorsement, at least a working relationship with the eventual future president, Barack Obama. Maybe the Sharpton brand name was too radioactive to compete for the White House, but he had helped a similar-minded candidate, and a black, get there.

Al Sharpton, though more refined, still exemplified the oft-used description of former British Prime Minister Margaret Thatcher, a "conviction politician," the problem in Sharpton's case being that his convictions were almost always wrong. Unfortunately, those convictions now defined virtually all of his party, and increasingly, the Republican Party as well. The Rev had nowhere to go but up. Who was going to stand in his way?

Sharpton was now past age 50, a psychological turning point in any man's life. More than ever, he polished his statesmanlike image, especially for those hopeful souls who longed for confirmation of his long-awaited "change." Not only was he a sharp-dressed man, but he also had slimmed down by about 150 pounds. With the election of Obama as president in 2008, the svelte Reverend Al was ready to hit the ground running. This was "morning in America" for real. And he was determined to soak up some of the sunshine. By behaving presidentially, Sharpton now could influence presidential decision-making. He was on top of his game. Mainstream media soon would take notice.

CHAPTER 23

NEW AND IMPROVED!

The rising Barack Obama tide lifted a lot of boats around him, and perhaps none more so than that of Al Sharpton. As long as Reverend Al behaved reasonably well, he could be a point man for the new administration – a de facto cabinet member – especially on race-related issues. Here, at last, was an administration willing to do things he had been advocating. He virtually had the keys to the White House, so frequent were his visits. This was not lost on news media.

An article in the popular webzine, *Politico,* dated August 21, 2014, revealed just how tight the Obama administration and Al Sharpton have been these past few years. The piece, written by Glenn Thrush, quoted an unnamed White House official. "There's a trust factor with The Rev from the Oval Office on down," the source said. "He *gets it,* and he's got credibility that nobody else has got. There's really no one else out there who does what he does."[1]

The ongoing crisis on Ferguson, Missouri, which began twelve days earlier, on August 9, 2014, has enabled Sharpton more than ever to serve as a conduit between the White House and "the streets." Thrush explained the situation this way:[2]

> *(T)he White House, as the crisis following (Michael) Brown's death seemed to flare out of control, worked extensively behind the scenes to maximize The Rev's doing what he does, using him as both a source of information and a go-between. After*

huddling with Brown's family and local community leaders, Sharpton connected directly with White House adviser and First Friend Valerie Jarrett, vacationing in her condo in the exclusive Oak Bluffs section of Martha's Vineyard, not far from where President Obama and his family were staying. Obama was "horrified" by the images he was seeing on TV, Jarrett told Sharpton, and proceeded to pepper him with questions as she collected information for the president: How bad was the violence? Was it being fueled by outside groups – and could Sharpton do anything to talk them down? What did the Brown family want the White House to do?

Whether or not *Politico* and its readers were too soft-headed to understand as much, the article was a stunning revelation. Here was a sitting U.S. president asking Al Sharpton, a man with a long history of mass incitement to riot, to defuse a riot. Even if the Rev's dispatches from the street were accurate – and inevitably, they were one-sided – it was highly significant that the White House would choose him, of all people, for the task. It says much about the character of this administration that it would lean on someone like Sharpton in a crisis.

Any lingering doubts about Al Sharpton's pull with the White House would be dispelled several weeks later on September 25 when Attorney General Eric Holder announced his resignation. At a press conference that day, Sharpton stated that he is "engaged in immediate conversations" with the Obama administration to name a successor.[3] Jesse Jackson, perhaps a bit enviously, verified this claim. "He's (Sharpton's) the man who's the liaison to the White House; he's the one who's talking to the Justice Department."[4]

The *Politico* article was one example of major media casting the Rev as a voice of moderation, humility and common sense. The *Wall Street Journal* already had weighed in sympathetically more than four years earlier. In its March 17, 2010 print edition, the Journal published an article by reporter Peter Wallsten titled, "Obama's New Partner: Al Sharpton."[5]

The piece argued that President Obama, stung by criticism from the Congressional Black Caucus and other sources of black political opinion that he wasn't "black" enough, wisely had turned to the Reverend Al for counsel. Wallsten assured the reader that Sharpton had cast off his flamboyant street provocateur ways, evolving into a constructive and pragmatic facilitator:

> *Mr. Sharpton has emerged as an important part of the White House response. On his national radio program, he is directly rebutting the president's critics, arguing that Mr. Obama is right to craft policies aimed at uplifting all Americans rather than specifically targeting blacks…Mr. Sharpton has been to the White House five times since Mr. Obama took office, most recently this month as part of a small group meeting with economics advisor Lawrence Summers.*

Sharpton, the author argued, was emblematic of an emerging post-racial generation of black leaders that has eclipsed the confrontational civil-rights style of the Sixties. The election of Obama as president marked the coming of age of this sensibility:

> *Well before Mr. Obama's victory, black leaders began to debate the limits of protest politics, a tradition steeped in the civil rights movement and aimed at highlighting the needs of African-Americans to white political leaders. A generation of fiery candidates, such as the Rev. Jesse Jackson in the 1980s and Mr. Sharpton later, was giving way to black politicians eager to build support beyond the African-American community and for whom the injustices that stoked the civil rights movement weren't as formative. The new generation included candidates such as Mr. Obama and Massachusetts Gov. Deval Patrick, who aimed for wide support and focused on broad remedies to social problems, rather than a race-based approach.*

Let us cut through the sanctimonious malarkey: What all this means is that shrewd black politicians, knowing blacks are a minority, realize that guile works better than confrontation in getting what they want, especially when one of their own is head of state and all too happy to give their leaders an audience.

It's interesting that the two exemplars of moderation here, Barack Obama and Deval Patrick, are two of the most-Left-leaning politicians in the country. That they seek to cultivate close relations with white progressives and even certain Republicans speaks of differences in style, not viewpoint, with their "fiery" predecessors. The views are virtually indistinguishable, and their partisanship is geared to advancing black interests. For good measure, the *Wall Street Journal* quoted Rev. Eugene Rivers, a Boston-based senior policy adviser to the Church of God in Christ, a major black Pentecostal denomination: "There's a philosophical power struggle going on in black America between the old-school protestors and the post-ideological pragmatists. Al Sharpton learned more quickly than many others that the ascension of Obama meant the end of protest politics. Al Sharpton has grown from the premier politician of protest to the ultimate political pragmatist."

It's hard to determine which is more insufferable, Rivers or the article quoting him. Let it be said: Al Sharpton has become a "pragmatist" *because it serves his interests.* Throughout the last decade, especially during his presidential run, he was adamant about articulating black grievances, while expanding the coalition of progressive true believers. No doubt in part due to aging, his tone is more measured. But his message remains the same. Sharpton, in fact, will be the first to state as much. He supports affirmative action, slavery reparations, and aggressive welfare state expansion as much as ever. And he remains explicitly unapologetic about his past protest campaigns. In its haste to celebrate the "new" Sharpton, the *Wall Street Journal* failed to see that the old one was always there.

Sharpton's stature would rise further with the publication of the August 2, 2010 cover story of *Newsweek* magazine, "The Reinvention of the Reverend Al."[6] In a fawning and highly misleading portrait, authors Allison Samuels and Jerry Adler elevated Sharpton to the status of moral conscience of America. Lead author Samuels, herself black, was no stranger to puffery in that magazine, having authored a post-election piece heralding the impending arrival of Michelle Obama as First Lady.[7] Interviewed by the authors, Reverend Al made clear he was the same man. "My mission, my message, and everything else about me is the same as always," he remarked. "The country may have changed, but I haven't."

Whether or not Samuels and Adler saw this as an accomplishment, their view of Reverend Sharpton was positively reverential. Consider the opening sentences:

> *If the Rev. Al Sharpton didn't exist, he would have had to be invented. In fact, the novelist Tom Wolfe has claimed he did invent him, in the character of Reverend Bacon, a supporting figure in The Bonfire of the Vanities. Each generation of black America gives birth to its own incarnation of the charismatic preacher-activist who confronts the white power structure in the streets and talks circles around it on Meet the Press. Just a few months after the fictional Bacon made his appearance in 1987, the real Sharpton burst onto the national stage as the fiery advocate for Tawana Brawley, a New York teenager who claimed to have been raped by a gang of white men, including a policeman.*

This is wishful thinking. If Al Sharpton, whose syntax all too often is jumbled, "talks circles" around the white power structure on "Meet the Press" or any other political TV talk show, it's hard to imagine anyone noticing. And Tawana Brawley, as this report has explained in great detail, didn't simply "claim" to have been gang-raped. She fabricated a massive hoax which Sharpton chose to believe against all sound evidence to the contrary, a fact acknowledged in a state grand jury report. Moreover, one hardly can imagine Tom Wolfe, an exceedingly sharp-eyed observer of the colliding social worlds of New York City, claiming that his composite literary creation, Reverend Reginald Bacon, "invented" Sharpton. If anything, it was the other way around. When *The Bonfire of the Vanities* appeared in bookstores in 1987, Sharpton *already* had become a national public figure, having led obnoxious demonstrations in the streets of New York in an effort to send "subway vigilante" Bernhard Goetz into prison and do likewise to those even tangentially involved in the death of Michael Griffith in Howard Beach, Queens. Sharpton, having absorbed first-hand the convictions and theatrical styles of his mentors, from Jesse Jackson to James Brown, invented his own persona and ran with it. He needed no help from Tom Wolfe.

The authors' snow job is even more blatant in their assessment of his various campaigns:

> *Sharpton has been right much more often than wrong in his choice of causes, dating back at least to the 1989 murder of Yusuf Hawkins, a black teenager who paid with his life for the mistake of walking down the wrong block in Brooklyn. Many African-Americans will be forever grateful to Sharpton for taking on the thankless task of defending the victims of Bernhard Goetz, who opened fire on four unarmed black teenagers in the subway. But he also has made some grave missteps. In 1991, during a tense confrontation between blacks and Orthodox Jews in Brooklyn, he notably failed to calm tensions with a remark about "the diamond merchants in Crown Heights." In 1995 his reference to "white interlopers," at a protest against the eviction of a popular Harlem music store, was followed by a fatal arson attack on the white-owned business that held the lease.*

Each of these statements is a misinterpretation, if not in letter, then certainly in spirit. It is worth encapsulating prior chapters to explain why.

The phrase "right much more often than wrong" is a huge stretch. The authors give just two cases – Yusuf Hawkins and Bernhard

Goetz – of his being "right." Neither example holds water. In the case of Hawkins, his fatal shooting at the hands of a young Bensonhurst resident that August evening in 1989 was indeed a crime. But the sequence of events leading up to it reveals that this was as much a case of mistaken identity as of wanton violence. Only a few people among the crowd of white male teens even remotely were involved in any way. And what caused the crowd to form in the first place was a highly troubled, temperamental local white female who for weeks had terrorized certain local residents and, more immediately, had threatened to sic a mob of black and Hispanic drug-dealing friends on them. The young whites had every reason to be nervous when they encountered Mr. Hawkins and his three black companions. They surmised that these must have been the people of whom the trashy neighborhood chick had spoken. It was a wrong guess, and it led to tragedy. But it was an understandable guess. In any event, the shooter's actions did *not* necessarily reflect the character of the Bensonhurst area or that of his friends. Oblivious to cause and effect, Sharpton and his servile rent-a-mob for many months after that made life miserable for the area.

The case for Sharpton as a hero in the arrest and prosecution of Bernhard Goetz is even more preposterous. By any reasonable definition, Goetz had acted in self-defense when he shot four young menacing black males in a New York City subway car on the afternoon of December 22, 1984. His four "victims" already by then had amassed a combined nine criminal convictions. Two of the "unarmed" youths were packing sharpened screwdriver shanks. Their intent, as one of the would-be attackers, Darrell Cabey, stated at Goetz's civil trial, had been to rob Goetz. To describe Bernhard Goetz, a mild-mannered white electronics repairman, as having "opened fire" on these criminals is true only in the narrowest sense. Any number of blacks, as explained earlier in this book, defended Goetz, including civil rights leader Roy Innis.

As for the two cases in which Sharpton was "wrong," the authors likewise provide disingenuous summaries. While admitting their hero had left something to be desired, they parse their language so as to minimize his culpability. The "tense confrontation" between blacks and Orthodox Jews in Brooklyn's Crown Heights in August 1991 was a case of predators fitfully encountering resistance from prey. Roving bands of blacks had gone on a rampage in the wake of the death of a local black boy accidentally struck and killed by a passing car occupied by Jews. What ensued was a full-fledged riot, not simply a confrontation. One of the rioters stabbed an unarmed Jew to death. To say that Sharpton "failed to calm tensions" gives him far too much credit. He helped to create and escalate those tensions. And his post-riot protest march through the neighborhood to the Orthodox Jews' headquarters was an act of provocation that could have led to another riot.

The authors, if it is possible, are on even shakier ground in referring to the fatal arson attack on Freddy's Fashion Mart in December 1995. They conveniently omit the fact that the attack, a combination of arson and gunfire, was committed by a black and that it claimed the lives of seven innocent people plus the murderer. They also omit the fact that Freddy's, which subleased (not leased, as the authors note) space to the black-owned record store, was white (and Jewish)-owned. *That's why it was targeted in the first place.* And Sharpton did more than simply denounce a "white interloper" on a radio broadcast months earlier. He sent out a lieutenant, Morris Powell, a man with a history of criminal arrests and mental instability, to organize menacing pickets in front of Freddy's to prevent the "racist" eviction of the record store.

In a disingenuous bow to modesty, the authors admitted Sharpton has his faults. But on balance, they concluded, his legacy is noble:

> *It is, of course, the fate of people like Sharpton to be misunderstood, and his own tendency to get carried away while addressing a crowd has contributed to it at times…He is out there alone, still standing on the same principle he first enunciated in his housing project in Brooklyn: poor people have the same rights as rich ones, to justice in the streets and in the courts. If he didn't exist, we might, in fact, need to invent him.*

The only thing missing at this point are the handkerchiefs.

The *Wall Street Journal, Newsweek* and *Politico* haven't been the only publications to indulge in this wish-fulfillment. In December 2011 the *Huffington Post* ran this laudatory post: "At 57, the Rev. Al Sharpton is a long way from the young, overweight firebrand and street activist, known for his perfectly coiffed 'do and his closetful of multicolored jogging suits – the provocateur whom some people wanted dead...Today he is a lean and dapper multimedia activist, who has carved out a public and political niche that few if any black activists have ever enjoyed."[8] The website Factmonster.com noted: "His (Sharpton's) reputation took a blow in 1987 when he was the spokesman for Tawana Brawley, an African-American teenager who accused a group of white men of rape – a charge a grand jury deemed a hoax. In later years Sharpton has refashioned himself as a more mature spokesman for the downtrodden."[9] And on April 6, 2011, only hours before President Obama took the stage that evening to speak at the annual National Action Network conference, *Washington Post* reporter Jonathan Capehart, a black, rhapsodized in a blog:[10]

> *If you've followed Sharpton's career the way I have you'll understand how extraordinary tonight will be. He was once seen as the rabble-rousing, portly preacher in jogging suits with a James Brown hairdo. Actually, some people still see him as the hub of the Tawana Brawley hoax that inflamed racial tensions far beyond Wappinger Falls (sic), N.Y. Today, Sharpton is a slimmed-down, savvy and pragmatic civil rights leader in business suits – and a James Brown hairdo.*

The Rev had come a long way. It now was hard to find anyone in print media outside of the conservative blogosphere who could bring themselves to criticize him – and even the conservative blogosphere, accustomed to facile preaching to the converted, failed to lay a glove on him. By 2011, it was more than just print media that thought well of Sharpton. Indeed, one major news outlet wanted him on their roster.

CHAPTER 24

ANCHORMAN

If print media has heralded the arrival of a refined, mature Al Sharpton, one major television network has gone further: It hired him. Starting on August 29, 2011, Sharpton has been a full-time anchorman delivering six o'clock news and commentary for MSNBC on an hour-long weeknight show, "PoliticsNation." Given the nature of the program, a left-of-center equivalent of Fox News' "The O'Reilly Factor" (on which, by the way, Sharpton was a frequent guest), he has been relatively restrained. His vocal delivery sounds more like that of an aging bluesman than a world-class verbal arsonist. Yet his presence as a network anchorman is significant all the same – and for two reasons.

First, at least in theory, there is a clear bright line between reporting the news and making the news. Journalistic ethics would appear to dictate that if Sharpton wants to rouse the masses into action, he should not be holding down a job that involves daily reporting on highly sensitive stories, especially those with a racial angle. Conversely, if he wants to provide TV news and commentary, he should refrain from hitting the streets. He shouldn't have it both ways. Al Sharpton delivering the news is as surreal as imagining Tom Brokaw, Dan Rather and Peter Jennings in the Nineties leading public demonstrations with bullhorns. There ought to be a division of labor. MSNBC thinks otherwise.

The blurring of the line between reporting and political advocacy, by the Right as well as the Left, is a disturbing media trend of the last couple decades. Yet with Sharpton, one strains to see *any* line, much less a blurred one. The Ferguson, Mo. police shooting and its aftermath offers any number of examples. On August 29, 2014, he conducted an interview with Reginald Greene, an attorney representing five Missouri residents who filed the $40 million lawsuit in federal court alleging "unnecessary and unwarranted force" by Ferguson police. Here is an online transcript of the opening portion of that conversation:[1]

Sharpton: Attorney Greene, what message do your clients want to send with this lawsuit?

Greene: First of all, thank you for having me on your show. I have been watching you for many years. And I applaud you for the things you do and continue to do on the front line for justice in America, particularly for African-Americans. So, I want to thank you for having me on your show.

Sharpton: Thank you.

Greene: You're welcome. With respect to the question, Reverend Al Sharpton, we are not necessarily trying to send a message per se. We have filed a lawsuit in federal court. Our role is to vindicate the rights of our clients whose rights we believe were violated.

Sharpton: Well said. And so, this is not a message. This about really trying to seek justice for the violations they felt that they experienced during the protest around Michael Brown's death.

Greene: Yes, sir. I am with Malik Shabazz, Black Lawyers for Justice, and Greg Latimer, who is the other attorney that works with us on this file. And Mr. Latimer has many, many years of experience with these cases. Malik Shabazz has been on the front line as a civil rights lawyer and lead for years. And I have 20 years of experience myself. Our goal is to put the experience and expertise to bear so we can do things like shed light on the situation, take action, and pursue justice. And what we are doing is, in fact, in a court of law, pursuing justice.

Many people are speaking about no justice, no peace. Many people are speaking about how the injustices and the atrocities that occurred. But we have decided to take it one step further and take action, identify victims and assist them in vindicating their rights.

Note that Sharpton does not acknowledge that these "injustices" and "atrocities" were committed against people who were involved in, or in close proximity to, a riot. In other words, these were people who may have looted and destroyed property. Note as well that Sharpton does not question the reasonableness of the $40 million figure, which would seem exorbitant even for a blatant ambulance chaser like Greene. And finally, note that he does not question the account of events in Ferguson by "civil rights" activists who assume the shooting of Michael Brown to be a product of ingrained police brutality and racism.

This, of course, is but a very brief segment of one show. But it is indicative of a larger pattern of Sharpton inviting guests onto his show whose views reinforce his own. Moreover, while on air, he doesn't challenge those views in any meaningful way. If this is MSNBC's idea of "fair and balanced," the term needs some redefinition.

The second and less visible problem with Sharpton sitting behind the anchor desk is how he landed the job in the first place. The process that led MSNBC to hire Sharpton, in fact, provides a fascinating window into the minds of his corporate benefactors – and not just at the network. It also says much about the degree to which media enterprises are at the mercy of federal regulators and Congress when they seek to expand operations.

MSNBC for the last few years has been a subsidiary of cable TV and Internet provider Comcast Corp. The Philadelphia-based Comcast, which in 2013 employed roughly 125,000 employees and generated $65 billion in revenues, back in January 2011 paid $13.75 billion in cash and stock to acquire a 51 percent-majority stake in NBC Universal following approval of the proposal by the Federal Communications Commission (FCC). NBC's previous majority owner, General Electric, retained a 49 percent interest following its acquisition of the 20 percent stake held by

French multimedia giant Vivendi. The merger, worth a grand total of $30 billion, had been proposed in December 2009.[2]

This complex transaction, as it turned out, had plenty to do with Al Sharpton. Comcast, one must realize, isn't shy about the fact that it gives preferential treatment to nonwhites in all phases of its operations. While virtually all major U.S. corporations now commit themselves to "diversity," Comcast goes that extra mile. In the official brochure for National Action Network's 2009 convention, the company welcomed attendees with the following message:

> We live and breathe innovation every day. By embracing diversity of thought, philosophy and experience, we have become the nation's leading provider of entertainment, information and communication products and services. By embracing diversity of communities, we have become an employer and a provider of choice. Our diversity is our strength.

> Comcast proudly supports the National Action Network.

This support was more than rhetoric. From 2009 to the summer of 2011, when Sharpton became an anchorman, Comcast had contributed a combined $140,000 to National Action Network.[3] The company has been a sponsor for any number of recent NAN extravaganzas. This may have been related to an ethically-challenged quid pro quo necessitated by the FCC and accompanying "civil rights" monitoring.

Reverend Sharpton long had established himself as an MSNBC presence as both a guest and host. And in 2011 he frequently served as a substitute host for Cenk Uygur's 6 P.M. (EST) news hour, a slot bracketed by 5 P.M. and 7 P.M. airings of Chris Matthews' "Hardball" show.[4] But in July of that year, Uygur, himself relatively new to the job, departed from the network on less than amicable terms. This opened the door for Al Sharpton. MSNBC President Phil Griffin, for one, saw potential. Griffin said of him before a meeting of the Television Critics

Association: "He (Sharpton) fits in with the MSNBC…sensibility."[5] At that meeting, Chris Matthews stated, "He's done really well at 5 and 7… If he (Sharpton) does really well, I think the job is his."[6]

As a matter of company policy, Comcast refrains from influencing MSNBC hiring decisions. In July 2011 MSNBC issued a statement: "There is no agreement with Mr. Sharpton to host a program; however, it is important to note that Comcast plays no role in either the independent editorial decision-making of MSNBC or the selection of its hosts."[7] But that hardly was the end of the story.

In 2010, Comcast reportedly approached Rev. Sharpton in an effort to pave the way for its takeover of NBC Universal, a transaction requiring FCC approval. Comcast, hoping for a thumbs-up, happened to be in the process of developing a racial/ethnic minority "diversity" plan. In lieu of such a plan, approval would be unlikely. Sharpton, among a number of black civil rights leaders consulted, eventually signed a Memorandum of Understanding (MOU), which amounted to an endorsement of the merger. The NAACP and the National Urban League also would sign an MOU. The tide turned when FCC Member Mignon Clyburn, daughter of black South Carolina Democratic Congressman James Clyburn, gave a green light. She had concluded that Sharpton's approval "will serve to keep the new entity honest in promoting diversity." Clyburn's statement in turn won over FCC Chairman Julius Genachowski, not to mention Jesse Jackson, various black organizations, and several top black members of Congress, including then-House Judiciary Committee Chairman John Conyers, D-Mich., and Rep. Maxine Waters, D-Calif. All initially were opposed to the deal because it wasn't sufficiently supportive of diversity. The FCC on January 18, 2011 voted 4-1 to approve the merger; Commissioner Michael Copps dissented on grounds that it failed to promote consumer choice.

Diversity is what Comcast and especially MSNBC might have been thinking about in an effort to revamp its 6 P.M. news slot. MSNBC had initiated a shakeup in January 2011, the month of the merger. Keith Olbermann, whose "Countdown with Keith Olbermann" show had run continuously since March 2003, left the network (or was fired, as many assert)[8] and took his show to Current TV. Ed Schultz, like Olbermann, combative in a hard-Left way, had his program, "The Ed Show" (which Sharpton had guest-hosted a number of times), moved from 6 P.M. to 10 P.M.; and Cenk Uygur, a Left-leaning lawyer with a wide appeal to younger viewers, took over Schultz' slot. But the new arrangement didn't last long. Ratings for Uygur were lower than expected. And rather than change his tone or format, the Istanbul-born Uygur left, choosing instead to focus his energy on his long-running Sirius Satellite Radio-video streaming talk show, "The Young Turks."

Al Sharpton now was poised to take over the 6 P.M. slot full time. A tipoff had occurred in April 2011 at the National Action Network banquet (at which President Obama spoke) in New York. Rev. Sharpton handed MSNBC President Phil Griffin a "Keepers of the Dream" award. Small surprise – Chris Matthews and other network top guns were seated at Griffin's table. On August 23, 2011 Griffin made the official announcement: Sharpton would be taking over the 6 P.M.-7 P.M. slot on a full-time basis on a new show called "PoliticsNation." Six days later, Reverend Al made his debut. The following month, Griffin defended his decision. "We are breaking the mold," he told the *New York Times*. "Anything he does on the streets, he can talk about on the air. We won't hide anything."[9] Audiences, for better or worse, responded favorably. Nielsen data showed that Sharpton's show attracted 767,000 viewers in November 2011, up from 655,000 viewers the previous month.[10]

Al Sharpton may be a news anchorman in a choice time slot, but underneath it all, he is the same person. What is different is the context in which he operates. Prodded by the federal government, especially in the Obama era, ethno-racial diversity has been enshrined as a cardinal virtue. Unlike the old days, Sharpton doesn't have to knock down doors to influence the higher reaches of American society. The doors have been opened for him. His ascent testifies to the power of mass media and its implied motto: "Image is everything." But money, too, is everything. Sharpton helped grease the wheels for a $30 billion corporate merger. That's clout. Other companies surely have taken notice. For the right price, Reverend Al can be their friend, too. He's on top of the world.

CHAPTER 25

LIFE AT THE TOP: THE LARGER MEANING OF AL SHARPTON

Al Sharpton is far more than a hustler on the make. He is that, of course. But so are lots of people across a wide range of races, ages and conditions. Hustlers come a dime a dozen and always will. Yet Sharpton stands far taller than the competition, gaining respectability that nobody, perhaps not even himself, had envisioned 10 or 15 years ago. His rise to become one of the most influential persons in this country reveals not just the sycophants willing to indulge him, but also a distorted political culture that made it possible.

From the Reverend Al's standpoint, his rise to the top is evidence of things gone right, an affirmation of our nation at least trying to live up to its best ideals. This view is entirely wrong, but in one way, if unintended, it hits on something: Sharpton is not "out for himself." He is an idealist. All of his campaigns, political or otherwise, have sprung from his idealism, a commitment to create a more just society. He may avoid paying his taxes or hotel bills, but his ulterior motive is to leave money over to fight "injustice." *His views, within the frame of reference of contemporary black civil rights activism, are quite conventional.* It is a frame of reference that assumes blacks are noble sufferers of white racism and its institutions. It is a frame of reference long on accusations and short on cause-and-effect reasoning, and in which lawbreaking, even of a lethal sort, can be rationalized as a cry for justice. Arguing with such activists is futile. And Sharpton, an aggressive version of this, has a politician's gift for deflecting criticism toward an overarching narrative.

Sharpton has an undeniable charisma that has carried him a long way. He knows how to win friends and influence people. There is no way he could have survived months, much less decades, in the national spotlight without a reasonable degree of charm, however superficial. Very few people have his ability to mix church, street and suite in a distinctly black voice. And very few people have his knack for hitting media hot buttons that shape public opinion. Call him a buffoon, an embezzler or a power broker, but he is a man certain of his mission. He defines himself as a champion for justice, and his audiences define him in the same way. The White House visits, media showboating, inflammatory speeches, tax evasion and other seeming acts of self-promotion and law-breaking are but means to an end.

In Sharpton's world, the religious and the racial operate in tandem. Many of his critics miss that connection, preferring to believe that he simply is "using Christianity" to get his way. While perhaps understandable, such a view is wrong. Black Protestantism, as a belief system and a style of discourse, defines him. "Everything I've tried to do," he notes, "has been a Christian walk, an effort to live the gospel, to live the sermons I preached when I was young, the feed the hungry, shelter the homeless, comfort the afflicted."[1] But he is selective in his loyalties. When it comes to the Christian walk, he walks with blacks. He makes it pretty clear, too:[2]

> *Those people, blacks, are my people. I set out to serve them when I started preaching at the age of four, and that is all that I've ever wanted to do. Those people, the lower class, the lower part of the middle-income class, trust me. I was their child prodigy; those working black folks, the maids and janitors, cooks and doormen, watched me grow up. They know me; I carry many of their aspirations. Those people chart my progress and treat me like a grandson. They're there every Saturday at my rallies, every Sunday at the churches. That's why they give me their money, which doesn't come easy, because they believe in me and the things I stand for.*

There is nothing innately wrong with standing up for one's own kind. All people have their loyalties. Families, communities and nations would be impossible without intra-group loyalty. The problem is that Sharpton is espousing more than simply black mutual aid. He is promoting disinformation and aggression in order to shift public opinion against innocent non-blacks, dressing up demagoguery and character assassination as "justice." Sharpton knows the psychology of his audience because he is a part of that audience – first among equals, as it were. That's why he should be treated far more seriously than some garden-variety crackpot. Without his followers, he could not have achieved prominence. And without Sharpton to lead them, his followers would less prone to violent outbursts. The speaker and the audience need each other to function.

This kind of symbiotic reinforcement long has been recognizable in a variety of contexts. For centuries, crowds, as opposed to individuals or small groups, have served as a natural feeding range for demagogues. Crowds enable a demagogue to substitute subconscious for conscious action, to generate panic over "enemies" onto which great grievances, real or imagined, can be projected. Though first published in 1895 in the backdrop of the Dreyfus Affair, French social philosopher Gustav Le Bon's classic tract, *The Crowd*, speaks to present-day America. Defining a crowd as "a servile flock that is incapable of ever doing without a master," he explains why its masters so often connect with their audiences:[3]

> *The leader has most often started as one of the led. He has himself been hypnotized by the idea, whose apostle he has since become...The leaders we speak of are more frequently men of action than thinkers. They are not gifted with keen foresight, nor could they be, as this quality generally conduces to doubt or inactivity. They are especially recruited from the ranks of those morbidly nervous, excitable, half-deranged persons who are bordering on madness. However absurd may be the idea they uphold or the goal they pursue, their convictions are so strong*

*that all reasoning is lost upon them. Contempt and persecution
do not affect them, or only serve to excite them the more. They
sacrifice their personal interest, their family – everything. The
very instinct of self-preservation is entirely obliterated in them,
and so much so that often the only recompense in martyrdom.
The intensity of their faith gives great power of suggestion to
their words.*

Could any words better describe Al Sharpton? Here is a man of
one undeniable lifelong skill: preaching to audiences. His application
of that skill, whether in a religious or secular context, has made him a
leader of the top rank. For in his world, there is no shortage of blacks
who cling to the official civil-rights narrative of "white oppressor, black
victim." For them, suspicion equals proof, and rumors suffice as facts.
It doesn't matter that Tawana Brawley's claim to being "assaulted" and
"raped" had no basis in fact. She is black and her accused oppressors
were white, *and for that reason alone,* she must be believed. An orator like
Al Sharpton tells his audiences exactly that – and in their voice. By plug-
ging into their fears, resentments and hopes, he transforms them into
a force of nature.[4] Sometimes these audiences respond by doing bad
things – such as assault, vandalism and murder.

Sharpton demands reparations, welfare state expansion, affirmative
action and special prosecutions of ordinary or nonexistent crimes – and
with no accountability if the would-be beneficiaries are black. Whites
must pay their "debt" to blacks before they can expect absolution for
their sins. His view on racial reparations – he's all for them – is telling.
He wrote in *Al on America*:[5]

*Let's start there with reparations. Let's start with the fact that
there is a debt owed. Then we negotiate how we can repair it.
What's fair? We can start with creating an even playing field.
But we can't even get there until we recognize that there is a problem. We cannot bring up the discussion of how we will repair*

250

this, or what brings us up to par, because America still will not recognize officially or even unofficially that the dead are owed… America must admit its sins in Africa and its sins against people of African descent. It's the first step toward healing.

The idea that America needs a national conversation on race as part of a "healing" process is thoroughly disingenuous. We have been having such a "conversation" for decades. And the script has been unchangingly one-sided. Blacks talk, accuse and threaten; whites listen, grovel and hand over money. It is verbal abuse and extortion by any other name. As for reparations, there is no "debt owed." Supporters of the idea see such payments as a necessary step toward closure. It is nothing of the sort. It is a classic example of a velvet glove covering an iron fist. And the payments, once disbursed, will never end. Affirmative action originally was intended to be "temporary," too.

Sharpton isn't the only advocate of such extortion. Black writer Ta-Nehisi Coates, in a cover story for the June 2014 *The Atlantic,* also laid out an elaborate case for reparations.[6] It was a piece of demagoguery, but in a tone credible enough for well-meaning, naïve whites to nod their heads in agreement. The argument for reparations, quite simply, must be challenged at every turn. This is one campaign that will never end. Black civil rights radicals, recognizing the persistence of inequality, will see to it that no amount of compensation from whites will be enough. Far from being a vehicle for healing, a reparations program, if taken far enough, could trigger an all-out race war.

Al Sharpton is not going to change. To the very end of his life, he will hold firm to his conviction that blacks are still second-class citizens and that he, a servant of God, is carrying out His will by publicly demanding that whites pay for their crimes. The crimes almost always are imagined, or if real, wildly exaggerated and taken out of context. Notwithstanding, his loyal audiences will hang onto his every word. Surely the years since 2009 have shown how popular he is. How else can one explain a sitting U.S. president, not once, but twice, speaking at National Action Network's premiere annual event? The idea that Sharpton is socially or politically isolated is nothing short of ridiculous.

The burden of change ultimately lies with the pillars of American society who support him. That means corporations, labor unions, philanthropies, churches, media outlets, employee pension funds, both major political parties, and the current presidential administration. They subsidize his coffers, give him moral credibility, and facilitate his drive for power, effectively enabling him to continue doing the things he has been doing for decades. His rise to the apex of American society would not have been possible without this support. And unless his enablers withdraw their support, Sharpton's influence may grow further, and with few checks upon that influence. Unfortunately, that isn't likely to happen anytime soon. Reverend Al is on the side that is winning. And in America, everyone loves a winner.

It wasn't always like this. For years, virtually all his revenues came from black supporters of modest means.[7] But that was before Sharpton made his move to ingratiate himself with America's top-tier institutions and individuals. As with Jesse Jackson, his bid for respectability has been successful. Company officials readily give Sharpton money because it is a relatively inexpensive way of buying their way out of bad publicity while proclaiming to be champions of Diversity – a real twofer. Moreover, a number of corporate leaders respect and even admire the man. H. Lee Scott, then-CEO of Walmart, speaking on July 24, 2007, at the annual conference of the National Council of La Raza, praised Sharpton, also present at the event, as a "dynamic leader," adding that he was "someone you can sit down with, talk with and build a relationship with." Scott said that he was "pleased to share the podium" with Sharpton.[8]

Mr. Scott must have been short on friends at the time. That Sharpton is "dynamic" or able to "build a relationship" may be true, but it is irrelevant. He should not be exempt from public scrutiny. Even some critics on the Left, such as Wayne Barrett and the late Jack Newfield, have recognized as much. Newfield, who knew practically every street, park and neighborhood in New York City, had cautioned at one point that Sharpton is "dangerous because he is so likable."[9] The "likable" part may be debatable. The "dangerous" part isn't.

Al Sharpton's image as a noble visionary inevitably runs up against his track record. His institutional supporters believe that he has "changed," or at the very least, that if they donate funds to his organizations, he will go away. But that's true only in the short run. Sooner or later, Sharpton will come back to demand more alms. And he'll use that money to launch more misleading campaigns for "justice." Self-delusion has come at a high price. The moral and financial support is bad for the benefactors and even worse for the country. A withdrawal of support will go a long way in stopping this demagoguery.

Those benefactors, however, must understand the character of the man and his mission. He is the essence of the civil rights radical driven by deep religious convictions. Changing the public mind will prove very difficult. Sharpton, even more than the typical black civil rights leader, is adept in the use of emotionally loaded language to convey moral outrage. He also knows how to divert attention away from the outcomes of words such as "justice," "inclusion" and "diversity," and attract attention toward the ostensibly good intentions. Economist and ethnic historian Thomas Sowell, himself black, understands why noble-sounding language, without a reality check, often leads to social disaster. He observed in his book of some 25 years ago, *Preferential Policies: An International Perspective*:[10]

> *We may or may not be able to agree on what the ideal, or even a viable, policy may be. What we can agree on is far more fundamental: We can agree to talk sense. That will mean abandoning a whole vocabulary of political rhetoric which pre-empts factual questions by arbitrarily calling statistical disparities "discrimination," "exclusion," "segregation," and the like. It will mean confronting issues instead of impugning motives. It will mean that goals have to be specified and those specifics defended,*

rather than speaking in terms of seeking some nebulously unctu-ous "change" or "social justice." Perhaps more than anything else, talking sense will mean that policies must be examined in terms of the incentives they create, and the results to which these incentives lead, rather than the hopes they embody. It will mean that evidence must take precedence over assertion and reiteration.

What Sowell called for, in other words, is a political culture *in which people like Al Sharpton no longer are able to exert influence.* If people, especially those now in power, recognized the importance of "talking sense," at whatever the cost to their bottom line or reputation, Sharpton and his supporters would become obsolete. Unfortunately, the personal cost for many is too high.

Al Sharpton is now 60. He may have altered his style, but he hasn't changed his positions over the last 30 years. And he isn't going to change over the next 30 years, assuming he lives that long. But his benefactors can change. If nothing else, they should know by now that supporting him, monetarily or otherwise, makes him stronger – and free societies weaker.

Notes

Chapter 1 – "The Rev"

1 Carl F. Horowitz, *Mainstreaming Demagoguery: Al Sharpton's Rise to Respectability*, Special Report, Falls Church, Va.;   National Legal and Policy Center, 2009.

2 Annie Karni with Erin Durkin, "Stars Shine at Rev. Al's 60th," *New York Daily News*, October 2, 2014.   The Four Seasons party was held on the evening of October 1.

3 Edith Honan, "NY Police Cleared in 50-Bullet Wedding Day Shooting," Reuters, April 25, 2008.

4 Peter Flaherty, "Colgate-Palmolive Denies Supporting Sharpton Group in Wake of Rush Limbaugh/NFL Controversy," National Legal and Policy Center, October 19, 2009.

5 Quoted in Dana Milbank, "Al Sharpton's Second Act: Power Player," *Washington Post*, April 13, 2012.

6 See Adam Lisberg, "$110K Grant Kept Rev. Al Sharpton Quiet about Mayor Bloomberg Changing Term Limits," *New York Daily News*, August 15, 2010; Carl F. Horowitz, "Sharpton's Finances in Disarray despite Bloomberg Support," Falls Church, Va.:   National Legal and Policy Center, September 10, 2010.   The foundation had made separate

contributions to NAN of $50,000 and $60,000 during October 2008. New York City Mayor Bloomberg made this possible. His spokesman, Stu Loeser, while not discussing specifics, confirmed to the *New York Daily News* that his boss had donated funds to the project that year. Financial records showed that revenues for the Educational Equality Project in 2008 consisted of two anonymous donations of $250,000. In other words, Michael Bloomberg gave at least $250,000, and very likely $500,000, to the project, a generosity arguably not unrelated to his desire to seek a third term in office.

7 For the full transcript of the speech, see Black Entertainment Television, "Transcript of the President's Speech at the National Action Network Gala," April 7, 2011.

8 Reverend Al Sharpton and Anthony Walton, *Go and Tell Pharaoh: The Autobiography of the Reverend Al Sharpton*, New York: Doubleday, 1996; Reverend Al Sharpton (with Karen Hunter) *Al on America*, New York: Dafina Books (Kensington Publishing Corp.), 2002; Reverend Al Sharpton (with Nick Chiles), *The Rejected Stone: Al Sharpton and the Path to American Leadership*, New York: Cash Money Content, 2013. For a wealth of information on Sharpton from a highly critical perspective, see Thomas Clough, "The Saga of Al Sharpton," *Weird Republic*, 2002, http://www.weirdrepublic.com/episode35.htm.

9 Chuck Bennett and Lois Weiss, "Rev. Al's Half-Price Deal on $1.8M Taxes," *New York Post*, March 28, 2009. This article came out over two years prior to his becoming an MSNBC news anchor-commentator. A source close to Sharpton in 2011 put his annual network salary at about $500,000. See Alan Feuer, "As an MSNBC Host, Sharpton Is a Hybrid Like No Other," *New York Times*, September 18, 2011.

10 See "Al Sharpton Net Worth," www.celebritynetworth.com.

CHAPTER 2 – AL SHARPTON AS CIVIL RIGHTS RADICAL

1 See, for example, Stephan Thernstrom and Abigail Thernstrom, *America in Black and White: One Nation, Indivisible*, New York: Simon & Schuster, 1997; Karlyn Bowman, "Racial Progress: Black and White Attitudes Towards Racial Discrimination," *The American Enterprise*, Vol. 12, No. 5, July/August 2001. Even as early as 1963, survey data had shown white attitudes toward blacks, especially on integration, had grown a good deal more favorable over the previous two decades. See Paul B. Sheatsley, "White Attitudes Toward the Negro," in *The Negro American*, Talcott Parsons and Kenneth B. Clark, eds., Boston: Beacon Press, 1966, pp. 303-24.

2 Ample evidence can be found in Caroline Wolf Harlow, Ph.D., *Hate Crime Reported by Victims and Police*, Washington, D.C.: U.S. Department of Justice, Bureau of Justice Statistics, Special Report NCJ 209911, November 2005. The study combined data from the FBI's Uniform Crime Reports and the Bureau of Justice Statistics' National Crime Victimization Survey (NCVS). The author estimated that an annual average of 210,000 "hate crimes" occurred during July 2000-December 2003 based on information provided by the victim. The annual rate of hate-related victimizations per 1,000 persons was 0.9 for whites and 0.7 for blacks; for violent acts, the respective figures were 0.8 and 0.5. Even more telling, in crimes in which the victim cited "hate" as a factor (typically committed with a verbal threat indicating disgust over race or other observable status), a black or group of blacks had been the offender in 38.8 percent of all cases, even though blacks were only around 12 to 13 percent of the U.S. population.

NCVS data during that time showed that black-on-white felonies are far more common than vice versa. In 2005, 17.2 percent of the estimated (and reported) 3,201,320 single-offender crimes of violence involving a white victim were perpetrated by blacks. By contrast, 10.4 percent of the 507,210 single-offender crimes involving a black victim were perpetrated by whites. In other words, whites committed roughly 53,000 crimes of violence against blacks, while blacks committed around 550,000 crimes of violence against whites – slightly more than ten times the white rate against blacks. See *Criminal Victimization in the United States, 2005*, Report NCJ 215244, Table 42, "Personal Crimes of Violence, 2005," Washington, D.C.: U.S. Department of Justice, Bureau of Justice Statistics, December 2006, http://www.ojp.usdoj.gov/bjs.

3 James Q. Wilson, "The Negro in Politics," in *The Negro American*, pp. 438-39.

4 Godfrey Hodgson, *America in Our Time: From World War II to Nixon, What Happened and Why*, New York: Vintage Books, paperback edition, 1978, p. 189.

5 See transcript of phone interview, "Rev. Al Sharpton: Jena Rally Marks 'Beginning of a 21st Century Rights Movement,'" Democracy NOW! (www.democracynow.org), September 21, 2007.

6 Reverend Al Sharpton with Karen Hunter, *Al on America*, New York: Dafina Books (Kensington Publishing Corp.), p. 266.

7 Even Sharpton's urging of blacks to avoid using "racism" as an all-purpose excuse for failure has an undercurrent of anti-white sentiment. He writes in *Al on America* (p. 265): "We have internalized the decadence that was imposed on us. We have taken that inferior moniker that was placed on us throughout slavery and Jim Crow, and we keep it around our neck as if it actually belongs to us. It's like a security blanket. A convenient excuse just in case things don't work out." In other words, Sharpton is saying that it's white racism that ultimately explains unjustified complaints by blacks about white racism.

8 Richard Lowry, "Sharpton's Victory," *National Review Online*, December 3, 2003.

9 *Al on America*, p. 186.

10 This speech can be found in a number of sources on the Web, including www.blackpast.org.

11 Quoted in Freddie Allen, "Latt March on Washington More Diverse," www.blackvoicenews.com, August 26, 2013.

12 *Ibid.*

13 *Ibid.*

14 The part of the poem most explicitly immersed in the "Rainbow" language reads: "So say the Asian, the Hispanic, the Jew/The African and Native American, the Sioux/The Catholic, the Muslim, the French, the Greek/The Irish, the Rabbi, the Priest, the Sheikh/The Gay, the Straight, the Preacher/The privileged, the homeless, the Teacher/They hear. They all hear/The Speaking of the Tree."

15 Martin Luther King Jr. "Letter from Birmingham Jail," 1963, reprinted in *The American Idea: The Best of the Atlantic Monthly*, Robert Vare, ed., New York: Doubleday, 2007, p. 172.

16 E. Franklin Frazier, *The Negro Church in America*, New York: Schocken Books, 1964; see revised 1974 edition, p. 36. Frazier also believed that the two-parent family was crucial to black assimilation into white America. That black families are now predominantly female-headed for at least several years during the child-rearing phase is a key reason, though not the only one, for the lack of assimilation. See Clovis Semmes, "The Sociological Tradition of E. Franklin Frazier: Implications for Black

Studies," *Journal of Negro Education*, Vol. 55, No. 4, Autumn 1986, pp. 484-94.

17 Adam Nagourney, "Say It Loud," review of *Al on America*, *New York Times*, December 1, 2002.

18 Quoted in American Legend Interviews, "Ed Koch On: Rudy Giuliani," http://www.americanlegends.com/Interviews/ed-koch.html. The interview was held in conjunction with the release of Koch's new book, *Giuliani: Nasty Man*, New York: Barricade Books, 2007.

CHAPTER 3 – EARLY YEARS, DEFINING INFLUENCES

1 Al Sharpton and Anthony Walton, *Go and Tell Pharoah: The Autobiography of the Reverend Al Sharpton*, 1996, New York: Doubleday, p. 17.

2 Quoted in Jay Nordlinger, "Power Dem," *National Review Online*, March 20, 2000, www.nationalreview.com.

3 Sharpton has been less than clear about historical dates on this issue. In his first autobiography, *Go and Tell Pharoah* (p. 27), he indicates his father left the family when he was nine and a half years old. Simple math says that if he was born in October 1954, this event occurred in or around the spring of 1964. Yet in Sharpton's latest autobiography, *The Rejected Stone: Al Sharpton and the Path to American Leadership*: New York: Cash Money Content, 2013, p. 16, he recalls this disruption as happening in 1963.

4 Kenny Sharpton thus at once was Al Sharpton, Jr.'s half-brother and nephew.

5 Sharpton, *The Rejected Stone*, p. 16.

6 Due to post-Census redistricting, Powell represented three districts in the U.S. House of Representatives during 1945-71. The seat Rangel holds is New York's 13th Congressional District.

7 Reverend Al Sharpton with Karen Hunter, *Al on America*, New York: Dafina Books (Kensington Publishing Corp.), 2002, pp. 183-84.

8 *Powell v. McCormack*, 395 U.S. 486 (1969). The defendant in this case was House Speaker John William McCormack. At issue was the authority of Congress to add qualifications for its membership on top of those indicated in the U.S. Constitution (i.e., age, length of citizenship and state residency). The court held by a 7-to-1 margin that Congress, in this context, was not justified in excluding Powell.

9 *Al on America*, p. 187.

10 Quoted in Nordlinger, "Power Dem."

11 Operation Breadbasket actually originated in the early Sixties with a Philadelphia black Baptist minister, Reverend Leon Sullivan. King soon adopted this program for the Southern Christian Leadership Conference and expanded it nationwide. Rather than distance themselves from Sullivan, corporations courted him; General Motors even placed him on its board of directors. The "Sullivan principles," a voluntary code of conduct for investment in apartheid-era South Africa, also were a legacy of Leon Sullivan, who died in 2001.

12 *Al on America*, pp. 179-81.

13 Black critics of Sharpton who think like this include Shelby Steele, *The Content of Our Character: A New Vision of Race in America*, New York: HarperCollins, 1990; Juan Williams, *Enough: The Phony Leaders, Dead-End Movements, and Culture of Failure That Are Undermining Black America – and*

What We Can Do About It, New York: Three Rivers Press (Crown), 2007; Michael Meyers and Juan Williams, "How Al Sharpton Struck Out," *New York Daily News*, July 14, 2007.

14 Clarence B. Jones, "King and the Jews," *Wall Street Journal*, April 30, 2008.

15 Lowry, "Sharpton's Victory," *National Review Online*, December 3, 2003. Sharpton's visit to the Four Seasons Hotel in Los Angeles managed to soak up five percent of the cash donations NAN raised during the third quarter of 2003.

16 Martin Luther King III heads the Atlanta-based civil-rights organization that his father headed, the Southern Christian Leadership Conference.

17 Martin Luther King Jr., "Letter from Birmingham Jail," 1963, reprinted in *The American Idea: The Best of The Atlantic Monthly*, Robert Vare, ed., New York: Doubleday, 2007, p. 174. It is worth noting that these words bear a strong resemblance to those of the late Chicago-based community organizer, Saul Alinsky. Virtually all conservatives today revile Alinsky, a man whom they regard as the First Cause of Barack Obama. Yet apparently they have little or no problem with revering King, who pursued a very similar course of direct action.

18 For numerous examples of this delusion, see John Blake, "Why Conservatives Call MLK Their Hero," *www.cnn.com*, January 19, 2013. Though arguing from the Left, Blake effectively demolishes the idea that King somehow was a Republican conservative.

19 Many laudatory books on King have appeared over the decades attesting to his fusion of Christianity and progressivism. Taylor Branch's magisterial three-volume series stands out. See Taylor Branch, *Parting the*

Waters: America in the King Years, 1954-63, New York: Simon & Schuster, 1988; *Pillar of Fire: America in the King Years, 1963-65,* New York: Simon & Schuster, 1998; and *At Canaan's Edge: America in the King Years,* 1965-68, New York: Simon & Schuster, 2006.

20 King wrote in his 1964 book, *Why We Can't Wait,* Penguin Group, New American Library, Signet Classics, 2000, p. 165: "Among the many vital jobs to be done, the nation must not only radically read-just its attitude toward the Negro in the compelling present, but must incorporate in its planning some compensatory consideration for the handicaps he has inherited from the past...Wherever the issue of com-pensatory treatment for the Negro is raised, some of our friends recoil in horror. The Negro should be granted equality, they agree, but he should ask nothing more. On the surface, this appears reasonable, but it is not realistic. For it is obvious that if a man is entered at the starting line in a race three hundred years after another man, the first would have to perform some impossible feat in order to catch up with his fellow runner." This passage is the essence of advocacy of both af-firmative action and reparations – the principle that however much blacks achieve as individuals, so long as those achievements *collectively* do not match those of whites, true justice would still elude our nation. Operation Breadbasket, in this context, can be seen as a dry run for federally-enforced affirmative action. SCLC staffers, in fact, had gath-ered data on hiring patterns of various corporations doing business in black communities across the country. As an aside, it was none other than Jesse Jackson who wrote the Afterward to the 2000 edition of *Why We Can't Wait.*

21 Sharpton began as a Pentecostal, but eventually became a Baptist.

22 *Al on America,* p. 191. Sharpton states here that he and Jackson first met when he was 12. Yet in *Go and Tell Pharoah* (pp. 47-48), he described their first meeting as occurring in 1969. Sharpton would have been at

least 14 and possibly 15. As the account in *Go and Tell Pharoah* was more detailed, it is more likely the accurate one.

23 *Ibid.*, p. 192.

24 Howard Kurtz, "State Calls Sharpton Group a Façade," *Washington Post*, March 30, 1990. Genecin's comment was part of an opening statement for the prosecution in a New York State trial court that Sharpton had used National Youth Movement as a front to embezzle more than $250,000 (he would be declared not guilty). This and other examples of Sharpton's shady financial dealings will be discussed later in this report.

25 *Ibid.*, p. 197.

26 *Go and Tell Pharoah*, p. 48.

27 See Thomas Clough, "The Saga of Al Sharpton," *Weird Republic*, 2002, http://www.weirdrepublic.com/episode35.htm.

28 See Ernest R. House, *Jesse Jackson & the Politics of Charisma: The Rise and Fall of the PUSH/Excel Program*, Boulder, Colo.: Westview Press, 1988.

29 Kenneth R. Timmerman, *Shakedown: Exposing the Real Jesse Jackson*, Washington, D.C.: Regnery Publishing, 2002, p. 29.

30 See *Shakedown*, which on page 428 provides a chart showing the formal structure of the El Rukn organization.

31 Operation PUSH originated in late 1971 when Jackson had a falling out with Ralph Abernathy, Martin Luther King's successor at the SCLC helm. Its founding goals were similar to those of Operation Breadbasket.

32 *Shakedown*, p. 30.

33 Ray Gibson, "Noah Robinson Seized in Employee's Slaying," *Chicago Tribune*, September 21, 1988. The other defendants – Charles Green, Jeff Boyd, Sammy Knox and Melvin Mays – were convicted of various acts of murder and intimidation for the purpose of helping the El Rukn gang control drug trafficking on Chicago's South Side during the 1970s and 80s. As for the murder of Barber, gunned down by two men at a commercial development owned by Robinson, the arrest warrant for Robinson alleged that the defendant "caused or directed other individuals to act as agents or employees" to commit the murder.

34 Matt O'Connor, "Noah Robinson Is Found Guilty Again in Retrial," *Chicago Tribune*, September 27, 1996. Actually, there were three murders or attempted murders in all, those of Leroy Barber, a former business partner, and the female witness. Only Barber had died.

35 *Ibid.*, p. 288.

36 *Ibid.*, p. 209.

37 See Edwin S. Rubenstein, ed., *The Right Data: The Conservative Guidebook to Busting Liberal Economic Myths*, New York: National Review Press, 1994.

38 Released nationwide on August 1, 2014, the movie was co-produced by none other than Mick Jagger.

39 Reverend Al Sharpton with Nick Chiles, *The Rejected Stone: Al Sharpton and the Path to American Leadership*, New York: Cash Money Content, 2013, p. 76.

40 After high school, Sharpton attended Brooklyn College, but dropped out after two years. Touring with James Brown had taken up too much of his time to remain in school.

41 *Al on America*, pp. 204-05.

42 Quoted in Cynthia Rose, *Living in America: The Soul Saga of James Brown*, London: Serpent's Tail, 1991.

43 *Al on America*, p. 206.

44 Accounts may differ as to what triggered Brown's rampage or how police reacted, but this much is accepted across the board: The singer, high on PCP ("angel dust"), burst into an insurance seminar held next to his office in Augusta, Ga. Toting a gun, he expressed outrage that one or more attendees apparently had used his private bathroom. Soon after, someone called the police. Upon the cops' arrival, Brown fled in a truck, leading law enforcement officers in hot pursuit onto I-20 in a chase extending into South Carolina, where police managed to shoot out more than one tire. Brown then circled back toward Augusta, eventually driving his vehicle into a ditch. Police quickly arrested him and administered a sobriety test. They stated Brown was incoherent and attempted to sing and dance during the test. The singer countered that police had used excessive force, pointing to nearly two dozen bullet holes in his truck. Less known is that Brown, out on bail, the very next day was pulled over and arrested for driving under the influence of PCP. A somewhat altered version of this incident, though fully accurate in spirit, served as the back story in *Get on Up*.

45 The reason for the long elapse may have been Hollander's deteriorating condition. She claimed that stress from the assault had caused her to contract Grave's Disease, a thyroid disorder.

46 Her official cause of death was a PCP overdose while on prescription medicine – and in the aftermath of facial cosmetic surgery.

47 Brown stated that he thought Eubanks was an intruder. But based on the evidence, Brown's perception was not only erroneous, but also demented. Eubanks rang the doorbell upon arrival, whereupon Brown greeted him and told him to wait. When Brown returned, he had a suit on a hanger and told the electrician that he (Brown) was a government agent and could incarcerate him for trespassing. At that point, Eubanks stated, Brown brandished a steak knife and moved toward him. Making this tantrum all the more inexplicable was the fact that South Carolina Electric & Gas had received no reports from anyone else in the area at that time concerning power outages. A company spokesman could not determine who had called from Brown's estate. See "Really Randoms," *Rolling Stone Online*, July 18, 2000, www.rollingstone.com; www.zoominfo.com/people/Eubanks_Russell_14158650.aspx.

48 See "The James Brown/Joe Tex Feud," www.lipstickalley.com, October 1, 2013. Accounts vary as to what happened, but the following is pretty much accepted as fact: An angered Brown walked into the nightclub with a shotgun, looking for Joe Tex. He found him. But another patron also was armed – and ready for a showdown. Brown and the other person exchanged gunfire, and then kept reloading and shooting. Though neither was hit, several members of the audience were. Tex, rightly fearing for his life, had run outside the club and hid behind the trees and bushes. Having made his statement, Brown ran outside, took control of his tour bus, and drove off. Not long after, someone in Brown's entourage gave each of the injured patrons $100 to keep quiet. As a historical aside, the band on stage featured a little-known Otis Redding.

49 Quoted in Spectropop Remembers, "James Brown (1933-2006): The Godfather of Soul," http:/www.spectropop.com/remembers/JamesBrown.htm.

50 Some accounts assert that Sharpton's apprenticeship lasted a decade (see Errol Louis, "Al Sharpton Is No Rat," *CNN.com*, April 9, 2014). Others, such as Sharpton's Wikipedia entry, say that it ended in 1980, the year he married Kathy Jordan. The reason for the divergence is that Sharpton wasn't always James Brown's tour manager in the formal sense. He was more a business partner and surrogate son rolled into one. This was true even when Brown wasn't on tour. It's understandable why Sharpton spent much less time with Brown after 1980, but the pair remained professionally close.

CHAPTER 4 – MUSIC, MICROPHONES AND THE MOB

1 William Bastone with Andrew Goldberg and Joseph Jesselli, "Al Sharpton's Secret Work as FBI Informant," *www.thesmokinggun.com*, April 7, 2014. Much of the discussion in this chapter is taken from that report and my own summation of it. See Carl Horowitz, "Al Sharpton Revealed as FBI Mob Sting Informant," National Legal and Policy Center, April 8, 2014.

2 "Donnie Brasco" was the alias of Joseph Pistone, an FBI agent who during 1976-81 worked deep undercover to infiltrate the Bonanno and Colombo crime families for the purpose of breaking up a massive East Coast theft ring. The evidence gathered by Pistone led to over 200 indictments and 100 convictions of Mafia members. Pistone later retold his experiences in *Donnie Brasco: My Undercover Life in the Mafia* (New York: New American Library, 1988). The book would serve as the source material for the acclaimed 1997 movie, "Donnie Brasco," starring Johnny Depp and Al Pacino.

3 Fredric Dannen, *Hit Men: Power Brokers and Fast Money Inside the Music Business*, New York: Random House, 1990; see also the Vintage paperback edition released in 1991.

4 Don King, born in 1931, was the king of the Cleveland numbers racket, recording lottery-style bets from neighborhood people. Enforcing his territorial and financial claims on two occasions led him to kill. On December 2, 1954, King shot and killed a man, Hillary Brown, after Brown and two associates tried to rob one of King's gambling houses. He would have gone to prison, but the presiding judge in that case had ruled that King acted in self-defense even though he had shot Brown in the back. King proceeded to expand his numbers empire. Unfortunately, he couldn't shrink his temper. On April 20, 1966, King brutally beat and stomped to death a former employee, Sam Garrett, over a $600 debt. In a disputed trial, King was convicted for second-degree murder, but following an *ex parte* meeting with King and his lawyer, the judge reduced the conviction to manslaughter. He spent less than four years in the slammer, eventually receiving a pardon from Ohio Republican Governor James Rhodes in 1983. In the early Seventies, within a year of his release, King put together his first fight. The rest was history. His killing days were behind him, but his hustling days were not. King ripped off any number of boxers, including Muhammad Ali, out of their promised share of the gate and then intimidated them into waiving their right to sue. Almost all sued him for fraud, but King settled out of court each time, thus avoiding another stretch in prison. Mike Tyson, for one, sued King for $100 million, but settled for $14 million. Al Sharpton long has had ethical clouds hanging over him, but his close relationship with King ranks among the most egregious. For a good description of King's life and times up to the present, see Jay Caspian King, "The End of Don King," *Grantland*, April 4, 2013. See also Jack Newfield, *The Life and Crimes of Don King: The Shame of Boxing in America*, New York: William Morrow, 1995.

5 Tommy James with Martin Fitzpatrick, *Me, the Mob, and the Music: One Helluva Ride with Tommy James & the Shondells*, New York: Scribner, 2011.

6 Frank Rosario, "Sharpton was 'Eager to Get Slice of 1980s Coke Deal': Pal," *New York Post*, April 12, 2014.

CHAPTER 5 – SUBWAY VIGILANTE

1 The primary sources for this section are Mark Lesly, *Subway Gunman: A Juror's Account of the Bernhard Goetz Trial*, Latham, N.Y.: British American Publishing, 1988; William Tucker, *Vigilante: The Backlash against Crime in America*, New York: Stein and Day, 1985, pp. 19-35; Jason Manning, "The Subway Vigilante," in *The Eighties Club: The Politics and Pop Culture of the 1980s*, 2000, http://eightiesclub.tripod.com/id311.htm; and Doug Linder, "The Trial of Bernhard Goetz, http://law2.umkc.edu/faculty/projects.

2 It turned out to be a good guess, too. Police already had tried to contact Goetz at his Greenwich Village apartment.

3 Lars-Erik Nelson, "Goetz in Light of Jefferson and Lincoln," *New York Daily News*, January 16, 1985.

4 Mike Royko, "They Deserved It, Sure as Shooting," reprinted in *New York Daily News*, January 16, 1985.

5 Quoted in Tucker, *Vigilante*, p. 23.

6 Quoted in *ibid.*, pp. 23-24.

7 Quoted in "Self-Defense Bill Needed More than Ever," *The Gun Owners*, June 1996, www.gunowners.org/news/nws9606.htm.

8 Quoted in Thomas Clough, "The Saga of Al Sharpton," *Weird Republic*, 2002, http://www.weirdrepublic.com/episode35.htm.

9 In 2004, Goetz stated in an interview on CNN's "Larry King Live" that he hadn't paid any of the money.

10 Reverend Al Sharpton with Karen Hunter, *Al on America*, New York: Dafina Books (Kensington Publishing Corp), 2002, p. 268.

CHAPTER 6 – A DEATH IN HOWARD BEACH

1 Indeed, his musician son, Arlo Guthrie, frequently has copyrighted his own songs as "Howard Beach Music, Inc."

2 For Sharpton's account, see Reverend Al Sharpton with Karen Hunter, *Al on America*, New York: Dafina Books (Kensington Publishing Corp.), 2002, pp. 92-95. Derrick Geter should not be confused with just-retired New York Yankees baseball star Derek Jeter.

3 Thomas Clough, "The Saga of Al Sharpton," *Weird Republic*, 2002, http://www.weirdrepublic.com/episode35.htm.

4 *Al on America*, p. 93. Sharpton is faulty with his facts. The infamous murder of a black adolescent boy, Emmett Till, in a small Mississippi town occurred in 1955, not 1950.

5 Ward, appointed by Mayor Koch in December 1983, took the office the following January.

6 Ronald Smothers, "Hynes Is Selected to Be Prosecutor in Queens Attack," *New York Times*, January 14, 1987.

7 The eventually selected jury panel, including four alternates, consisted of the following: two American blacks, seven whites, two Asian-Americans, three Latinos, a Caribbean-American and a native of Guyana of Indian descent. See John J. Goldman, "Trial Starts in Howard Beach Race Clash," *Los Angeles Times*, October 8, 1987.

8 See Lorrin Anderson, "Race, Lies, and Video Tape – TV Docudrama 'Howard Beach': Making the Case for Murder," *National Review*, January 22, 1990; Jared Taylor, *Paved with Good Intentions: The Failure of Race Relations in Contemporary America*, New York: Carroll & Graf, 1992, pp. 85-86.

9 The made-for-TV movie airbrushed incendiary material out of the script. For one thing, it did not depict Al Sharpton at all. For another, it depicted the Alton Maddox and C. Vernon Mason legal team as a composite character, "Jason Barry," who appeared in only one scene. While Daniel Travanti ("Hill Street Blues") adequately played Special Prosecutor Charles Hynes, the presentation wound up only hinting at the extraordinary tension created by black activists.

10 For a brief summary of instances of legal misconduct on the part of Maddox and Mason, see Nicolaus Mills, "Howard Beach – Anatomy of a Lynching," in Jim Sleeper, ed., *In Search of New York*, New Brunswick, N.J.: Transaction Books, 1987, pp. 73-79.

11 Quotes here can be found in Mills, *ibid*.

12 Sam Roberts, "A Racial Attack That, Years Later, Is Still Being Felt," *New York Times*, December 18, 2011.

13 See Constance L. Hays, "Key Figure in Race Case Is Arrested," *New York Times*, July 5, 1988; Joseph Fried, "Prison for Howard Beach Victim," *New York Times*, April 7, 1989.

CHAPTER 7 – THE GIRL WHO CRIED "WOLF"

1 Dwight Garner, "Al Sharpton's Second Act," The Salon Interview, 1999, http://www.salon.com/weekly/sharpton1.html.

2 Reverend Al Sharpton with Karen Hunter, *Al on America*, New York: Dafina Books (Kensington Publishing Corp.), 2002, pp. 229-30.

3 The context of the interview was Sharpton's apparent double standard in condemning anti-black comments made by radio talk-show host Don

Imus while refusing to apologize for his own role in the Tawana Brawley affair. David Gregory, a substitute host for Chris Matthews, was persistent in the exchange. Sharpton insisted Imus' "crime" was far worse than anything Brawley had done. Imus, he argued, castigated "an entire race," whereas Brawley merely made a statement "about an individual." But this was patently absurd. Imus hadn't leveled *any* accusation, much less a false one, at blacks as a whole in his remark about the Rutgers University women's basketball team. The worst that could be said of him (see later discussion) is that he was gratuitously crude in expressing an opinion about black females, an opinion commonly held by black males themselves. Miss Brawley, on the other hand, *did* make a fraudulent accusation, and against more than one individual. More crucially, her deception, under less favorable circumstances, could have inflicted lengthy prison sentences and ruined the lives of quite a few innocent persons. As it was, Brawley and her allies cost New York taxpayers at least $1 million and falsely inflamed anti-white passions among blacks.

4 *Report of the Grand Jury Concerning the Tawana Brawley Investigation*, available on the Web at http://www.courttv.com/archive/legaldocs/news-makers/tawana/part4.html.

5 Robert D. McFadden, Ralph Blumenthal, M.A. Farber, E.R. Shipp, Charles Strum and Craig Wolff, *Outrage: The Story Behind the Tawana Brawley Hoax*, New York: Bantam Books, 1990.

6 The Town of Wappingers and the Village of Wappingers Falls are two distinct entities, though occasionally confused with one another.

7 While King was convicted of manslaughter, by any reasonable account his crime was murder. See McFadden, *Outrage*, pp. 93-95. During the previous year, in April 1969, King had stabbed his estranged wife, Wanda King, with a stiletto knife 14 times after breaking into her Poughkeepsie apartment. His wife somehow survived that attack. In July 1970, Ralph

King killed her with four .38 caliber bullets to the head. Needless to say, King was abusive to Tawana Brawley's mother, Glenda King, *and* to Tawana Brawley. The mother was viciously abusive to her daughter as well. (See *Outrage*, pp. 96-97).

8 For the Sharpton and Maddox quotes, see Jay Nordlinger, "Power Dem," *National Review Online*, March 20, 2000.

9 Various persons testifying before the grand jury indicated that Crist was despondent over matters unrelated to the Tawana Brawley case. Still, that fact alone should not exonerate her. All of us inevitably at some point experience frustration in love and in work. It is too much of a coincidence that Crist happened to commit suicide practically as soon as he was identified as an "assailant." Sharpton and his supporters insisted either that his self-inflicted death was a de facto admission of guilt or that he really had been murdered before he could testify. But since the case was a hoax from the start, it is reasonable to suggest that while Crist might have committed suicide anyway in lieu of Brawley's accusations, fear of bad publicity pushed him over the edge.

10 Nordlinger, "Power Dem."

11 For a full account of what went on that day, see McFadden et al., *Outrage*, p. 275-77.

12 *Outrage*, pp. 371-88.

13 "Duke Case: Where Is Tawana Brawley?" *Johnsville News*, September 19, 2006. See http://johnsville.blogspot.com. In point of fact, Sharpton and his brain trust aided in the flight, arranging to hide Glenda Brawley inside Ebenezer Baptist Church in Queens, N.Y., rather than have her testify. The church deacons, to their credit, told Sharpton to take his fugitive somewhere else. Soon enough, Sharpton transported her to

Bethany Baptist Church in Brooklyn, evading police detection all the while. Then they called TV talk-show host Phil Donahue, who conducted a live broadcast from the church.

14 Quoted in John Perazzo, "The Nine Lives of Al Sharpton," *Front Page Magazine*, (www.frontpagemag.com). See also E. R. Shipp, "Abrams Backs a New Witness in Brawley Case," *New York Times*, June 18, 1988. Prompting the federal probe was U.S. Attorney Rudolph Giuliani's concern that Sharpton and his allies were collecting funds for Brawley's defense under false pretenses.

15 Quoted in *Outrage*, pp. 309.

16 The original suit had claimed the trio knowingly had made 22 false statements. The jury wound up being deadlocked on four of the statements, while finding eight others non-defamatory. "Winner in Brawley Suit Says Victory is Bittersweet," *CNN.com*, July 14, 1998.

17 Pagones originally had sought $395 million from the defendants. Granted, he stood no real chance of collecting anything resembling this sum. Yet the suit can be justified as a righteous rebuke to Sharpton.

18 Maddox and Mason were in the process of paying their share. Tawana Brawley, on the other hand, was not cooperating. "She has been difficult to locate and her assets have been impossible to locate," said Pagones' lawyer, Garry Bolnick. See Alan Feuer, "Sharpton's Debt in Brawley Defamation Is Paid by Supporters," *New York Times*, June 15, 2001.

19 Quoted in "Tawana Brawley Ordered to Pay $185,000 for False Rape Claim," *Los Angeles Times*, October 10, 1998.

20 For accounts of Brawley's speech, see Jim Yardley, "After a Decade, Brawley Reappears and Repeats Charges," *New York Times*, December

3, 1997; Tara George, et al., "'I'm not a Liar' – Tawana Stands by Her Account of Kidnap, Rape in '87," *New York Daily News*, December 3, 1997.

21 *Outrage*, p. 370.

22 John W. Barry, "Tawana Brawley Begins to Repay Prosecutor She Accused," *Poughkeepsie Journal*, August 5, 2013.

23 Maddox was indefinitely suspended from practicing law in May 1990 by the Appellate Division of the New York State Supreme Court in Brooklyn for refusing to answer allegations regarding his ethical conduct in the Brawley case. He remains filled with the politics of racial grievance. In the pages of the *Amsterdam News* (June 21, 2007), he reacted to the not-guilty verdict of three Duke University lacrosse players falsely accused of the "rape" of a local black woman and the disbarment of disgraced lead prosecutor Michael Nifong this way: "North Carolina's disbarment of Durham District Attorney Michael Nifong on June 16, 2007 is akin to the December 2, 1858 hanging of John Brown, a white freedom fighter, for conducting a raid on the United States Arsenal at Harper's Ferry, Virginia (sic) on October 16, 1858." Maddox's resentments die hard, as do his misstatement of facts – Harper's Ferry is in West Virginia.

24 The New York State Appellate Court, in disbarring Mason, cited 66 instances of professional misconduct with 20 clients over a six-year period, including "repeated neglect of client matters, many of which concerned criminal cases where a client's liberty was at stake; misrepresentations to clients [and] refusal to refund the unearned portion of fees." Unlike the Maddox case, the court did not cite the Tawana Brawley controversy.

25 Interestingly, the organization has the same West Side Manhattan street address as the National Council of Churches and its prominent

offshoot, the Interfaith Center on Corporate Responsibility (ICCR): 475 Riverside Drive. National Legal and Policy Center has published a lengthy paper on the ICCR's ongoing campaign to impose price controls on the pharmaceutical industry in the name of social justice. See Carl F. Horowitz, *The Interfaith Center on Corporate Responsibility: The Religious Left vs. Health Care Markets*, Special Report, Falls Church, Va.: National Legal and Policy Center, 2008.

CHAPTER 8 – GOING WILD IN CENTRAL PARK

1 David E. Pitt, "Gang Attack: Unusual for Its Viciousness," *New York Times*, April 25, 1989. A "wilding" should not be confused with another practice known as "whirling," where a gang chooses a female at random at a public swimming pool and sexually assaults her.

2 *Ibid.*

3 Salaam initially lied to police by claiming to be 16. He and his attorneys used that claim to argue that the case against him should be thrown out, since in New York anyone 16 and older no longer has the right to have a parent or guardian present during police questioning. Salaam did not have either present. But by lying to police, as an appellate court later ruled, he effectively had forfeited that right. Police later allowed his mother to be present after his attorney informed than of his true age.

4 Quoted in J.D. Podolsky, "As the Central Park Jogger Struggles to Heal, Three Attackers Hear the Bell Toll for Them," *People*, September 3, 1990.

5 Quoted in Jay Nordlinger, "Power Dem," *National Review Online*, March 20, 2000.

6 Lorrin Anderson, "Crime, Race, and the Fourth Estate," *National Review*, October 15, 1990.

7 Prosecutors were highly reluctant to work out a plea bargain with Lopez, acknowledged to be the most brutal of the six attackers. They worked out a deal only because they thought the case could have resulted in an acquittal.

8 Quoted in "'It Was Fun' – Robert K. Tanenbaum vs. The Central Park Five, 25 Years Later," www.vdare.com, April 19, 2014.

9 The District Attorney homicide bureau chief, Robert K. Tanenbaum, an experienced prosecutor who had won every murder case that went to trial, was so disgusted by Morgenthau's surrender to mob rule that he resigned his position. He eventually wrote an extensive critique, "The Injustice of a Rush to Judgment – The Central Park Jogger Case," www.blevinswordworx.com.

10 Sean Gardiner, "Central Park Case Settlement Could Cost City Millions," http://online.wsj.com, March 23, 2014.

11 For an effective debunking of the documentary, see Nicholas Stix, "Ken Burns' THE CENTRAL PARK FIVE: The New TO KILL A MOCKINGBIRD – Fiction Designed to Induce White Guilt," www.vdare.com, May 14, 2014. What is especially disturbing is that Ken Burns, of all people, would be involved in this. Over the years he had made highly acclaimed documentaries on baseball, jazz and, most importantly, the Civil War.

12 "New York Reaches $40M Settlement in Central Park Jogger Case," www.nbcnews.com, April 20, 2014. The article originally had been reported by Associated Press.

13 Quoted in *ibid.*

14 Trisha Meili, *I Am the Central Park Jogger,* New York: Scribner, 2003.

CHAPTER 9 – THE SIEGE OF BENSONHURST

1 For an effective, if ideologically skewed (to the Left) full-length narrative of this incident and its aftermath, see John DeSantis, *For the Color of His Skin: The Murder of Yusuf Hawkins and the Trial of Bensonhurst,* New Orleans: John DeSantis (self-published), 2013. The author had covered this case for United Press International. Many of the details in this chapter are taken from this book.

2 Reverend Al Sharpton with Karen Hunter, *Al on America,* Dafina Books (Kensington Publishing Corp.), 2002, p. 226.

3 See DeSantis, *For the Color of His Skin,* pp. 72-82.

4 Jared Taylor, *Paved with Good Intentions: The Failure of Race Relations in Contemporary America,* New York: Carroll & Graf, 1992, p. 86.

5 This raises the issue of why New York City officials allowed the marches to happen anyway. Why did they not arrest all demonstrators on sight? The only plausible answer is that they were terrified that Sharpton and his people would turn on them and create a far worse crisis. By their inaction, then, local officials helped light the fuse.

6 The parent company of WLIB is Inner City Broadcasting. The group long had been headed by Percy Sutton. Sutton, who died in 2009, had served as Malcolm X's lawyer back in the Sixties, and as mentioned earlier, helped retire Sharpton's outstanding civil damages in the Tawana Brawley case.

7 DeSantis, *For the Color of His Skin*, pp. 56-57. Moses Stewart, born Frederick Stewart, also was a problem drinker and a domestic abuser; the latter problem had caused him to be arrested more than once. Upon accepting the "teachings" of Farrakhan, he changed his first name to Moses, an odd move when one thinks about it. When his two younger sons were born, he gave them Muslim names.

8 Robert D. McFadden, "'Day of Outrage' March Ends in Violence," *New York Times*, September 1, 1989.

9 Taylor, *Paved with Good Intentions*, pp. 86-87. Plummer was a piece of work in her own right. Back in 1985, she stood trial with seven co-defendants for plotting a prison break to free two members of the radical gang who pulled off the 1981 Brink's armored car robbery in Rockland County, N.Y. She was acquitted of the most serious charges, but was convicted on falsely identifying herself to gain admission to a prison so she could visit Nathaniel Burns (aka Sekou Odinga), a Brink's job principal, later arrested after a shootout with cops in Queens. Her son, Robert Taylor, was among those convicted of possession of dynamite and machine guns. In this decade, she served as chief of staff to New York City Council Member Charles Barron, a former Black Panther and ally of Al Sharpton. As a council aide, she openly called for the assassination of a black City Council member, Leroy Comrie, whose "offense" had been to abstain from voting on a proposal to rename a stretch of Gates Avenue in Brooklyn after the late black activist and career criminal Sonny Carson, whose exploits are indicated elsewhere in this book. In response, New York City Council Speaker Christine Quinn in July 2007 fired her. Plummer promptly filed a $1 million lawsuit against Quinn, claiming "discrimination." In January 2008, Manhattan Federal Judge William Pauley, in a partial blow for common sense, dismissed Plummer's claim of discrimination, but refused to toss out the suit altogether.

10 Huey Newton was killed on an Oakland street on August 22, 1989 by Tyrone Robinson, a drug-dealing member of the Black Guerrilla Family (BGF), a breakaway faction of the Black Panthers. Newton, who had been feuding with the BGF for years, had just left a nearby crack house. Robinson was convicted of the murder in 1991. He received a 32-year prison sentence.

11 Thomas Clough, "The Saga of Al Sharpton," Weird Republic, 2002, http://www.weirdrepublic.com/episode35.htm.

12 Fama has insisted along all that he was framed. In fact, he has a plausible case. See Jen Fiorentino, "Twenty-Three Years after a Notorious Murder, the Convicted Killer Speaks," *The Brooklyn Link* (http://the-brooklynlink.com), December 10, 2012.

13 Arnold Lubasch, "Vento Acquitted of Murder in Bensonhurst Case," *New York Times*, December 7, 1990.

14 Andrew Maykuth, "Key Bensonhurst Witness: Accused Bragged of 5 Guns," *philly.com*, April 24, 1990.

15 Arnold H. Lubasch, "Juries Acquit 2 in Murder Case in Bensonhurst," *New York Times*, February 8, 1991. Sharpton had been in the courtroom when the jury announced its verdicts. He was so incensed over the not-guilty verdicts for Mondello's most serious offenses that he and the Hawkins family stormed out of the courtroom before the full verdict could be read. See DeSantis, *For the Color of His Skin*, pp. 270-71. Later on, Sharpton vowed to press the Justice Department to file federal civil-rights charges against all defendants, guilty or not. Nothing, thankfully, came of this.

16 In an odd turn of events, Sharpton appealed to the judge for leniency at sentencing. He even visited Riccardi in prison. Riccardi served

nearly nine years of his sentence before being released in January 2001. Sharpton's charitable instincts were less on display in a lawsuit he'd filed against the City of New York for failing to protect him. He settled, belatedly, in December 2003 for $200,000, plus exemption from a $7,447.76 unpaid hospital bill. Thomas J. Lueck, "City Settles Sharpton Suit over Stabbing," *New York Times*, December 9, 2003.

17 Lueck, "City Settles Sharpton Suit over Stabbing."

CHAPTER 10 – RUNNING RIOT IN CROWN HEIGHTS

1 This discussion draws heavily upon Edward S. Shapiro, *Crown Heights: Blacks, Jews, and the 1991 Brooklyn Riot*, Waltham, Mass.: Brandeis University Press, 2006. See also Philip Gourevitch, "The Crown Heights Riot & Its Aftermath," *Commentary*, January 1993, pp. 29-34.

2 Genocidal hatred against Jews also was in evidence at the funeral of Gavin Cato. One banner read, "Hitler did not do the job."

3 See discussion in Jeff Dunetz, "Recalling Al Sharpton's Role in 1991 Crown Heights Riots," *www.thejewishstar.com*, July 18, 2013.

4 Apparently, it also made an impression on a future U.S. president. On their first date, young Barack Obama took his future wife, Michelle Robinson, to see the movie. In 2014, in a special video message commemorating the film's 25th anniversary, President Obama said: "'*Do the Right Thing*' still holds up a mirror to our society, and it makes us laugh and think, and challenges all of us to see ourselves in one another."

5 For a good account of the Korean green grocer boycott and the thug who had engineered it, see Tamar Jacoby, "Sonny Carson and the Politics

of Protest," *NY: The City Journal*, Volume 1, Number 4, Summer 1991, pp. 29-40. Carson had a long history of incitement to riot. During the bitter 1967-68 academic year battle over proposed community (i.e., black community) control of public schools in the Ocean Hill-Brownsville section of Brooklyn, he and a group of radical black activists terrorized Jewish teachers. Carson's gang invaded school buildings and accosted teachers in the hallways, greeting them with such pleasantries as "The Germans did not do a good enough job with you Jews." He also bullied Albert Shanker, the Jewish head of the United Federation of Teachers, the New York City affiliate of the American Federation of Teachers. Carson died of natural causes in 2002. Among civilized people, at least, he would not be missed.

6 Much has been written about Leonard Jeffries and the furor he created. Arguably the most informative are Philip Gourevitch, "The Jeffries Affair," *Commentary*, March 1992, pp. 34-38; Peter Pringle, "Frozen Out by the Ice People," *The Independent*, August 9, 1993; Eric Pooley, "Doctor J: The Rise of Afrocentric Conspiracy Theorist Leonard Jeffries and His Odd Ideas about Blacks and Whites," *New York*, September 2, 1991, pp. 32-37; and David Horowitz, et al., *The Professors: The 101 Most Dangerous Academics in America*, Washington, D.C.: Regnery, 2006, pp. 234-37.

7 Jeffries' comments were outrageous enough to induce complaints from CUNY faculty. In March 1992, the university board of trustees voted to remove him as head of the black studies department, though he would be permitted to remain as a professor. This in turn triggered a legal challenge from Jeffries. The battle lasted until 1995, with Jeffries' dismissal upheld in Manhattan federal circuit court.

8 Exit polls showed Dinkins received about 90 percent of the black vote, and more crucially, about a third of the white vote. See Garrett McGrath, "Love/Hate: New York, Race, and 1989," *The Wilson Quarterly*, Summer 2014.

9 Shapiro, *Crown Heights*, p. 43.

10 *Ibid.*, pp. 53-54.

11 Alison Mitchell, "Suspect in Crown Heights Killing Was Released from Prison in October," *New York Times*, February 12, 1992; Arnold Lubasch, "Man Guilty of Murder of Woman in Brooklyn," *New York Times*, November 25, 1992. There was no doubt prosecutors had the right man in LaFond, who had left his own bloody palm print on the wall next to Mrs. LaPine's body.

12 Old habits apparently have died hard. In June 2008, four adolescent blacks were arrested on hate crime charges for throwing rocks at a school bus in Crown Heights full of Jewish toddlers. See Associated Press, "Teens Stone Jewish Children's Bus in Brooklyn," reprinted in www.ynetnews.com, June 28, 2008. More recently, there have been a number of incidents in which local Crown Heights black youths have sucker-punched Jewish residents. These assaults, often described by newspapers as "random assaults," are emblematic of what is known as the "knockout king" game. Here, black youths target a white pedestrian for no other reason than that person being white and beat him. Jonathan Mark, "Knockout Comes to Crown Heights," *The Jewish Week*, November 26, 2013.

13 Richard H. Girgenti et al., *A Report to the Governor on the Disturbances in Crown Heights, Vols. 1 and 2*, Albany, N.Y.: State of New York, Division of Criminal Justice Services, July 1993.

14 See William McGowan, "Race and Reporting," *City Journal*, Vol. 3, No. 3, Summer 1993, pp. 48-56, especially pp. 54-56.

15 Anna Quindlen, "The Graffiti on the Wall," *New York Times*, September 7, 1991.

16 Felicia R. Lee and Ari L. Goldman, "Tension in Brooklyn; the Bitterness Flows in 2 Directions," *New York Times*, August 23, 1991.

17 Reverend Al Sharpton and Anthony Walton, *Go and Tell Pharaoh: The Autobiography of the Reverend Al Sharpton*, New York: Doubleday, 1996, p. 195.

18 Reverend Al Sharpton (with Karen Hunter), *Al on America*, New York: Dafina Books (Kensington Publishing Corp.), 2002, pp. 217-218.

19 Quoted in Shapiro, *Crown Heights*, p. 13.

20 Quoted in Dunetz, "Recalling Al Sharpton's Role."

21 *Ibid.*, p. 14.

22 Quoted in Gourevitch, "The Crown Heights Riot & Its Aftermath," p. 31.

23 Dunetz, "Recalling Al Sharpton's Role."

24 *Go and Tell Pharoah*, p. 199.

25 "Sharpton Pays Quick Visit to Visit, but Fails to Serve Summons on Hasid," www.jta.org, September 20, 1991.

26 Even Judge Trager issued a ruling forbidding Nelson from ever possessing a weapon, as he was a "danger to the community" and had shown no remorse.

27 Shapiro, *Crown Heights*, p. 191.

28 *Ibid.*, p. 13.

CHAPTER 11 – FUNERAL PYRE AT FREDDY'S FASHION MART

1 A Harlem-based black nationalist, Jesse Gray, had organized a major rent strike among black tenants. On July 19, 1964, the day after the six-day riot began, Gray called for "100 skilled black revolutionaries who are ready to die" to solve "the police brutality situation in Harlem." While the trigger for the riot was the shooting by a white cop of an unarmed black teenager, the rent strike had sufficiently inflamed passions by that time. And Gray had more than established his credentials as a community leader.

2 Powell himself had quite a past. Early in 1996, forensic experts at the City of New York's Office of Mental Health put together a list of patients who had walked away from local mental institutions and found that in July 1974 Powell had escaped from Bellevue Hospital. What actions had he committed to be sent to the facility? On October 16, 1973, court records show, Powell had been hiding behind some garbage cans at 1683 Madison Avenue when he observed Police Officer William Hidelberger walking by. Powell, carrying a lead pipe and a pair of scissors, attacked the officer for no apparent reason. A struggle ensued, and Powell managed to seize the cop's gun and yell, "I am going to kill you, pig." Fortunately, he didn't, and Officer Hidelberger arrested him. Then-State Supreme Court Justice Martin Strecher on March 26, 1974 ruled that Powell was insane and sent him to Bellevue. Since his escape, he had been arrested on a half-dozen occasions. That Powell roamed the streets all that time says much about the shortcomings of the City's mental health system and even more about the character of the man who hired him, Al Sharpton. See Mike McAlary, "Harlem Hate Vendor Fled Psych Ward," *New York Daily News*, February 7, 1996.

3 There was a reason for using the medium, too. In Reverend Al Sharpton and Anthony Walton, *Go and Tell Pharoah: The Autobiography of*

the Reverend Al Sharpton (New York: Doubleday, 1996, p. 146), Sharpton called WLIB and WWRL, and their respective DJs, "the drums of the contemporary black community." The audiotapes of those broadcasts were released by the New York-based Jewish Action Alliance. A number of tapes were transcribed in "When Al Sharpton Invited a Massacre at Freddy's Fashion Mart," http://yidwithlid.blogspot.com, March 28, 2012. All quotes from Sharpton's radio broadcasts in this chapter are taken from this source.

4 Pam Belluck, "Prominent Freddy's Protestor Was Record Store Employee," *New York Times*, December 19, 1995.

5 Mr. Smith/Mulocko was a part-time street vendor selling African artifacts. Like many such peddlers selling their wares along 125th Street, he operated without a City license. These peddlers might look charming from a distance, but they were anything but that to store owners who saw their revenues bleed. One of those owners was Sikhulu Shange, who complained that peddlers of counterfeit records and tapes were severely cutting into his business. Sharpton's right-hand man, Morris Powell, happened to be tight with the vendors, heading an entity called the 125th Street Vendors Association. Many of the protestors at the site were there in support of Shange, but that hardly meant they were wrathful toward the street peddlers. The common enemy was Fred Harari, who was white and Jewish. See Dan Barry, "Death on 125th Street: The Neighborhood," *New York Times*, December 11, 1995.

6 *Al on America*, pp. 216-17.

7 Jeri Hester et al., "Rev. Al's Caught on Protest Tape Called Mart Owner a 'White Interloper,'" *New York Daily News*, December 13, 1995.

8 *Ibid.*

9 *Ibid.*

10 Cited in Belluck, "Prominent Freddy's Protestor Was Record Store Employee." Hardy inadvertently revealed what a criminal and suicidal sociopath Ligon really was. According to Hardy, "He (Ligon) said: 'I went through a lot of my life knowing that I was ready to die to rip somebody off or steal something. But after being in prison for 12 years, I realized I had to die for something positive, so I started getting involved in the community and the movement.'" Dying for something positive, in other words, meant killing innocent shoppers so long as they weren't black.

11 Peter Noel, "'Freddy's Not Dead,'" *Village Voice*, December 29, 1998.

CHAPTER 12 – GIULIANI-ERA POLICE CONTROVERSIES: RUBBING WOUNDS RAW

1 Reverend Al Sharpton with Karen Hunter, *Al on America*, New York: Dafina Books (Kensington Publishing Corp.), 2002, p. 21.

2 *Ibid.*, p. 269.

3 For thorough accounts of this event and its aftermath, see Marie Brenner, "Incident in the 70th Precinct," *Vanity Fair*, December 1997, www.vanityfair.com; Jim Dwyer, "No Way Out," *New York Times*, June 23, 2002; Sewell Chan, "The Abner Louima Case, 10 Years Later," *New York Times*, August 9, 2007. This chapter relies heavily on these accounts, especially that of Brenner.

4 Brenner, "Incident in the 70th Precinct."

5 Lynette Holloway, "Sharpton Says Brutality Issue Will Propel Him to a Victory," *New York Times*, August 31, 1997.

6 Mindful of Louima's suffering, it should not go unmentioned that for a while he pulled off a hoax or at least had made a thoughtless statement. On August 13, 1997, one of his lawyers, Brian Figeroux, told reporters that his client (i.e., Louima) had told him that one of the offending officers during the interrogation taunted him with a racial slur and stated: "Dinkins is no longer in power. Now it's Giuliani time." In January 1998, however, Louima retracted that comment under questioning by federal prosecutors. His defenders have said that he made this statement while in recuperation and thus likely was unaware of what he was saying. While the retraction would have no bearing on the criminal cases, it did cast some dispersion on his character. The phrase "Giuliani time" would stick, serving as a campaign prop for Ruth Messinger and the title of a documentary film, released commercially in 2006, about Rudy Giuliani's political career. See John Kifner, "Louima Says His Attackers Did Not Yell 'Giuliani Time,'" *New York Times*, January 15, 1998.

7 Very recently, Rubenstein has been in legal trouble himself. Having attended Sharpton's pre-60th birthday party on the evening of October 1, 2014, at Manhattan's Four Seasons restaurant, he and two women took a limo back to his East Side apartment. After one of the women left, Rubenstein and the other woman had sex and spent the night together. But the sex, charged the woman in a subsequent police statement, was coerced. While Rubenstein was not arrested and vehemently denies the rape charge (and appears to have a strong case), it was enough for Sharpton to terminate his relationship with the lawyer. For a detailed description of the incident, see Carl F. Horowitz, "Party out of Bounds: Sharpton Lawyer Rubenstein Accused of Rape," Falls Church, Va.: National Legal and Policy Center, October 9, 2014.

8 *Ibid.*, p. 242.

9 This section relies heavily upon Heather Mac Donald, "Diallo Truth, Diallo Falsehood," *City Journal*, Summer 1999; Thomas Clough, "The

Saga of Al Sharpton," *Weird Republic,* 2002, http://www.weirdrepublic.com/episode35.htm.

10 Mac Donald, "Diallo Truth, Diallo Falsehood."

11 See, for example, John J. DiIulio, "My Black Crime Problem, and Ours," *City Journal,* Vol. 6, No. 2, Spring 1996, pp. 14-28; William Wilbanks, *The Myth of a Racist Criminal Justice System,* Belmont, Calif.: Brooks/Cole Publishing Co., 1986.,

12 See data in *ibid.*

13 Steven K. Smith, Greg W. Steadman, Todd D. Minton and Meg Townsend, *Criminal Victimization and Perceptions of Community Safety in 12 Cities, 1998,* Washington, D.C.: U.S. Department of Justice, Bureau of Criminal Justice Statistics and Office of Community Oriented Policing Services, Special Report NCJ 173940, May 1999. See report online at http://www.ojp.usdoj.gov/bjs/abstract/cvpcs98.htm. The proportion of residents of all races reporting either being "satisfied" or "very satisfied" ranged from 78 percent in Washington, D.C. to 97 percent in Madison, Wisconsin.

14 Patrick Dorismond's older brother, Charles Dorismond, was a minor celebrity himself. Born in Port-au-Prince in 1964, Charles is a reggae musician who has recorded and performed under the stage name, "Bigga Haitian." He and his parents migrated to the U.S. in 1972 to escape the Jean-Claude ("Baby Doc") Duvalier regime, settling in Brooklyn. Patrick Dorismond was born two years later. See Michael R. Hall, *Historical Dictionary of Haiti,* Lanham, Md.: Scarecrow Press (Rowman & Littlefield), 2012.

15 Quoted in Robert Ingrassia, John Marzulli and Corky Siemaszko, "Man Slain by Drug Cop," *New York Daily News Online,* March 17, 2000.

16 *Ibid.*

17 David Barstow, "In Fatal Shooting, 2 Sides Clash in Portraying Victim and Officer," *New York Times*, March 19, 2000.

18 Igrassia, Marzulli and Siemaszko, "Man Slain by Drug Cop."

19 With the obvious support of Mayor Bloomberg, the City Council in 2008 voted to extend this limit to three terms.

20 *Ibid.*

21 Samuel Maull, "No Indictment in Dorismond Shooting," ABC News, July 28, 2000.

22 Brian Blomquist, "Sharpton Angling for Justice Probe of Dorismond's Rap-Sheet Release," *New York Post*, March 30, 2000.

23 Ron Howell and Sean Gardiner, "Mourning, Outcry over Shooting," *Newsday*, March 18, 2000.

24 "No Trial for Dorismond Shooter," CBS News, March 25, 2000, www.cbsnews.com.

25 There was a fairly high likelihood that Giuliani would have withdrawn from the Senate race anyway, given that his marital travails had become front-page news. But Sharpton's campaigns, in a sense, sealed the deal.

26 James Fulford, "Christopher Dorner, The Rampart Scandal, and the Real Problem with the LAPD," *vdare.com*, February 17, 2013. The late Christopher Dorner was a black LAPD officer who was kicked off the police force for lying about another officer's alleged racially-based

comments and acts of violence against him. Filled with vengeance, Dorner would go on a shooting spree against Los Angeles cops and family members early in February 2013, killing four persons and wounding three others. Days later, on February 12, 2013, he died of a self-inflicted gunshot wound at a San Bernardino Mountains hideout, having been tracked down in a massive LAPD manhunt.

CHAPTER 13 – HAVING IT HIS WAY: THE BURGER KING AFFAIR

1 For a recent example of Jackson's style of moral extortion, see Carl Horowitz, "Silicon Valley Capitulates to Jesse Jackson Shakedown," Falls Church, Va.: National Legal and Policy Center, May 29, 2014.

2 "Sharpton Threatens Boycott of Burger King," Associated Press, reprinted in *St. Augustine Record*, September 11, 2000.

3 Tom Stieghorst, "Battle Looms over Boycott," *sun-sentinel.com*, October 6, 2000.

4 Quoted in "Burger King Minority Franchisees Respond to Boycott," *www.qsrmagazine.com*, September 14, 2000.

5 Stieghorst, "Battle Looms Over Boycott."

6 Lee Uehara, "Sharpton Boycotts Burger King, Plans Class-Action Suit," *Jacksonville.com*, December 18, 2000.

7 Glenn Singer, "BK Will Buy Back Restaurants," *sun-sentinel.com*, January 10, 2001; Nathan Skid, "Serving off the Menu: Bistro Opens with La-Van Hawkins, Questions, but No Liquor License," *Crain's Detroit Business*, October 24, 2012.

8 Peter Noel, "Is Jesse for Sale?" *Village Voice*, December 27, 2000-January 2, 2001. Jackson's decision proved to be a sharp one, at least from his own standpoint. Burger King continues to be a prominent donor to Jackson's main nonprofit organization, Rainbow/PUSH Coalition.

9 Reverend Al Sharpton (with Karen Hunter), *Al on America*, New York: Dafina Books (Kensington Publishing Corp.), 2002, pp. 198-99.

10 "Hawkins, La-Van," *www.encyclopedia.com*, Contemporary Black Biography, 2006.

11 "Ex-Detroit-Area Pizza Man La-Van Hawkins Sentenced to Prison," *www.mlive.com*, July 9, 2009.

12 Marty Stempniak, *Austin Weekly News*, December 14, 2011. "Austin" in this case refers to a neighborhood on Chicago's Far West Side, not far from the suburb of Oak Park, Ill.

CHAPTER 14 – MICHAEL JACKSON AGONISTES

1 See "Michael's Immortal Money Machine," *Forbes*, June 16, 2014, pp. 14-15.

2 Here's how Alvin Malnik, a former Jackson financial adviser explained it in 2006: "I think that Michael never had any concept of fiscal responsibility...He was an individual that had been overindulged by those that represented him or worked for him for all of his life. There was no planning in terms of allocations of how much he should spend. As a businessman, you can forecast your spending for the next six months to a year. For Michael, it was whatever he wanted at the time he wanted." Quoted in Timothy O'Brien, "What Happened to the Fortune Michael Jackson Made?" *New York Times*, May 14, 2006.

3 In January 1994 Jackson settled a civil suit for $22 million with Evan Chandler whose boy, Jordan Chandler, allegedly had been molested by Jackson the previous year. It had been common practice for Jackson to have children as sleepover guests at his Neverland Ranch, where the sexual activity ostensibly occurred. Jackson denied having sex and was never charged with a crime. Opinion remains divided as to whether Jackson was covering up real crimes or avoiding further lawsuits over imaginary ones. The high settlement suggests the first view is plausible.

4 Quoted in Jennifer Vineyard, "Michael Jackson Shocks Al Sharpton by Calling Tommy Mottola a Racist," *MTV News*, July 8, 2002, http://www.mtv.com/news/articles.

5 Reverend Sharpton with Nick Chiles, *The Rejected Stone: Al Sharpton and the Path to American Leadership*, New York: Cash Money Content, p. 241.

6 Quoted in Jennifer Vineyard, "Michael Jackson Shocks Al Sharpton By Calling Tommy Mottola a Racist," *MTV News*, July 8, 2002.

7 Quoted in "Michael Jackson & Sony Relationship for Dummies," Part 5, http://muzikfactorytwo.blogspot.com, December 14, 2010. See also Lynton Guest, *The Trials of Michael Jackson*, Glamorgan (Wales), UK: Aureus Publishing, 2006. As an aside, Sharpton's statement about Otis Blackwell writing all of Elvis Presley's hits was a wild exaggeration, not to mention an implied pitch for racial reparations. It's true that Blackwell, who died in 2002, did write a few of Presley's early hits ("All Shook Up," "Don't Be Cruel"). Yet these songs represented only a portion even of Elvis' *early* output. Fifties-era Presley singles "Jailhouse Rock," "King Creole," "Love Me," and "Don't," for example, each were written by the white (and Jewish) Jerry Leiber-Mike Stoller duo.

8 Actually, the break was not complete. Though the contract was inactive, Sony wound up releasing any number of anthologies of previously released Jackson recordings.

9 These figures, which exclude singles/digital downloads, can be found on Michael Jackson's official website, www.michaeljackson.com. As they represent worldwide sales as of July 31, 2010, the numbers no doubt are a good deal higher today. Discrepancies also may be due to definition of a unit sale. Some industry people include web downloads as part of total sales; some don't. The above-mentioned Forbes magazine "Leaderboard" feature ("Michael's Immortal Money Machine") puts the worldwide sales figure of *Thriller* at 100 million copies.

10 In large measure, the prosecution bungled the case. During the trial, Santa Barbara County District Attorney Tom Sneddon made derogatory public statements about Jackson, leading the defense and a sympathetic public to believe Jackson was a victim of a personal vendetta. Sneddon, in fact, had tried to prosecute Jackson back in 1993, but Jackson and the Chandler family reached a settlement before the wheels could be set in motion.

11 O'Brien, "What Happened to the Fortune Michael Jackson Made?"

12 "Michael Jackson Becomes a Muslim and Changes Name to Mikaeel," *Daily Mail Online*, November 21, 2008, http://www.dailymail.co.uk/ tvshowbiz/article. Jackson and his siblings were raised as Jehovah's Witnesses. One of his older brothers, Jermaine, became a Muslim in 1989.

13 In the late Nineties, Seagram purchased PolyGram Records, which it then merged with another Seagram subsidiary, MCA Inc., to form Universal Music Group. The revived Casablanca has no formal connection with the original Casablanca label, which in the Seventies had

launched the careers of Donna Summer, Kiss and other top-selling recording artists. Tommy Mottola simply liked the name.

CHAPTER 15 – THE TROUBLES IN JENA, LOUISIANA

1 See transcript of phone interview, "Rev. Al Sharpton: Jena Rally Marks 'Beginning of a 21ˢᵗ Century Rights Movement,'" *Democracy NOW!*, September 21, 2007.

2 Testimony of Reverend Al Sharpton, House Committee on the Judiciary, Subcommittee on Crime, Terrorism and Homeland Security, Hearing, "Jena 6 and the Role of Federal Intervention in Hate Crimes and Racial Violence in Public Schools," October 16, 2007. The mere title of the proceedings was a dead giveaway that the committee had little sympathy with anyone who demurred from the view expressed by Sharpton. Reps. Sheila Jackson-Lee, D-Texas, and Keith Ellison, D-Minn., for example, bitterly castigated Donald Washington, the black U.S. Attorney who had not secured the release of the six blacks accused of attempted murder of a white student.

3 See, for example, Craig Franklin, "Media Myths about the Jena 6," *Christian Science Monitor*, October 24, 2007.

4 Marcus Epstein, "Media Manufactured Noose Mania," www.vdare. com, April 8, 2008.

5 Quoted in Craig Franklin, "DA/School Officials Grant Exclusive Interviews," *Jena Times*, October 3, 2007.

6 "The Jena Six," Editorial, *New York Times*, September 23, 2007.

7 Walters had every reason to try these defendants as adults, and indicated as much in a guest editorial for the *New York Times*. See Reed Walters, "Justice in Jena," *New York Times*, Opinion, September 26, 2007.

8 Quoted in Carl F. Horowitz, "The Jena Defendants: Is Thuggery a New Right?," *Townhall.com*, October 30, 2007.

9 "Jena Six Case Wrapped Up with Plea Bargains," Associated Press, June 26, 2009, reprinted in www.nbcnews.com, June 26, 2009. The Barker family filed its civil suit against the parents of the accused, the adult members of the Jena Six (i.e., adults at the time of the attack), an additional student named Malcolm Shaw, and the LaSalle Parish School Board. The settlement later was revealed to be $29,000, of which $22,000 went for medical bills and $7,000 went for damages. See Mary Foster, "5 Years later, Jena 6 Move On," Associated Press, www.nbcnews.com, August 25, 2011.

10 See especially "Some 'Jena Six' Defendants Have Recent Legal Problems," *www.thetowntalk.com*, May 30, 2008; "The Jena 6 and Barker: Where Are They Now?" *www.thetowntalk.com*, September 21, 2008.

11 According to police, Bell tried to steal several shirts and a pair of jeans from a Monroe, La. department store and fled when a security guard and an off-duty police officer tried to detain him. After they found him hiding under a car, Bell "swung his arms wildly"; one of his arms struck the security guard with a glancing blow. See "'Jena Six' Teen Shoots Self," Associated Press, December 30, 2008.

12 See articles about the SPLC in *The Social Contract*, Special Issue, Spring 2010.

13 Jamie Kizzire, "'Jena Six' Teen Now an SPLC Community Advocate," *www.splccenter.org*, December 17, 2012.

14 *Ibid.*

CHAPTER 16 – HOLY WAR ON DON IMUS

1 Sharpton, it should be noted, has spoken out often against rap lyrics that he finds degrading to black women. And he isn't imagining things; many of these lyrics are degrading. While this book does not advocate censorship in any way – every artist has a method to his madness – it is significant that Sharpton has no problem censoring Imus for making far tamer comments than those often found on such records. In other words, the issue is the double standard: "Free speech for me, but not for thee." Sharpton, for one, is an adherent.

2 Quoted in David Carr, "Networks Condemn Remarks by Imus," *New York Times*, April 7, 2007.

3 Quoted in "Rutgers Players Describe How Imus' Remarks Hurt," *CNN. com*, April, 10, 2007. Coach Stringer, pouring on the high-octane sanctimony, described her players this way: "Before you are valedictorians of their class, future doctors, musical prodigies, and yes, even Girl Scouts. They are young ladies of class, distinction; they are articulate; they are brilliant; they are gifted. They are God's representatives in every sense of the word."

4 "Don Imus on Al Sharpton's Radio Show," Transcript, *New York Times*, April 9, 2007.

5 David Bauder, "Racist Remarks Cost Imus CBS Radio Job," Associated Press, April 12, 2007.

6 Bill Carter and Jacques Steinberg, "Off the Air: The Light Goes Out for Don Imus," *New York Times*, April 13, 2007.

7 Jacques Steinberg, "Source: Imus Back on Air in Early December," *New York Times*, November 14, 2007.

8 Interview with Al Sharpton, conducted by David Shankbone, *Wikinews*, December 3, 2007.

CHAPTER 17 – SEAN BELL AND FRIENDS: REBELS WITHOUT A CASE

1 See especially Heather Mac Donald, "Time for the Truth about Black Crime Rates: The Lessons of the Sean Bell Case," *City Journal*, April 2, 2007, http://www.city-journal.org.

2 Quoted in Sewell Chan and Daryl Khan, "Sharpton and Jesse Jackson Lead Angry Group to Site of Deadly Police Shooting," *New York Times*, November 30, 2006.

3 *Ibid.*

4 Diane Cardwell and Sewell Chan, "Mayor Calls 50 Shots by the Police 'Unacceptable,'" *New York Times*, November 28, 2006.

5 Chan and Khan, "Sharpton and Jesse Jackson Lead Angry Group."

6 See "New York Mayor Promises 'Fair and Thorough' Investigation of Groom's Death," Fox News Channel, November 27, 2006; Emily Vasquez and Daryl Khan, "Pastor Remembers a Confident Family Man Looking Forward to His Marriage," *New York Times*, November 27, 2006.

7 Ernie Naspretto and Alison Gendar, "Dealer: I Was Shot by Bell," *New York Daily News*, March 27, 2007.

8 Murray Weiss, Ikimulisa Livingston and Andy Geller, "50-Shot Victim Held as 'Beater' – Says Sharpton Pays Him to Loaf," *New York Post*, September 27, 2007. Prosecutors stated Benefield was busted after undercover cops, working on a separate case, by chance had witnessed him punching his girlfriend, Nyla Page Walthrus, 19, in the face, and after that, slamming a car door against her and grabbing her by the throat outside her South Jamaica (Queens) home. Walthrus was the mother of Benefield's son, at the time nine months old. Benefield was released on his own recognizance at his Queens Criminal Court arraignment where he had been charged with attempted assault and harassment. He pleaded guilty the following month to disorderly conduct and agreed to undergo therapy. For her part, Ms. Walthrus's had refused to cooperate. Indeed, after Benefield's guilty plea the beaming pair held hands – psychiatrists would call this "traumatic bonding." See Nicole Bode, "Sean Bell Friend Pleads Disorderly Conduct in Assault Try," *New York Daily News*, October 12, 2007.

9 Weiss, Livingston and Geller, *ibid.*

10 See Michael Wilson, "Dramatic Testimony from Bell Shooting Survivor," *New York Times*, April 2, 2008; "Commentary: Testimony of Sean Bell's Friends Sank Case," CNN.com, April 25, 2008.

11 Denis Hamill, "For a Star Witness in Sean Bell Case, Benefield Has Tough Time with his Lines," *New York Daily News*, April 1, 2008.

12 See John Marzulli and Bill Hutchinson, "New York City Settles for $7.15 Million in Sean Bell Shooting," *New York Daily News*, July 27, 2010. Under the agreement, the City would pay $3.25 million to Sean Bell's estate, which was controlled by his would-be wife, Nicole Bell (she took

his last name following his death), $3 million to Joseph Guzman and $900,000 to Trent Benefield. Michael Palladino, president of the New York City detectives union, rightly called the settlement "an absolute joke." He explained: "The police were doing their duty. Bell was intoxicated and tried to run them over. The taxpayers are now on the hook for $7 million. There's something seriously wrong with that picture."

13 Matt Flegenheimer and Al Baker, "Officer in Bell Killing Is Fired; 3 Others to be Forced Out," *New York Times*, March 23, 2012.

CHAPTER 18 – VILIFYING GEORGE ZIMMERMAN, SANCTIFYING TRAYVON MARTIN

1 Joseph Cotto, "Revenge, Misconduct, and Injustice: The Scary Story of Angela Corey," *Washington Times*, July 23, 2013; "Lies, Abuse, and Absolute Power: The Scary Story of Angela Corey," *Washington Times*, July 24, 2013.

2 Jeff Weiner, Jon Busdeker and Martin Comas, "Trayvon Martin: Thousands in Sanford Park Join Rev. Al Sharpton Calling for 'Justice,'" *Orlando Sentinel*, March 22, 2012. Actually, the incident had occurred 25 days earlier, even allowing for the fact that 2012 was a leap year.

3 *Ibid.*

4 There are any number of references that contradict the Trayvon-as-victim narrative, beginning with two lengthy articles I did for National Legal and Policy Center on the subject, "Obama Fails 'Uniter' Test on Trayvon Martin Incident" (April 3, 2012) and "Obama, Holder Sharpton Misrepresent Facts in Trayvon Martin Case; Seek Federal Charges" (July 24, 2013). There are several other sources that recount the events as they most likely had happened, several of which these two articles

referenced. See especially Rene Stutzman, "Police: Zimmerman Says Trayvon Martin Decked Him with One Blow then Began Hammering His Head," *Orlando Sentinel*, March 26, 2012. The British press also offered a reasonable account. See "Trayvon Suspended Three Times for 'Drugs, Truancy, Graffiti and Carrying Burglary Tool' – Did He Attack Bus Driver Too?" *Mail Online*, March 27, 2012.

5 Cited in Lisa Iannucci, "Neighborhood Watch versus Professional Security: What You Need to Know," *South Florida Cooperator*, December 2013, sofl.cooperator.com.

6 See Sanford Police Department, Public Version, March 6, 2012. The full report and quote from Officer Smith is linked in pdf form to Debbie Schlussel, "If Barack Obama Had a Son, Would He Be a Violent Thug Like Trayvon Martin?" *www.debbieschlussel.com*, March 26, 2012.

7 Matt Gutman and Seni Tienabeso, "ABC News Exclusive: Zimmerman Medical Report Shows Broken Nose, Lacerations After Trayvon Martin Shooting," *http://abcnews.go.com*, May 15, 2012.

8 See quotes from black members of Congress in Horowitz, "Obama Fails 'Uniter' Test."

9 *Ibid.*

10 Formally, Zimmerman was on trial for second-degree murder only. But in the event of a "not guilty" verdict, the jury in this case had the option to convict him on a lesser manslaughter charge.

11 See video and transcript of "Dershowitz: Zimmerman Special Prosecutor Angela Corey Should Be Disbarred," *Real Clear Politics*, July 14, 2013.

12 John Fund and Hans von Spakovsky, *Obama's Enforcer: Eric Holder's Justice Department*, New York: Broadside Books (HarperCollins), 2014.

CHAPTER 19 – DEATH BY POLICE CHOKEHOLD?

1 Michael Winter, "NYPD Chokehold Death Ruled Homicide," *www.usatoday.com*, August 1, 2014.

2 Harry Bruinius, "Staten Island Marchers Protest Police Killing of Eric Garner," *www.csmonitor.com*, August 23, 2014.

3 Natasja, Sheriff, "Thousands March in New York City to Protest Police Chokehold Death," http://news.yahoo.com, August 23, 2014.

4 Joseph Goldstein and Nate Schweber, "Man's Death After Chokehold Raises Old Issue for the Police," *New York Times*, July 18, 2014.

5 Jim Meyers, "11 Facts About the Eric Garner Case the Media Won't Tell You," www.frontpagemag, December 5, 2014.

6 According to the New York State Department of Taxation and Finance (www.tax.ny.gov), the current state excise tax on cigarettes is $4.35 per package of 20 cigarettes. On top of that, the City of New York imposes an excise tax of $1.50. And the federal government levies a rate of $1.01 per pack, raising it from 39 cents a pack, effective April 1, 2009. In other words, a street-legal pack of cigarettes in New York City is taxed at nearly $7.00.

7 Bernard Kerik served as New York City police commissioner during August 2000-December 2001; i.e., the latter months of the second Giuliani administration.

8 Quoted in Todd Beamon, "Ex-NYPD Chief Kerik on Garner Case: 'You Cannot Resist Arrest,'" *NewsMax*, December 3, 2014.

9 Quoted in Meyers, "11 Facts About the Eric Garner Case."

10 Quoted in Abby Ohlheiser, Elahe Izadi and Cameron Barr, "Holder Opening Federal Probe in Chokehold Case," *Washington Post*, December 4, 2014.

11 Meyers, "11 Facts About the Eric Garner Case."

12 J. David Goodman, "Man Who Filmed Fatal Police Chokehold Is Arrested on Weapons Charges," *New York Times*, August 3, 2014.

13 Jen Chung, "Ramsey Orta '100 Percent Sure' Cops Arrested Him as Revenge for Filming Fatal Chokehold," *gothamist.com*, August 5, 2014.

14 Sarah Wallace, "Man Who Took Eric Garner Cell Phone Video Arraigned on Weapons Charge," ABC 7, WABC-TV, New York City, August 4, 2014.

15 "Sgt. Kizzy Adoni: Cop on Scene Who Ordered and Supervised Step-by-Step Takedown of Eric Garner Was a Black Woman," http://patdollard.com, December 5, 2014.

16 Marc Santora, "Eric Garner's Family to Sue New York City over Chokehold Case," *New York Times*, October 7, 2014. The announcement took the form of a claim filed with the City Comptroller, which is the first formal step prior to an actual lawsuit.

17 Cited in Bruinius, "Staten Island Marchers." It hardly would be going out on a limb to assert that the "unnamed" U.S. attorney was Loretta Lynch, who managed to be nominated as Eric Holder's successor as attorney general only weeks later. Political common sense virtually would dictate as much.

18 Michael Scotto, "Garner Family, Sharpton Call on Justice Department to Take over Garner Case," Time Warner Cable News, http://manhattan.nyl.com, October 5, 2014.

19 John Fund and Hans von Spakovsky, *Obama's Enforcer: Eric Holder's Justice Department*, New York: Broadside Books (HarperCollins), 2014.

20 See Andrew Siff and Jonathan Dienst, "Grand Jury Declines to Indict NYPD Officer in Eric Garner Chokehold Death," www.nbcnewyork.com, December 3, 2014. Of the 23 members of the grand jury, 14 were white and nine were nonwhite; of the nonwhites, five were black. Under New York state law, to formal indict someone with a crime, at least 12 grand jurors who heard all the evidence and legal instructions must agree that there is sufficient evidence and reasonable cause to believe a crime had been committed.

21 Ohlheiser, Izadi and Barr, "Holder Opening Federal Probe in Chokehold Case."

22 "Rev. Al Sharpton, Relatives of Eric Garner Vow to Continue Fight," www.silive.com, December 3, 2014.

23 Quoted in Sari Horwitz, "Attorney General Nominee Lynch to Spearhead Civil Rights Investigation in Garner's Death," *Washington Post*, December 4, 2014.

24 For an extensive discussion of Lynch's racially-based ideological enthusiasm, see "Loretta Lynch," www.discoverthenetworks.org.

25 Scotto, "Garner Family." The article stated the role of Al Sharpton this way: "Sharpton said he is already in conversations with the White House about Holder's eventual successor." That the Obama administration would feel a need to consult with Sharpton about an appropriate Attorney General nominee is a telling commentary on its character.

CHAPTER 20 – ST. LOUIS FUSE

1 The discussion in this chapter draws primarily from two articles that the author wrote for National Legal and Policy Center: "Sharpton Creates Tension in Wake of St. Louis-Area Rioting" (August 15, 2014); "Is Eric Holder Trying to Railroad Ferguson Cop?" (August 26, 2014).

2 See, for example, Sandhya and Kimbriell Kelly, "What Was Michael Brown Doing?" *Washington Post*, November 30, 2014.

3 See Ben Kesling, Pervais Shallwani and Mark Peters, "Ferguson Beefs Up Response," *Wall Street Journal*, November 26, 2014; Chico Harlan, David Montgomery and Kimberly Kindy, "Assessing Damage, Bracing for Unknown," *Washington Post*, November 26, 2014.

4 Quoted in Jessica Chasmar, "Al Sharpton Says No Indictment for Darren Wilson 'An Absolute Blow,'" *Washington Times*, November 25, 2014. Sharpton's comment reveals a genuine ignorance of the workings of our criminal justice system, to say nothing of English grammar. A grand jury hearing is not a "trial." It is a fact-finding mission. The purpose is to determine whether enough evidence exists to warrant a formal prosecution, not to pronounce anyone guilty or not guilty. As for the hearings not being "open," grand juries, as a matter of course, meet in secret so as to avoid intimidation, bribery and other forms of undue influence.

5 "Rev. Al Joins Mo. Protest," *New York Daily News*, July 13, 1999; Associated Press, People in the News, reprinted in *www.cjonline.com*, December 13, 2000.

6 An excellent and detailed summation of the testimony and the evidence (and discrepancies between them) can be found in Marc Fisher, Kimbriell Kelly, Kimberly Kindy and Amy Brittain, "Two Lives Collide, A Nation Divides," *Washington Post*, December 7, 2014.

7 Quoted in Colin Campbell, "'America Is on Trial': Al Sharpton on Ferguson Protests," *Business Insider*, August 17, 2014.

8 *Ibid.*

9 *Ibid.*

10 Bradford Thomas, "Sharpton Heckled at St. Louis Presser," *TruthRevolt.org*, August 13, 2014.

11 Chris Hayes, "Police Investigating Assault & Felony Robbery Following Fight among Michael Brown's Family," Fox 2 News, http://fox2now.com, November 5, 2014.

12 Jessica Chasmar, "Michael Brown's Parents to Speak at U.N. Committee on Torture," *Washington Times*, November 5, 2014. A professor at St. Louis University, Justin Hansford, helped arrange the trip. Ms. McSpadden sounded as absurd in Switzerland as she had back home in suburban St. Louis. On the eve of the conference, on November 11, she told the committee that her son's death amounted to torture. See Susan Jones, "Michael Brown's Parents Tell UN His Death Equals Torture," CNS News, November 11, 2014.

13 "Attorney General Holder Arrives in St. Louis to Meet with Community Leaders, FBI," Fox 2 News, http://fox2now.com, August 20, 2014.

14 Kimberly Kindy and Sari Horwitz, "Holder Announces Ferguson Probe," *Washington Post*, September 5, 2014.

15 Christopher Caldwell, "No Law, No Order," *The Weekly Standard*, September 1, 2014, p. 23.

16 Wesley Lowery, "Protest Tries to Shut Down I-70 in an Act of Civil Disobedience," *Washington Post*, September 11, 2014.

17 One uses the word "reportedly" here because there is substantial evidence that a fracture did not occur and that the original report, first published on The Gateway Pundit blog site, operated by one Jim Hoft, was based on bad information. That said, it is almost indisputable that Brown, without provocation, punched Officer Wilson in the face, which is a felony. And that blow might have incapacitated Wilson to the point of being unable to prevent his gun from being removed by Michael Brown. Those in the Leftist blogosphere who smugly chortle about the initial report of the broken eye socket being a "hoax" would do well to look at the larger picture.

18 Gilbert Bailon, "Reporter Clarifies Controversial Twitter Post," www.stltoday.com, August 19, 2014.

19 Emily Wax-Thibodeaux, DeNeen L. Brown and Jerry Markon, "County Autopsy: Michael Brown Shot 6 Times from the Front, Had Marijuana in His System," *Washington Post*, August 18, 2014.

20 Quoted in Nicholas Stix, "Joyce Carol Oates' Scorched-Earth Campaign for a Nobel Prize," *vdare.com*, September 12, 2014.

21 Typically, a potential defendant is not called as a witness by a grand jury. Significantly, Officer Wilson did not even have an attorney present. He was taking a real risk by testifying. That he did testify is a sign of how confident he was that his version of events was accurate.

22 One did not have to wait long for champions of Michael Brown to seize upon Officer Wilson's "demon" comment as embodying latent white racism. See Eugene Robinson, "Ferguson Dehumanized," *Washington Post*, November 28, 2014. Perhaps Robinson, who is black, has not encountered a murderous thug about to attack. Let it be said that such a person is a frightening sight, regardless of race.

23 See Julie Bosman, Campbell Robertson, Erik Eckholm and Richard A. Oppel Jr., "Ferguson Grand Jury Faced Mass of Evidence, Much of it Conflicting," *New York Times*, November 25, 2014.

24 Bosman et al., "Ferguson Grand Jury Faced Mass of Evidence."

25 Kimberly Kindy and Sari Horwitz, "Witnesses Are Said to Bolster Ferguson Officer's Account," *Washington Post*, October 23, 2014.

26 Carey Gilliam, "St. Louis Grand Jury Term Extended as It Hears Ferguson Evidence," Reuters, September 16, 2014. The term was set to expire on September 10, 2014.

27 Devlin Barrett and Ben Kesling, "Civil Rights Case Is Seen as Difficult to Bring," *Wall Street Journal*, November 26, 2014.

28 Another riot happened soon enough. On the night of September 23, and extending into the following morning, black mobs in Ferguson smashed windows of a store, rocked cars, set fires, and threw rocks and bottles in response to reports that a fire had destroyed a makeshift street memorial to Michael Brown. Aside from the fact that the riot was indefensible, the "memorial," such as it was, likely had caught fire as a result of surrounding burning candles. This was not even the main memorial to Brown. Two police officers were injured in the melee. Mark Berman, "Police, Protestors, Clash Once More Again in Ferguson," *Washington Post*, September 25, 2014.

29 Quoted in Ron Christie, "As Michael Brown Grand Jury Winds Down, Is Ferguson on the Brink of War?" *The Daily Beast*, November 16, 2014, http://www.thedailybeast.com.

30 David Montgomery and Wesley Lowery, "Signs of Hope, Healing Emerge in Ferguson," *Washington Post*, December 1, 2004.

CHAPTER 21 – WHERE'S THE MONEY?

1 Quoted in Russ Buettner, "As Sharpton Rose, So Did His Unpaid Taxes," *New York Times*, November 18, 2014.

2 *Ibid.*

3 *The Buying of the President 2004*, "Al Sharpton," Washington, D.C.: Center for Public Integrity, 2004. The report, in the center's own words, is a "quadrennial investigation of how money shapes presidential campaigns."

4 Cited in "Audit: Sharpton's National Action Network in Shambles," www.eurweb.com, September 8, 2010.

5 See John T. McQuiston, "After 6 Hours, Jury Acquits Sharpton of All Charges," *New York Times*, July 3, 1990.

6 For a discussion of this affair, see "FBI Investigating Sharpton," *Ethics Watch*, Vol. XI, Number 2, Summer 2005, pp. 1, 7; "Sharpton Indictment Looming?" *Ethics Watch*, Vol. XIV, Number 1, Spring 2008, pp. 1, 7. *Ethics Watch* is a publication of the National Legal and Policy Center.

7 Ian Bishop, "Feds Probe Rev. Al Sharpton's Campaign $$ Under Scrutiny as New Video of Hotel Meeting Emerges," *New York Post*, April 12, 2005. Wiretaps showed that White and Hawkins supported Sharpton because they believed that Reverend Al could get them approval for future business plans, especially a pending $40 million deal that would use New York City public pension funds to bankroll a chain of fried chicken restaurants.

8 Kevin Chappell, "How La-Van Hawkins Rose from the Projects to a Private Jet and a Multimillion-Dollar Empire," *Ebony*, April 2003.

9 "FBI Investigating Sharpton," p. 7.

10 The 1997 "fire" was cited in NLPC Staff, "Sharpton Fined $285K by FEC as a Result of NLPC Complaint," National Legal and Policy Center, April 19, 2009.

11 Quoted in Greg B. Smith and Larry McShane, "Subpoenas for Sharpton's Aides," *New York Daily News*, December 13, 2007.

12 In the indictment, the federal government claimed Hawkins helped White bribe Corey Kemp, former treasurer for the City of Philadelphia, lavishing cash and gifts upon him, including a trip to the 2003 Super Bowl and a party at an upscale restaurant in Detroit that Hawkins controlled. In exchange, Kemp did favors for White, Hawkins and their associates, in some cases using his position to get them business with the City. Hawkins was acquitted at least of conspiracy charges, if not others. See Keith Reed, "Hawkins Found Guilty of Perjury: B.E. 100s CEO Awaits Sentencing in Connection with Philadelphia Corruption Scheme," *Black Enterprise*, July 2005.

13 Luke Rosiak, "Al Sharpton, Seeking Justice for Trayvon Martin, Stiffed the FEC," *Washington Examiner*, July 17, 2013.

14 Cited in Isabel Vincent, "Feds Hit Rev. Al with Record 285G Elex Fine," *New York Post*, April 19, 2009.

15 Kevin Sack, "Guilty Plea by Sharpton in Tax Case," *New York Times*, January 6, 1993.

16 "Sharpton Owes IRS $1.5 Mil in Back Taxes," Associated Press, May 9, 2008.

17 Revals Communications Inc., located at 1776 Broadway, Suite 503, New York, NY 10019, formally was dissolved on July 29, 2009 after having

operated for a little over a decade (its filing date with the State of New York was March 15, 1999). See http://www.businesslookup.org. Revals Communications Inc. It is unclear whether Revals Communications is the same company as the also-defunct Rev-Al Communications, though there is every reason to believe that they are. The businesslookup.org website indicates no record for Rev-Al Communications.

18 *Ibid.*

19 Chuck Bennett & Lois Weiss, "Rev. Al's Half-Price Deal on $1.8M Taxes," *New York Post*, March 28, 2009.

20 Isabel Vincent, "Rev. Al Deep in the Red," *New York Post*, December 11, 2011.

21 Jonathan Berr, "Al Sharpton Can't Shake His Money Problems," http://money.msn.com, July 23, 2013.

22 Quoted in *ibid.*

23 Melissa Klein and Michael Gartland, "Sharpton Demands Accountability, but Still Owes Millions in Back Taxes," *New York Post*, August 3, 2014.

24 Dareh Gregorian, "Rev. Al Furor – Accused in 200G Credit Rip-Off," *New York Post*, August 21, 2003.

25 Andy Meek, "Peabody Sues Sharpton Group for $88K," *Memphis Daily News*, June 12, 2009. The complaint read as follows: "The plaintiff (i.e., the Peabody Hotel) furnished and sold services, room rentals, materials and merchandise to the defendant at its specific instance and request and…(the) amount remains past due and unpaid after demand for payment has been made and payment has been refused." It is no coincidence that the situation got to this point. Sharpton very explicitly chose

Memphis as the site of NAN's 2008 annual conference, held during the first week of that April, as a 40th anniversary memorial to the assassination of Martin Luther King Jr. and a "recommitment" to King's ideals. By refusing to pay the tab owed to the white-owned hotel, Sharpton was exacting his revenge on that city. It is almost impossible to miss the symbolism.

26 Vincent, "Rev. Al Deep in the Red."

27 Cited in Meek, "Peabody Sues Sharpton Group."

28 "Trade Association Claims Al Sharpton Group Owes $28,000 in Unpaid Rent," *Washington Post*, November 28, 2012. See also Carl Horowitz, "Sharpton Way Behind on Washington, D.C. Rent; Faces Eviction," Falls Church, Va.: National Legal and Policy Center, December 4, 2012.

29 Berr, "Al Sharpton Can't Shake His Money Problems."

CHAPTER 22 – A PRESIDENTIAL CAMPAIGN... AND ANOTHER

1 Sharpton had told *Time* magazine: "I feel that the Democratic Party must be challenged in 2004 because it didn't fight aggressively to protect our voting rights in Florida. I would be available." This statement was cited in a number of publications. See, for example, Philip Delves Broughton, "Sharpton to Take Tilt at Presidency," *The Telegraph*, May 22, 2001. It's also worth noting that Jesse Jackson's political stock at the time had been damaged by recent revelations that he had sired a love child with a female researcher and then used money from a nonprofit group to pay her to keep quiet. Without a viable black alternative in the party, Sharpton saw an opportunity to fill the void.

2 Messinger received 39 percent of the vote in that Democratic primary, while Sharpton got a respectable 32 percent. New York State law had required that the minimum threshold in a mayoral primary to avoid a runoff is 40 percent. A subsequent recount showed Messinger had barely cleared that hurdle. Sharpton went to court to force a runoff, but later relented and endorsed Messinger, though more than anything else out of a disdain for the Republican opponent and incumbent, Rudolph Giuliani. In the general election, Giuliani defeated Messinger by 59-41 percent.

3 Reverend Al Sharpton with Karen Hunter, *Al on America*, New York: Dafina Books (Kensington Publishing Corp.), 2002, Introduction, p. xix.

4 *Ibid.*, pp. 17-18.

5 "The Rev. Al Sharpton for President?," *CNN.com*, January 27, 2003.

6 Wayne Barrett, Adam Hutton and Christine Lagorio, "Sleeping with the GOP: A Bush Covert Operative Takes over Al Sharpton's Campaign," *Village Voice*, January 27, 2004.

7 Geoffrey Gray, "Where's Al amid the Obamania?" *New York Magazine*, June 22, 2008. After withdrawing from the presidential race in March 2004, Sharpton endorsed John Kerry.

8 Polls showed that Ryan was the underdog against Obama. But the race at least could have been competitive with Ryan staying in. Like Obama, Ryan was a Harvard law graduate with a bright political future. His undoing proved to be his 1999 divorce in California from his wife, TV actress Jeri Ryan. By mutual agreement, the records of the divorce were kept open, but those of the custody agreement (they had a son) were

sealed. Voyeurs in the Chicago media, especially the *Chicago Tribune* and WLS-TV, wanted to open the latter. They succeeded. On March 29, 2004, nearly two weeks after Ryan's victory in the Republican primary, Los Angeles Superior Court Judge Robert Schnider ruled that a portion of the custody records should be released to the public. That June, based on a referee's report, Judge Schnider ordered specific records to be released in the best interests of the child. The details, some of them dealing with Ryan's private sex life, proved embarrassing. Ryan withdrew from the race the following month. GOP national and state party leaders who had demanded his heave-ho were now hyping Alan Keyes, a proven dud in Maryland U.S. Senate races of 1988 and 1992, and again in presidential races in 1996 and 2000. If nothing else, the results of the 2004 Illinois senatorial general election should have dispelled the notion that most blacks will vote Republican if only the party "reaches out" to them.

9 *Ibid.*

10 See www.nationalactionnetwork.net/html/press_releases.html.

11 Quoted in Bill Levinson, "Tell Obama and Clinton What You Think." *War to Mobilize Democracy*, June 28, 2007, netwmd.com/blog.

12 Janny Scott, "Iowa Caucus Results Put Pressure on Black Leaders for Endorsements," *New York Times*, January 7, 2008.

13 Reverend Al Sharpton (with Nick Chiles), *The Rejected Stone: Al Sharpton and the Path to American Leadership*, New York: Cash Money Content, 2013, p. 181.

14 Quoted in "Al Sharpton: Black Voters Should Punish GOP," *NewsMax*, July 26, 2007.

15 In essence, Sen. D'Amato bought Sharpton's endorsement by promising a U.S. Department of Housing and Urban Development grant of $500,000 for a drug treatment center for Sharpton's "ministerial group." HUD approved the funds about a month after the endorsement. When NBC News' Tim Russert asked Sharpton why he endorsed D'Amato, the Rev answered: "We did not feel that he was going to be a conservative Republican." Given that the alternative was Mark Green, a liberal Democrat and former Gary Hart speechwriter, such a response was hard to accept. See "Why Did Al Sharpton Endorse Senator Al D'Amato (R-NY) in 1986?," *http://archive.democrats.com*. Interestingly, the drug treatment center never opened. A few years after the campaign, Green filed complaints with the Senate Ethics Committee calling for an investigation of "possible D'Amato misconduct." Green had cited articles indicating that D'Amato back in 1984 and 1985 had gotten in touch with the U.S. Attorney's Office in Manhattan, asking him to review the sentences of two convicted mobsters, Genovese family capo Mario Gigante and Gambino family boss Paul Castellano, the latter of whom would die in an infamous December 1985 hit ordered by Gambino underboss John Gotti. Eventually, in 1991, the Ethics Committee reprimanded Senator D'Amato, but on an entirely unrelated matter – his brother, Armand D'Amato, a defense contractor lobbyist, had sent letters to the Department of Defense via unauthorized use of the senator's stationery. See Leslie Maitland, "D'Amato Cited in Another Brief Filed by Green," *New York Times*, December 14, 1989; "D'Amato's Conduct Found 'Improper, Inappropriate,'" *CQ Almanac 1991*, 47th ed., pp. 42-43, Washington, D.C.: Congressional Quarterly, 1992.

16 Deb Riechmann, "Bush: Noose Displays 'Deeply Offensive,'" Associated Press/ABC News, February 12, 2008. As a former president, Bush continues to be a Sharpton admirer. He wrote on the back dust jacket of Sharpton's most recent book, *The Rejected Stone*: "Al cares just as much as I care about making sure that every child learns how to read, write, add and subtract."

17 Quoted in Jennifer Rubin, "Gingrich Has Embraced Sharpton," *Washington Post*, Right Turn, November 23, 2011.

18 Rachel Noerdlinger, born in November 1970, already had done a lengthy stint at the Terrie Williams Agency, one of the most important black-run public relations firms in the U.S., before going to work for Sharpton's 2004 campaign. Among her clients was lawyer Johnnie Cochran, who had represented Sharpton. Very arguably, more than anyone else, she has been responsible for Sharpton's rise to respectability in the public eye. Her own company, Noerdlinger Media, has a lengthy list of blue-chip clients.

19 Noerdlinger, a black whose German-Jewish last name owes to her adoptive parents, is a piece of work in her own right. For one thing, her boyfriend, Hassaun McFarlan, 36, has a criminal record that includes manslaughter (as a 15-year-old, he pleaded guilty to killing another youth over a jacket), conspiracy to run a cocaine trafficking ring, and vehicular assault against a police officer, the latter offense plea-bargained down to disorderly conduct. Then there is Noerdlinger herself. Back in February 2010, she was arrested for misdemeanor assault against another woman, Myasia Layne. Noerdlinger had visited the McFarlan home in the Mott Haven section of the Bronx when Layne answered the door. A fight – or rather, an assault – ensued. "There was pushing and shoving, and [Layne] fell to the ground," noted a police source. "There was cursing back and forth – 'You're a bitch.' 'You're a ho'…Rachel was the primary aggressor." McFarlan was not at home at the time of the incident. This wasn't Noerdlinger's first run-in with the law. Police sources say that she was arrested in April 2007 for attacking an ex-boyfriend, an act for which she was arrested but not charged. The record of the assault remains sealed. More recently, she had come under scrutiny for her failure to disclose her boyfriend's criminal record on the background questionnaire required for her $170,000 job as assistant to Mayor de Blasio's

wife. Ironically, on November 17, 2014, she reportedly took a leave of absence following her teenaged son's arrest for trespassing. See Jamie Schram, "Sharpton Aide in 'Cheesy Catfight,'" *New York Post*, February 22, 2010; Carl Campanile and Joe Tacopino, "McCray Aide Didn't Disclose Killer Beau in Background Check," *New York Post*, October 3, 2014; Russ Buettner, "As Sharpton Rose, So Did His Unpaid Taxes," *New York Times*, November 18, 2014.

CHAPTER 23 – NEW AND IMPROVED!

1 Glenn Thrush, "Revved Up," *Politico*, August 21, 2014.

2 *Ibid.*

3 Colin Campbell, "Al Sharpton Says He's Helping the White House Pick the Next Attorney General," *Business Insider*, September 25, 2014.

4 Quoted in John Fund and Hans von Spakovsky, "Al Sharpton Empowered," *National Review Online*, September 28, 2014.

5 Peter Wallsten, "Obama's New Partner: Al Sharpton," *Wall Street Journal*, March 17, 2010.

6 Allison Samuels and Jerry Adler, "The Reinvention of Reverend Al," *Newsweek*, August 2, 2010, pp. 32-37. All subsequent quotes and references by the authors are attributable to this article.

7 Allison Samuels, "What Michelle Obama Means to Us," *Newsweek*, November 21, 2008. A few years later the author wrote a book exalting the First Lady as a female role model. See Samuels, *What Would Michelle Do? A Modern-Day Guide to Living with Substance and Style*, New York: Gotham, 2012.

8 Trymaine Lee, "Al Sharpton Reinvents Himself for His Second Act," *Huffington Post*, December 18, 2011.

9 "Al Sharpton," www.factmonster.com/biography.

10 Jonathan Capehart, "President Obama Does Al Sharpton a Solid," *www.washingtonpost.com/blogs*, April 6, 2011.

CHAPTER 24 -- ANCHORMAN

1 "Politics Nation," *www.nbcnews.com*, August 29, 2014.

2 See, for example, "Comcast, NBC Universal Complete Merger," Reuters, January 29, 2011; "U.S. Approves Comcast-NBC Merger," *CNNMoney.com*, January 18, 2011; Karl Bode, "FCC's Baker Heads for Job at Comcast," *dslReports.com*, May 11, 2011. The latter story, whose title refers to ex-FCC Member Meredith Attwell Baker, a Republican and an Obama appointee, underscores the power of the proverbial "revolving door" between regulators and industry. Baker recently took over as CEO of CTIA – The Wireless Association, a Washington, D.C.-based trade group.

3 See comment by Comcast spokesperson cited in Wayne Barrett, "Sharpton's Affirmative-Action Win," *The Daily Beast*, July 27, 2011.

4 In August 2013, two years after Sharpton's show debuted, MSNBC management replaced the 5 P.M. Matthews slot with Ed Schultz' show, a sure sign that the network viewed Schultz, Sharpton and Matthews as a formidable triple play. Schultz for the last few years had broadcast during a series of time slots, most recently on weekend afternoons, a virtual dead zone in the world of political talk show TV. See Jack Mirkinson, "Ed Schultz Moves Back to Weekdays, Takes Chris Matthews' 5 PM Slot," *Huffington Post*, August 19, 2013.

5 Lisa de Moraes, "MSNBC Still Undecided on Plans for Guest-Host Sharpton," The TV Column, *Washington Post*, August 2, 2011.

6 Quoted in *ibid.*

7 Brian Stelter, "Sharpton's Push for Comcast Raises Issues about Possible MSNBC Job," *New York Times*, July 27, 2011.

8 MSNBC gave no official explanation as to why it had ended its contract with Olbermann. Yet it was discovered that on October 28, 2010, only days before the midterm elections, he had donated $2,400 each to three congressional candidates. In fact, one of them, Rep. Raul Grijalva, D-Ariz., had appeared on Olbermann's "Countdown" show immediately prior to the latter's donation. On November 5, MSNBC President Phil Griffin indefinitely suspended Olbermann without pay for violating a network policy that required prior network authorization for political donations. Thanks to an online petition, Olbermann returned to the airwaves. The return would be brief. On January 21, 2011, Olbermann announced his permanent departure from the network. Accounts differ as to whether this was voluntary or involuntary. The following month, he secured a slot for his show at Current TV, co-founded by Al Gore and Joel Hyatt. His tenure there likewise would be brief. He was fired on March 30, 2012; the network gave a terse and nonspecific explanation for the move. Olbermann sued the network for $50 million for termination without cause. In March 2013, he and the network settled for an undisclosed sum. For good accounts of Olbermann's travails, see James Joyner, "Keith Olbermann Fired from MSNBC," *Outside the Beltway*, January 21, 2011; Keach Hagey, "Current TV Fired Keith Olbermann," *Politico*, March 30, 2012.

9 Alan Feuer, "As an MSNBC Host, Sharpton Is a Hybrid Like No Other," *New York Times*, September 18, 2011.

10 Cited in Lee, "Al Sharpton Reinvents Himself for His Second Act."

CHAPTER 25 – LIFE AT THE TOP: THE LARGER MEANING OF AL SHARPTON

1 Reverend Al Sharpton and Anthony Walton, *Go and Tell Pharoah: The Autobiography of the Reverend Al Sharpton*, New York: Doubleday, 1996, back jacket quote.

2 *Ibid*, p. 5.

3 Gustave Le Bon, *The Crowd: A Study of the Popular Mind*, Introduction by Robert K. Merton, New York: Penguin Books, 1977 (originally published in 1895), p. 118.

4 New York City affairs author Jim Sleeper makes this point specifically about Sharpton. See summation of authors' interview with Sleeper in Stephan Thernstrom and Abigail Thernstrom, *America in Black and White: One Nation, Indivisible*, New York: Simon & Schuster, 1997, p. 511. The Thernstroms write: "New York writer Jim Sleeper makes another point. The message of Sharpton and other demagogues acts like drops of dye in water: The color quickly spreads. The views of their black listeners alter – especially because the will to believe is already there – the sense that the "system" is alien and "the powers that be" can't be trusted. Many of those affected won't take to the streets, and they won't show up in a courtroom to harass victims like the Central Park jogger. But their heightened sense of collective embattlement will reinforce an already dangerous culture of disbelief."

5 Reverend Al Sharpton with Karen Hunter, *Al on America*, Dafina Books (Kensington Publishing Corp.), 2002, pp. 82-83.

6 See Ta-Nehisi Coates, "The Case for Reparations," *The Atlantic*, June 2014, pp. 54-71. This lengthy cover story has attracted much attention and, regrettably, applause. Its case for mandatory compensation by

whites to blacks is every bit as indefensible as that put forth by Martin Luther King Jr., Al Sharpton or any other reparations advocate, past or present. Coates draws upon the now-familiar trope of white skin privilege. In this frame of reference, white achievement in this country has been made possible primarily by past exploitation of blacks. Factors such as individual intellect, social skills or moral character at best are of secondary importance – at least when they apply to whites.

7 *Go and Tell Pharaoh*, pp. 5-6.

8 "NLPC Criticizes Wal-Mart CEO Lee Scott for Endorsement of Illegal Alien Amnesty and Praise for Sharpton," PR Newswire, July 30, 2007.

9 Quoted in Jay Nordlinger, "Power Dem," *National Review Online*, March 20, 2000.

10 Thomas Sowell, *Preferential Policies: An International Perspective*, New York: William Morrow/Quill, paperback edition, 1990, pp. 168-69.

INDEX

BIOGRAPHY

Carl F. Horowitz since 2005 has been an author, editor and policy specialist with National Legal and Policy Center, a Falls Church, Va.-based nonprofit group dedicated to promoting ethics and accountability in American public life. He holds a B.A. in economics from the University of Kansas, and a master's and a Ph.D. in urban planning and policy development from Rutgers University. Prior to his assuming present position, he had been a professor of urban and regional planning at Virginia Tech, a policy analyst with The Heritage Foundation, and a Washington correspondent with *Investor's Business Daily*. His work has been published, among other places, in *National Review*, the *Wall Street Journal, Reason, Planning, Journal of the American Planning Association* and *The Social Contract*. Originally a native of New York City, he is a longtime Al Sharpton watcher.

Made in the USA
Middletown, DE
17 February 2015